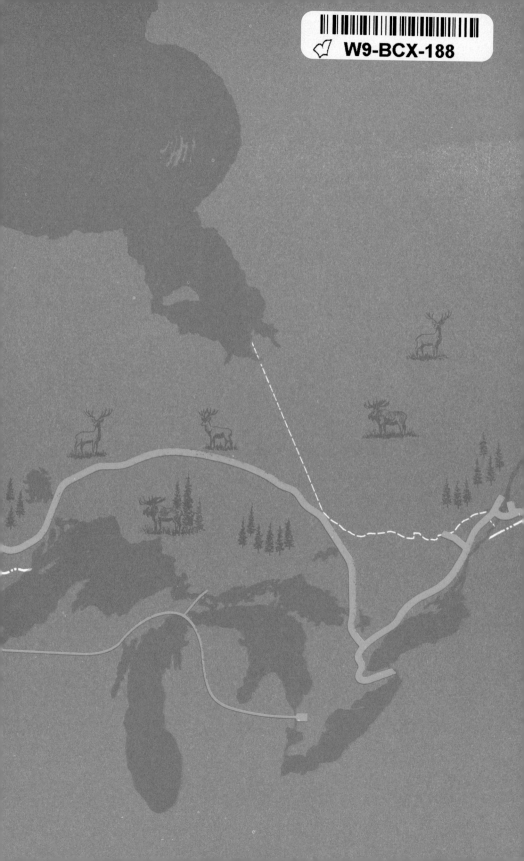

PipeLine

PipeLine

TRANSCANADA AND THE GREAT DEBATE
A HISTORY OF BUSINESS AND POLITICS

WILLIAM KILBOURN

CLARKE, IRWIN & COMPANY LIMITED   TORONTO, VANCOUVER, 1970

Designed by Hugh Michaelson Ltd.

Other books by the same author:

The Firebrand

The Elements Combined

The Restless Church

The Making of the Nation

Religion in Canada

Canada: A Guide to the Peaceable Kingdom

Contents

Who What When How

The pipeline debate of 1956 was the stormiest episode in Canadian parliamentary history. It shattered a quarter century of political quiet — the era of Mackenzie King, his chosen ministers and mandarins, who ran our national affairs the way it pleased them, with a benign and soundless efficiency that was the despair of anyone who believed in Parliament as the critical theatre of democratic government. Between the calm of the King-St. Laurent era and the present, over a decade of political excitement has intervened. There have been two party leadership battles which changed the style of Canadian politics; four minority governments; six general elections; the only major cabinet breakup and decisive Commons defeat in modern times; the phenomenal prairie grass fire campaign of 1958; and, the first act in it all, that wild month in the House of Commons from May Day to Black Friday, 1956. In retrospect, it is easy to see that somehow, sometime, a different issue would have come along to trigger the fall of the old régime. But, in fact, the agent was the pipeline debate.

There are other reasons for studying the history of Trans-Canada Pipe Lines however. Any account of its long struggle to be born inevitably raises most of the classic issues in Canada's survival as a nation: American economic influence and the nature of Canadian-American relations; the debate between north-south continentalism and east-west nationalism; the questions of transportation and national unity, of energy and national growth, of control over natural resources and their exploitation; the latent conflict between western producer and eastern consumer; dominion-provincial relations; the problem of public versus private enterprise and the compromise of

the crown corporation; the connections between business and politics, and the role of regulatory bodies between them; the rights of
Parliament; and the place of popular feelings, pressure groups and
the press in the difficult matter of making decisions on complex issues
of great national importance.

Trans-Canada's history also involves many of the prominent public figures of the 1950s: C. D. Howe, the Liberal cabinet and their
opponents in the House of Commons; four of the most powerful
provincial premiers in Canadian history — Manning, Frost, Duplessis
and Douglas; several key public servants such as Mitchell Sharp and
James Coyne; leading financial houses in New York, Toronto, Montreal and Winnipeg; oil tycoons from Texas and Alberta; Canada's
two largest banks; the world's largest insurance companies; several of
North America's leading businessmen; and on the margin of the
drama, a cast of characters that ranges from Dwight Eisenhower and
Dean Acheson to Allan Lamport and Jean Drapeau.

While this book attempts to evoke and illuminate the chief issues
and characters in Trans-Canada's history and the interplay among
them, it is obviously not an analysis of any one of them. Nor does
it intend to be an apologia or an exposé, a report or a judgement,
though it may offer material for all four, and in some places judge-
ments are obviously made. The central aim is to present a narrative
— a clear reconstruction of a complex event — with as much objectivity
as a decade's distance in time and access to most of the relevant
sources can give it. In the concluding section of the book there are
some reflections on certain of the issues involved in the narrative. In
the course of the narrative, especially in Chapter One, there is some
attempt to suggest the general atmosphere of the 1950s and to touch
on the surprisingly interesting folklore and early history of natural
gas, as well as some digression into Canadian social history and biography. But the focus of this book is upon a dramatic sequence of
events and decisions. It is the story of the attempt to bring an enterprise into being, from its conception in 1950 to the beginning of its
first full year of operation in 1959. The last chapter, necessarily more
of a subjective and tentative impression than a history, looks at the
company's development over the decade since that time and at
the major national and international conflicts that have shaped its
most recent fortunes.

Scene One: Shotgun Wedding

On a bitter January morning in 1954, two groups of men emerged at an interval of some forty minutes from beneath the green-capped castle towers and lengthening icicles of the Château Laurier Hotel. They were bound for the shanty end of Wellington Street, below the western slope of Parliament Hill, at what was then the outskirts of official Ottawa. No. 1 Temporary Building—dirty snow and peeling white paint and tarpaper roof without, noisy steam rads and school portable decor within—bespoke its origins. It suggested blackouts and war savings stamps, ration cards and Victory gardens and Carry On Canada. Through the grey years of World War II and Reconstruction and Korea, exhilarating as life itself to those iron souls who thrive on long hours and will power and impossible problems, the place had become one of the vital decision centres in the capital. Weathered though it was, the building had basically changed as little as its chief occupant.

As his visitors stood in attendance outside his office (he was impatient of wasting other people's time or his own and rarely kept anyone long), a knowledgeable observer might have recognized them as one of the most remarkable assortment of businessmen of all the many hundreds who had over the years made their pilgrimage to that place.

One group included representatives of three leading investment houses in Toronto, Montreal and Winnipeg, together with a small, alert, bejowled individual who had long been Alberta's leading man of affairs. Although by political affiliation he was a Tory, and was now waiting upon a Liberal, he had been a friend of Alberta premiers of every political stripe since the province was founded. The other group included three partners of Lehman Brothers of New York, the quintessential merchant bankers; a senior partner of the Ottawa law firm of W. D. Herridge, who had been Canadian ambassador to Washington during the prime ministership of his brother-in-law, Mr. Bennett; an astute Texas petroleum geologist with an intimate knowledge of Western Canada; and a casual old-fashioned little man with a frontier manner and a corn-pone drawl, by the name of Clint Murchison, who among other activities had recently helped his friend, General Eisenhower, to the Republican nomination for the Presidency of the United States.

Formidable though they were, and for all the weight of their years and fortunes and influence, there was in their conviviality a certain note of deference and a discernible anxiety as each of the groups in turn crossed the threshold into the sparsely furnished office.

Its occupant was about to render judgement, and the two groups were rivals for his favour. But more than that, all of them, either by acquaintance or reputation, had come to regard him as the one politician in the country who understood how things were accomplished in the world of business.

Clarence Decatur Howe, nearing seventy, and during the past two decades the member of cabinet chiefly responsible for the Canadian economy ("Minister of Everything," as an Opposition critic called him), was dedicated to the proposition that there should always be at least one great national enterprise under way and something stirring to get it done. In the end, it was he who decided who should do it and how it would be done, and he who used the weight of his own influence and drive and the power of the government of Canada to see that it was done well.

Sometimes the enterprises were imposed upon him, as when he undertook to marshal the resources of Canada at war, and so effectively that at its end this under-populated ex-colony was for a time the world's fourth largest industrial and military power. Or again, when Howe's post-war give-away reconstruction programme confounded the experts and the expectations of Canadian businessmen and helped the nation share so richly in the economic boom of the 1950s. But what this engineer tycoon-turned-politician loved most were the great public enterprises he initiated and watched over himself. Of them all his favourite was Trans-Canada Airlines—"*my* airline," as he once called it. Now in 1954, as he approached the end of his second career, there was one great national project he still wanted to accomplish, a last reason for waiting on in office beyond his time. This was the idea of a natural gas pipeline to bring western energy to the industrial east. It was big—a matter of billions of dollars of new investment in Canada. It was daring—nothing quite like it had been done before in engineering history. And it would be the longest line in the world. It was, he had convinced himself, comparable to the greatest of all our nation-making enterprises, the building of the Canadian Pacific Railway.

Howe met with each group of visitors separately for about twenty-five minutes. After the handshakes and the preliminary cordial noises were over, he sat behind his large bare desk and looked intently at his guests. His white hair and craggy black brows, his high olive-brown forehead, and the heavy purple-sepia patches under his eyes gave to his gaze and his raw north-east Atlantic accent a keenly penetrating quality. He remarked that he was meeting each group separately and that he would say exactly the same thing to both:

National policy was fixed. There was to be one east-west pipeline built entirely on Canadian soil. There was room for only one company to build it and that company would get all the support he could muster for it. But he would only issue a licence to them if the two parties could settle their differences and agree on a plan that both sides accepted. They had been manoeuvring around each other in negotiations for nearly a year, after three years of outright rivalry for favour. Now time was up. They must go back to the Château Laurier and meet. "Come back and see me at nine a.m. tomorrow morning. Together."

To the Canadian group (Western Pipe Lines), who protested that the Murchison scheme to construct the line straight across the Canadian Shield was not economically feasible until markets were built up in eastern Canada with imported American gas, Howe said, "The all-Canada line is national policy. I will *make* it feasible." To the group headed by Murchison and supported by the Herridge law firm and Lehman Brothers (Trans-Canada Pipe Lines), he said, "You

could not get involved with a better or stronger group of men in this
country. You should join them." One of the Western group, he reminded them, was an old wartime comrade of his and a colleague in
other great national undertakings.

Back at the hotel, after a phone call between the two headquarters,
it was decided that most obstacles to agreement were no longer serious
and that the chief stumbling block now lay in arrangements for financing the pipeline. Accordingly, Deane Nesbitt of Montreal and
Charles Gundy of Toronto, representing Western Pipe Lines, agreed
to visit the Murchison suite with a draft proposal by mid-afternoon.
They did so. Essentially they asked that their group be involved in
half the financing and that the Murchison's bankers, Lehman Brothers, take the other half.

They were listened to in stony silence. Then Lehman's senior
partner, Monroe Gutman, stated that, since the Canadian financial
market was one-tenth the size of the American, financing of the
corporation should not be divided on a fifty-fifty basis but on a split
of 90%-10%. Other arguments were presented: the Murchison group
had spent well over twice the money on the project spent by Western;
and furthermore their surveys, unlike Western's, showed that an all-
Canada route was financially feasible. Unspoken but powerfully
present was the fact that Howe and Murchison had taken an immediate liking to each other and that Howe's feeling for a project's
worth depended heavily on his instinctive judgement of the man in
charge. So that the presence of Howe's wartime colleague, Alan
Williamson, among the Western group was partially offset by that of
Murchison among their opponents. Afterwards, back at Western
headquarters, there were three hours of fruitless discussion in which
no counter-proposal could be worked out. Finally, despite the abhor-
rent idea of meeting Howe next morning only to confess failure, it
was decided to send Nesbitt back with a flat refusal of the 90%-10%
proposal. But in order to keep the door open for negotiation he was
instructed to add that the counter-proposal was "not even in the spirit
of a mutually acceptable agreement." Nesbitt's statement was received
by Gutman without comment, and the Canadian group then went
down to a gloomy dinner at the Château Grill.

About ten p.m., while still at their table, they were approached
by the only one of the Lehman partners who had said nothing during

the meetings at the Murchison suite, a stocky tough-looking individual who introduced himself again as John Fell. Unlike most Lehman partners who had won their way to the top by sheer ability, Fell partly owed his position to the fact that he came from one of old New York's Four Hundred families. In spite—or because—of his resemblance to one of Damon Runyan's rougher characters, he was an excellent diplomat—with his own unique brand of charm—and a shrewd observer of the human comedy. He invited Nesbitt and Gundy to come up to his private room for a nightcap. Once there, he advised his visitors that he was acting on his own and not on behalf of the group. He expressed some sympathy for their views and asked them what they thought he might do to reconcile the two opposing positions. After long and sometimes heated argument, they convinced him that Howe meant business and that both projects would fail if agreements were not reached by morning. They also reminded him that the New York money market was open to Canadian underwriters and that they themselves had placed many millions worth of corporate securities there without any American help.

As the argument wore on, Fell woke his two Lehman partners and brought them up to his room. By the small hours of the morning he had convinced them that a fifty-fifty agreement was fair, though Nesbitt and Gundy would likely have taken less if there had been any bargaining over a compromise percentage. The Lehman partners then left to wait upon Clint Murchison, who was always up and stirring by 5 a.m. anyway, and to greet him with the news that they now agreed with the Western proposal and would advise him to accept it.

At seven, Nesbitt received a call in his room. Trans-Canada agreed that the financing, like the ownership of the new company, should be split evenly. They would all proceed to Howe's office together to inform him.

The meeting went swiftly, and arrangements for the new company's creation were worked out over the next few weeks. It would be years before the new colleagues would meet Howe again with so much to be pleased about. Before the year was out the pipeline was well on its way to becoming the dominant political issue of the decade. Howe in the end got his way; the pipeline would perhaps be his lasting monument. But not quite in the way he expected.

PipeLine

Chapter 1 Once Upon a Time

A long time ago, back in 1950 A.D., Canadians lived in a world without jet travel and computers, super-highways and shopping plazas, metro government and pedestrian malls. Most of our vast new suburban cities were still farms and bushland, gravel roads and village stores. Towns like Kitimat and Thompson in the northern wilderness had not yet been conceived, let alone built. Television, transistors, tranquillizers, stereo, Stratford, Sunday sport, pot, the pill, long hair and abstract art were not yet part of Canadian culture. Names that would become a familiar part of the Canadian language – Pierre Berton, Harold Town and Marshall McLuhan, René Levesque, "Wacky" Bennett and Robert Stanfield – were no better known than that of an obscure lawyer called Trudeau, who was working in Ottawa for the new Prime Minister, Louis St. Laurent. Mackenzie King was still living. So were a dozen of the Privy Councillors appointed by Laurier and Borden. T. T. Shields still thundered against French-Canadian popery from his Jarvis Street pulpit as if the fires of the Inquisition had but recently been lit; and for Jehovah's Witnesses and Roman Catholic liberals in Duplessis's Quebec, Dr. Shields was not entirely wide of the mark.

At the turn of the half century, January 1950, a *Maclean's Magazine* article predicted that in the coming year, the British Labour Government would be re-elected with Sir Stafford Cripps telling people to eat less, that the French cabinet would reshuffle itself seven times, that the St. Lawrence Seaway project would be re-opened for discussion in a short time, only to be deferred once more, and that the Toronto subway would be two feet closer to completion. Canada's population, it went on, "now about 13 millions, would, owing to immigration, emigration, births, deaths and sheer exhaustion, increase to about 13 millions." The same article also looked ahead over the next half century to Monday, January 1, A.D. 2000, when, "with the Toronto subway completed and the housing shortage finally solved, some politician, speaking by ultra-radio to the entire population of Canada (thanks to immigration, emigration, etc. now about 13 millions) would affirm that 'the 21st century belongs to Canada.' "

The head of the Canadian State in 1950 was King George VI, represented in Ottawa by a British Governor General. Canada was a member of a United Nations with only half the members it had admitted two decades later, and of a Commonwealth dominated by Britain and the four white Dominions. As a member of NATO, Canada was taking the unprecedented step of sending troops to Europe in peacetime. But the idea of a Canadian presence in Korea or Vietnam, Cyprus, Africa or the Gaza Strip, would have seemed at the very least improbable – as improbable as a Russian victory over the American space programme, over Canadian hockey teams, or over the spirit of Joseph Stalin.

In 1950 more than half of Canada's present universities did not exist, and many of the rest had fewer freshmen back then than they had staff for 1970. In 1950, the average professor existed on a salary of $4000 a year and usually meant something to do with used cars when he talked about values. In 1970, the universities may not have changed their spiritual goals much, but they had become the new churches of an opulent society whose attitudes and way of life they were studying and changing beyond recognition — with the help of automation and electronics and a new industrial alchemy which seemed capable of turning any substance into anything else. In most fields, from mining and heavy industry to construction and the services, the pace of that new society's physical growth in Canada has been remarkable. But perhaps the most staggering economic change of all has occurred in the oil and gas industries, which have in the quarter century since World War II increased their average production some fifty times over.

Natural gas, as one of the commonplaces of Canadian life, is newer than the atomic age. In the early 1950s, with the exception of several centres in Alberta, it supplied only a miniscule amount of all the energy consumed in Canada. As a fuel and energy source it did not surpass wood until 1955, the year before the great pipeline debate. But since then its growth has been phenomenal. By 1960 it had become a greater source than hydro-electric power and in 1964 finally caught up with coal, the traditional staple of a modern industrial economy. In 1969 as a supplier of 20% of the nation's energy, natural gas was second only to crude oil. And there was every likelihood that this proportion would someday reach one third of the total. Proven reserves would soon be rising at a rate of three trillion cubic feet a year, an amount equal to the total of all established reserves in Canada just after World War II. It would be well into the twenty-first century before nuclear or solar energy appeared as a rival and longer still before the vast Canadian deposits of this fossil fuel showed signs of depletion.

Outside of the United States, the appearance of natural gas as one of man's two major sources of heat and energy was really only beginning in the 1960s. In certain areas of the Soviet Union natural gas supplies were used to rebuild that country's shattered economy after World War II, but even as late as 1959 its total annual production was less than two trillion cubic feet compared with the American total of twelve and a half. During the sixties, the Russians made plans for a giant fifty-inch pipeline from the gas fields of the Caspian Sea to Moscow, which might ultimately feed from there to the cities of the Baltic and as far south as the industrial complex of Northern Italy. Another network of European pipelines was beginning to tap reserves drawn from under the North Sea and the Sahara Desert. Liquid natural gas, refrigerated to little more than one-millionth part of its volume at consumption, was ferried regularly across the Mediterranean by the first of a fleet of tankers that would soon sail all the oceans of the world. The great reserves of the Arabian desert had not yet begun to flow across the Asian and African continents to help bring the great majority of the human race the energy needed for living above the level of mere subsistence.

In twentieth-century North America, the earliest important products of the petroleum industry, diesel oil, fuel oil and gasoline, later reinforced by natural gas, have already effected a revolution.

They have helped reshape the character of cities and their architecture, break down class structures, and eliminate great armies of domestic servants. They have changed patterns of leisure and travel and work, and transformed methods of producing and distributing everything from steel to frozen food.

In the long span of human history, the petroleum age of the twentieth century is the briefest of chapters. The discovery and application of revolutionary sources of energy has been the peculiar characteristic of that unique, technology-based civilization which began in western Europe during the dark ages; took a leap forward in the industrial revolution of eighteenth-century Britain; has been paced for the past hundred years by the United States; and is now spreading to every corner of the earth. This western civilization has had no parallel or precedent whatever for the quality or quantity of its dynamic social and economic change. That dynamic change in turn has been absolutely dependent on the use of new sources of energy. It began in the dark ages with the substitution of wind and water and animal power for human labour. Western Europe in the high middle ages had no slaves; at its growing edge, in the towns, even serfdom had been abolished. The most important social fact of the ancient world, and of all other higher civilizations, was the existence of slavery. Where democracy existed at all, it was only for a small, privileged class of males. But medieval Europe, with its revolutionary development of the blast furnace and the horse collar and the windmill, to name only three of the most important, began that process of change in the whole physical quality of human life of which the latest chapter is exhibited in the harnessing of petroleum and electric and atomic energy to the needs of man. The question of why this unique civilization emerged in medieval Europe cannot be discussed here. Its causes will never be agreed upon, though it does seem related to the gradual application of the Judaeo-Christian doctrine of human equality for all persons, first in the towns and monasteries of medieval Europe, and then to all men everywhere.

In this development of western civilization, the period called palaeotechnic by Lewis Mumford was dependent on the use of coal and iron. Just as wood was replaced by iron and steel as the chief industrial material, so steam from coal replaced the power of wind and water and animals as the chief source of energy. The nineteenth century was also, peculiarly, the age of manufactured gas, gas made from heating coal. Coal gas was first used for street lighting in 1807; by the end of the century it was being replaced by electricity.

It is hard to think of the Victorian age without the image of gaslight and the shadows it cast. The Victorians' vocabulary included such smart new phrases as "cooking with gas." The "gashouse gang" and the gas works were synonymous with the roughest and toughest part of town. Robert Louis Stevenson's lamplighter was a familiar figure in every town. So was the inspector who used to walk the late night streets to see that no gas lamps shone from the windows after a given hour, since home owners were charged at first not by meter, but by the number of outlets they possessed.

The first commercial use of gas occurred in 1802 when a Scottish engineer named William Murdoch, who had already lit his own house by means of a system of small gas pipes, illuminated the famous factory of James Watt, cradle of the eighteenth-century industrial revolution.

The first gas mains ever put down in a public street were pipes made of sheet lead laid by a German named Frederic Albert Winsor from Haymarket to St. James Street in London in 1806. In the following year Winsor lit up Pall Mall.

In 1817 Baltimore became the first city in the new world to light its streets with gas. Over the following generation the cities of Europe and North America became new environments by night. Little island areas of perpetual day glowed from every street corner in the heart of town. The era of curfew and torchlight was coming to a close. Among the products of progress and gaslight one might include the modern city police force. The British Home Secretary Sir Robert Peel's bobbies date from the same period as the London and Westminister Gas, Lighting and Coke Company, the first of its kind in the world. Though Jack the Ripper was never caught, the police patrolling the city streets at night left them no longer the free domain of footpad and criminal. Inside the homes of the more well-to-do, soon emulated by great numbers of the populace, the gas brackets flared in the family parlour. In the House of Commons, the candlelight era of Walpole and the Pitts gave way to the gaslit debates of Disraeli and Gladstone. Other products of the new age were explosions and fires and asphyxiations, and, until methods were found for reducing sulphur content, a nauseous smell emitting from the bracket's blue flame. Perhaps the most elusive effect of the gaslight era, but one of the most profound, was the new quality of light in which all man's seeing was bathed at night – the character of the flame and of the shadows cast in Victorian streets and shops, factories and homes.

Montreal was the first colonial town to build a gas works – in 1836, just in time to light the streets before Papineau's rebellion the following year. Canada's first incorporated city, St. John, New Brunswick, along with Halifax and the smaller, recently renamed city of Toronto in the far western interior of British North America, all followed Montreal's example early in the 1840s. By the time of Confederation in 1867, the homes and squares and taverns of over a dozen Canadian towns were lit by gas. By the end of the century, thanks to the ingenuity of American and Canadian inventors, many other uses had been found for manufactured gas, chiefly in home heating and cooking, and as early as 1887, in refrigeration. In 1898 Crane's of New York advertised such ornate conveniences and status symbols as gas griddles, gas irons, gas signs, gas crematories, gas plate warmers, gas radiators and every variety of gas stove from those used for soldering to those for making candy, stewing oysters, or warming feet. Every elegant twist of gooseneck and socket conceivable to the Victorian imagination had been conceived. And manufactured. And advertised, purchased, and *appreciated*. O gas! O progress!

Man's discovery of gas made from coal is relatively recent. It goes back only a couple of centuries before the first commercial use of the fuel. The father of modern chemistry, Robert Boyle, experimented with coal gas in the seventeenth century. The first record of it in English is said to be that of an Anglican priest some ten years after the founding of the Royal Society of London in 1660. Being interested in all forms of knowledge, but, unlike his fellow parsons George Herbert and Robert Herrick, untalented in the writing of verse, the Yorkshire rector John Clayton experimented with and recorded his distillation of the spirit of gas from coal. Later, Clayton met Boyle and told him about his experiment. The first man known to have produced coal gas was the sixteenth-century Flemish alchemist, Jan Van Helmont, who by chance one day among his mysteries and crucibles released an inflammable spirit, or "ghost," from some coal he was distilling. The origin of the word itself is variously ascribed to the Germanic *geist*, and to the Greek word χαos (chaos) meaning *a gaping void*. The Greek word when pronounced properly makes the sound of escaping and burning gas.

Like coal gas, natural gas is also a hydrocarbon. Its ultimate source is the life of the earth's primeval seas – myriads of tiny one-celled animals, algae and other marine creatures, which settled as they died, and decayed into the ooze of the ocean floor. As the earth's crust shrank and cooled and cracked, layers of this organic matter were trapped into pockets and domes of rock and under enormous pressure transformed into petroleum and natural gas. The waters moved over the earth, the younger mountains rose, and when the ocean which once covered the Canadian prairie receded for the last time, there was left a vast sedimentary basin of this buried treasure, bounded by the Rockies on the west and the Precambrian Shield on the east from the Mackenzie delta down to Lake Winnipeg. The same process took place in many of the other prairies and deserts of the world.

The record of man's first knowledge and experience of natural gas is lost in prehistoric time. Escaping from a rift in the earth's sur-face, burning sometimes in tall columns with tremendous flame and noise, sometimes gently hovering over rock fissures or spring waters, river or lake, natural gas has inspired more than one religious cult. In recorded annals, there was near the Caspian Sea a giant column of fire, reported to be as tall as a mountain, which travellers visited in the tenth century A.D. Some historians have connected burning gas in that region with the religion of Zoroaster or the Parsee worship of fire. Pilgrims to the Greek oracle of Delphi were supposed to have inhaled gas to make them light-headed and inspired.

The first record of natural gas used for a practical purpose occurs in ancient China and Japan. The Japanese word *kaza-kusodzu*, like the western words *gas* and *geist* and *chaos*, corresponds to the sound of the escaping and burning substance. The Chinese drilled wells in search of it and used to run it in bamboo pipes short distances to supply heat and light. The Byzantine emperor used natural gas liquids, probably naphtha, in the manufacture of Greek fire, the famous secret weapon of his day that helped maintain the military ascendancy of the Golden Horn and make Constantinople the world's greatest trading city of its time. There are records of a burning fountain in Caesar's time in Roman Gaul, and of natural gas being used in medieval Genoa.

In the new world the presence of a burning spring was recorded by Thomas Jefferson in his *Notes on Virginia*, at a spot on the Kanawha River, where it was seen by George Washington in 1775. The earliest historical record of the practical use of natural gas in the new world may well be that made by Governor Simcoe in Upper Canada, when he wrote on November 10, 1794, after visiting Niagara Falls that "among many other natural curiosities, a spring about two miles above the falls attracts the attention of the curious – emitting a gas or inflammable air which, confined in a pipe and flame applied to it, will boil the water of a tea kettle in fifteen minutes."

Most of the early glimpses of natural gas in North America, like those of General Washington and Governor Simcoe, seem to have occurred somewhere on the western slopes of the Appalachians or near their northern reaches, particularly in western New York and Pennsylvania. It was in the little town of Fredonia, New York, that, according to the famous scientist Alexander Von Humboldt, the eighth wonder of the world was to be found. From the 1820s Fredonia's lighting was done not by manufactured but by natural gas, fed from a twenty-seven foot well and carried through town in a one and a half inch lead pipe. When the American and French Revolutionary hero, General LaFayette, passed through Fredonia on his triumphal tour of the United States and Canada a crowd gathered to greet him in the old hotel which was entirely illuminated by natural gas. The general remarked that he had "better get away from [the] place . . . as it was evidently too near to Hades." Scientists and professional men and curiosity seekers came from all over the world to see the illumination of Fredonia, "unparalled on the face of the globe."

In Canada the first commercial use of natural gas appeared in Trois Rivières, Quebec. A newly arrived Scotsman named McDougall was impressed with stories about a gas that farmers mined in the area, and in 1853 he won a contract from the City Council to light the streets. His fifteen miles of cast iron pipe formed the first natural gas line in Canada and probably the longest in existence anywhere. Reserves became depleted about the time electricity came in, and a young native of the district named Maurice Duplessis recalled how local people lost money on natural gas – one reason he remained sceptical of plans fifty years later to bring it to Quebec from Alberta.

The use of natural gas remained peculiar to Trois Rivières and Fredonia until the dramatic arrival of the petroleum age in the 1860s. The sinking of the world's first commercial oil well occurred at Oil Springs, Ontario, in 1858. It was followed in 1859 by the more famous well of Colonel Drake at Titusville, Pennsylvania, and a host of others in western Pennsylvania, New York and Ohio during the next decade. The world's first oil pipeline was built between Petrolia and Sarnia, Ontario, in 1862. Natural gas was found in these areas in large quantities associated with the oil. In most cases it was now regarded as a nuisance. It was usually burnt off as expeditiously as possible. Even if short pipelines could be constructed for some local industrial use, heavy leakage and danger were taken for granted. However by the 1870s natural gas was being used in the manufacture of iron and steel and pottery in factories close to its source. In some towns natural gas was beginning to compete with coal as a source of home heating.

The first major commercial gas well in Canada was brought into production in Essex County, Ontario, by Eugene Coste in 1889. As technology improved, however, it gradually became possible to construct longer and larger pipelines which leaked less, and so to bring gas to larger industrial areas around the lower Great Lakes. The first Canadian gas export was made from Welland County in 1891. Later in the decade gas was also exported from Essex County wells in southwestern Ontario in a large, eight-inch pipeline under the Detroit River. Some of these Ontario fields soon showed signs of depletion and their chief value since has been in the storage of gas piped in from larger fields. The world's first successful underground storage of natural gas took place in Welland County in 1915. In 1907 the export of natural gas and electricity from Canada was placed under licence restriction. As it turned out, southwestern Ontario did not possess a great source of natural gas. But the history of natural gas in Alberta was a different story.

The first discovery in Alberta was made by accident. In 1883 in the little town site named for Cartier's colleague Hector Langevin, and now known as Alderson, a Canadian Pacific Railway construction crew was drilling for water to supply a stationary tank to feed their wood-burning locomotives. Down past a thousand feet, much to their annoyance, they hit not water but gas. They repeated the exasperating performance at a second site the following year.

In Medicine Hat thirty miles to the southeast, when crews found gas in 1890 during their search for coal, a small gas well was kept open and its product used commercially. In 1904 the Medicine Hat field was drilled systematically to supply the city with fuel for heating and industry and street lighting. The city's lights were left burning day and night, since it was cheaper to do so than hire someone to turn them off and on. It was these lights that prompted Rudyard Kipling during his visit there to compare the city to the infernal regions. During the western land boom of 1912, some real estate promoters laid out a town site near Medicine Hat, advertising it widely and promising natural gas almost free of charge. A rolling mill and some brick and glass plants were constructed, but the town was practically blown down by a sandstorm. Medicine Hat remained the premier gas city of Alberta.

In 1911 Calgary formed a public utility company to drill systematically in the area of Bow Island where the CPR had again hit gas. Soon there was enough to justify building a 180-mile pipeline into Calgary. The Canadian Western Natural Gas Light Heat and Power Company possessed the longest sixteen-inch pipeline in the world in 1912, and Calgary has had a good supply ever since. Again it was a breakthrough in pipeline technology, first exhibited in the successful completion of the slightly smaller gauge 183-mile line into Cincinnati in 1909, that made possible the supplying of a large Canadian city with natural gas.

Canada's first major gas and oil field was discovered in the Turner Valley in southern Alberta on January 26, 1913. For the next thirty-four years until Imperial Leduc #1 blew in just south of Edmonton, Turner Valley was the heart of the Canadian petroleum industry. Drilling there began when a rancher named William Herron noticed gas seeping out of a creek near a mine from which he used to haul coal. He persuaded a couple of Calgary businessmen to come with him to the spot, lit the gas coming out of a fissure in the rock with a match, produced a frying pan and fried some eggs. The businessmen promptly formed a company and began drilling. The wild excitement that followed in Calgary when this little company blew in a large well of wet gas in May 1914 may have won and lost as many fortunes as the Klondike gold rush. Thousands of paper shares and certificates were bought and sold. The Palliser Hotel which opened a few weeks later was jammed with fortune hunters. The Calgary *Herald* recalled that a list of regulations was posted in the hotel lobby which included such items as "Number 1: No well shall be drilled before 6 a.m. or after 3 p.m. Operations at that time are liable to disturb paying guests while in the midst of beautiful dreams of vast wealth and permanent gushers" and "Number 2: No more than one well shall be drilled in each leather chair or sofa during one time interval. It is exhausting to the furniture."

The next important discovery of gas and oil in the Turner Valley occurred in 1924, after Imperial Oil had taken over the company formed in 1913. The driller had just received orders from head office to stop but he decided to continue for several hours to finish the shift. A few moments later he hit a tremendous heave and burst of pressure. Royalite #4, as it was called, spewed out gas that could not be controlled for three weeks. Part of the time it was on fire, burning ten days out of control before being extinguished.

"The coming in of this well set off a chain reaction of drilling," Eric Hanson has written. "Dozens of rigs churned up the rolling countryside. More than two hundred wells were drilled in the next twelve years, mainly in search of naphtha," which was the chief high-grade product discovered in Royalite #4. In order to get the liquid naphtha, large quantities of natural gas, for which there was little market, were burned off. Observers reported that "the flames could often be seen in Calgary thirty miles away. The flares burned night and day and turned the country into a Hell's Half Acre, a yawning chasm that spouted flames for fourteen years." In 1938 Alberta established a Conservation Board with enough legal powers to force operators to produce naphtha and crude oil in an orderly fashion. "Until that time," Hanson continues, "it was difficult to persuade small independent operators to adopt scientific methods of production used by the larger companies. These latter had difficulty in applying such methods to their own properties since oil and gas are migratory and come to the surface in whatever holes are drilled in the field." Independent operators trying to get their money back in a short time drilled as many wells as quickly as possible. The result was that an old timer can recall "hunting rabbits at mid-night by the light of flares. Flowers bloomed the year round and during the depression homeless unemployed men huddled beside the fires' warmth in winter." It is estimated in the 1930s that one trillion cubic feet of gas were wasted in the Turner Valley, enough to have supplied all the energy needs of central Canada from Confederation until then.

The last and greatest of the Turner Valley booms arrived on June 16, 1936, when a very deep well was drilled as the result of the persistent efforts of R. A. Brown, founder of Home Oil Company, which was later to become the largest shareholder in Trans-Canada Pipe Lines. And again, gas was an unwanted by-product.

By the 1930s, however, pipeline technology had once more leapt ahead. The first 1,000-mile line was built from Texas and Oklahoma up to Chicago in 1930-31. Might not Alberta gas someday be piped to industrial centres of the east? Was it conceivable that the appalling waste of energy would continue? These were the questions put by the flaring night sky of Calgary.

Chapter 2 Rivals in the West

In 1931 a new Canadian who had given the better part of his professional life to working in his adopted country sat down to write a letter to Premier Brownlee of Alberta. He was a Belgian mining engineer named Jan Bilterijst who had come out to help mine coal in the Rockies. He wrote to say that the amount of natural gas wasted in the Turner Valley was sufficient to replace all the domestic fuels presently used in Ontario and Quebec. He was excited as he prophesied the building of a pipeline across Canada. His letter outlined in detail a practical plan for building it and making it economically feasible. He calculated that the gas reserves in Alberta were far higher than the three trillion cubic feet then considered to be proven. His analysis showed gas could be brought to Ontario for 30¢ per thousand cubic feet (mcf.) — a competitive price at that time, and in today's currency three or four times higher than that at which Alberta natural gas actually came east in 1958. He pointed out that the whole operation could be made efficient by storing the summer's surplus of gas in southwestern Ontario's depleted gas fields. The pioneering of this practice after all had begun in Ontario.

Bilterijst's scheme could be dismissed by sober and responsible Canadians as the product of an overheated imagination. Nevertheless the engineering of a trans-Canada pipeline was within the realm of possibility. Though its terrain presented few of the problems of the Canadian Shield, the line built from Texas to Chicago in 1931 did inaugurate the long distance transmission of natural gas. Bilterijst advocated public ownership of his pipeline, pointing to Ontario Hydro as a good example of the publicly owned utility, as opposed to the many competing private utilities in the United States which appeared to be more interested in means of fighting of government regulations or their rivals than in serving their customers or the public good.

Twenty years later Bilterijst sent a copy of his 1931 letter to the Prime Ministers of Canada and Ontario, Louis St. Laurent and Leslie Frost. His covering note proposed that the idea was now ripe for execution and that a single crown corporation – one big service rather than two or three rivals, as in the example of the transcontinental Canadian railways, would be the best way to build the line. By then both Frost and St. Laurent's general manager of the economy C. D. Howe were becoming interested in the possibility of using governmental aid and pressure to bring Alberta gas to Ontario by means of a single company. But the only reply Bilterijst received came from Ontario's Minister of Mines, who predicted that it would be five to ten years before Alberta gas reserves would be large enough to supply Ontario's needs.

A good deal happened to technology in the twenty years between the writing of these two letters. New methods of welding, strengthening and coating large-diameter pipe against high pressure and corrosion had been discovered. Pipelines had been run under water and over mountains, through muskeg and swamp. By the end of World War II it did seem feasible to build a line from Alberta to central Canada large enough to make the whole operation economically viable. The first Texas gas reached California in 1945. In 1948 the American Federal Power Commission (FPC) authorized a 1830-mile, 30-inch line, the longest and largest ever, from the Gulf states to New York City.

World War II made it clear that pipelines were to be one of the great public carriers of the future. The Big Inch and the Little Big Inch oil pipelines in the United States, and the Canol pipelines from Norman Wells, North West Territories, to Alaska had compensated for the critical shortage of shipping and the vulnerability of tankers to enemy submarines. Engineers were already thinking ahead to the transportation of solids. Soon it would be cheaper to send many materials, especially minerals, in a flux through pipelines than to ship them by rail or even by river barge or lake boat. Besides being a new and sophisticated form of transportation, the pipeline is also a very basic one, more primitive in a sense than the wheeled cart. The ultimate model is that of the ducts and arteries of the human body. One of the great symbols of Roman imperial glory was the aqueducts. Modern adaptations include pipelines for beer and sugar, and in the Valais region of Switzerland, a seven-mile plastic pipe from the Sanetsch Pass above the Rhone Valley which sends seven hundred gallons of milk a day from the cows up in their Alpine summer pastures to the creameries and cheese factories below.

As for piping natural gas from the field to centres of population, the post-war era in North America made the advantages of this fuel increasingly apparent wherever it was available. In contrast to other fossil fuels like coal and oil it requires no storing and no handling by the consumer; there is automatic delivery; its supply is independent of the weather; and there is no problem of dirt or smell. It could be one of the most important means of solving the problem of urban air pollution. Its flow can be regulated so exactly that natural gas is now deemed essential in many industries like glass-making which require extremely precise heat measurements. As with airplane accidents, its potential as a killer has been dramatized by such terrible incidents as the explosion of a school in East London, Texas, in 1937, when nearly four hundred children and teachers were killed. Yet statistically, compared to the death toll on the highways and in homes burned down by faulty stoves or overloaded wiring, the danger of natural gas is infinitesimal.

The advantages of gas as a fuel were as readily apparent in central Canada as anywhere in the world. The problem was to get enough of it, and at competitive prices. Ontario suffered a critical fuel shortage during World War II and afterwards. The Ontario Hydro system had been forced, for lack of new sources of water power and American coal, to ration electricity. In 1945 there was also a clamour in northern New York to keep all the precious American gas available in the United States and not export it.

Then in 1947 Imperial Leduc #1 south of Edmonton blew into operation as a commercial oil well. Leduc's development and that of the richer Redwater field clearly established Alberta as one of the

world's major sources of oil and gas. There were quantities far out-
stripping the imagination of the excited explorers of the Turner
Valley back in the twenties or thirties. Few fields the size of Leduc
or Redwater were being discovered in the United States any more or
could be expected in the future.

In the short run, gas again became a nuisance. No one in the first
couple of years after Leduc was even looking for it, because the means
of transport and the export market were not clearly established.
There were times when, if you hit sour gas — gas with sulphur in it,
unsuitable to immediate local consumption – there was nothing for
it but to go out and get drunk. But there were also potential advantages for big companies planning large and expensive exploration. If
they missed oil they might find gas. Or they might make a marginal
operation profitable on the gas they found associated with their oil
discoveries. Furthermore, if enough capital could be invested in ex-
ploiting it, the sour gas, through its sulphur by-product, could be the
foundation of a chemical industry.

What was needed now was someone to take hold of a plan for
collecting and processing the gas and piping it to a potential market.
If that could be done the oil companies would no longer have to cap
their gas discoveries.

Between 1947 and 1949 the five chief promoters seriously interested in piping Alberta gas to markets arrived on the scene. The
most obvious big market outside the province was the west coast.
The northwestern United States was the last major industrial area
in that country without a supply of natural gas. With the Pacific
War just finished and the Cold War begun, the United States was
particularly conscious of another possible fuel shortage there. Greater
Vancouver was the third largest metropolitan area in Canada. And
there would be such benefits on the way as supplying the great
smelter at Trail, British Columbia. So the first proposal by a New
York engineer named Faison Dixon was, logically enough, to bring
southern Alberta gas through Washington and Oregon with branch
lines up to lower British Columbia. The Canadian oil promoter
Frank McMahon also wanted to bring gas west, but he proposed a
longer line, from the Peace River district of northern Alberta and
British Columbia down to Vancouver and eventually from there to
the state of Washington. Though he had to get American permission

for the latter, and the financeability of his line appeared to depend on this, McMahon had the advantage of being a Canadian and of possessing a gas supply which was not immediately adjacent to the heavily populated centres of Alberta. Local resistance to the export of gas, until there was certainty of sufficient supplies for home consumption, was to be an important factor in the history of pipelining in Canada.

A third promoter, the Texas pipeliner Ray Fish, developed a plan similar to Dixon's, except that he planned to supplement it with a line from his own area in Texas up to the Pacific Northwest and eventually to link the whole of the west coast in a single system from northern Alberta down through Vancouver into California. He later added to his proposal a scheme for supplying gas to Ontario from Texas so that the difficult long route across Canada could be avoided and the then apparently limited supply of Alberta gas could be dedicated to west coast markets. Thus the last two industrial areas in North America without natural gas would both be served at once. Fish paid a visit to C. D. Howe and gave him the results of an engineering study he had commissioned showing that an east-west pipeline across Canada would be prohibitively expensive.

The other two serious applicants for a permit to export gas from Alberta were Western Pipe Lines and Clint Murchison's Canadian Delhi Oil Company, the two groups who were eventually forced into the shotgun marriage by C. D. Howe in January of 1954.

In 1948, as a result of the recent oil and gas discoveries, Alberta appointed the Dinning Royal Commission to help establish ground rules under which oil and gas might be gathered and exported from the province. The commission's report in 1949 contained no firm recommendations for export because it was not convinced that proven reserves were high enough for the future needs of Alberta as yet. However, in July 1949 the Alberta government authorized its Conservation Board to hear export applications from promoters. In its interim report of January 1951 the board came up with an excessively cautious estimate of 4.6 trillion cubic feet as the proven reserves of the province. Since this was not much larger than the thirty years' supply of gas Alberta was thought to need, the board recommended that no export permits be granted for the time being. The oil companies and the pipeline promoters were bitterly disappointed. The chief incentive to more exploration and the discovery of proven reserves was the prospect of a market outside Alberta. However the applicants were invited to return to the board before its final report was made, and to spend 1951 in exploring so that reserves could be built up to a point well beyond Alberta's projected future needs.

The caution of Premier Manning and his board can only be understood in terms of the role of natural gas in Alberta's history. From the beginning most Albertans who lived in towns and villages were able to count on an abundant supply of fuel at next to nothing. Though they lived in one of the coldest winter climates in the world, a farm family could expect to heat their homes and their water, do their cooking and keep the barn warm, for about sixty dollars a year. The price Albertans were paying for gas around 1950 was the equivalent of coal at about one dollar per ton. In districts where a major gas line was close, farmers were in the habit of simply going over to the line and hooking it in to their barn. Some of them managed to blow their heads off or burn their buildings down, but the right to a free fuel supply in many rural areas was considered as natural as the right of an American pioneer to carry his own gun and use it if molested.

Farm wives had 120-foot water wells around Camrose where the soil was so saturated with gas that if a match was applied to the hot water tap when it was turned on, it would immediately light up. Children skating on the South Saskatchewan River in winter noticed places where the natural gas bubbled up through the winter ice; they could light a fire and warm themselves before returning home. In the towns, seepage from gas mains frequently would poison a tree or a plot or blow up a basement. But gas kept the street lights on and the barn warm and the house cheerful. The vast caverns of natural gas beneath the farm or the thousands of cubic feet running by in a pipe was part of the everyday life and folklore of Alberta. God had put it there for the enjoyment of His people. Woe betide the politician who sold such a birthright. It would be a hardy man indeed who would risk exporting Alberta gas without a sure supply for the future.

In case Premier Manning and his Social Credit government needed any guidance in the matter, the Edmonton Chamber of Commerce in 1950 issued a brief demanding that all export of gas be deferred for five years. The Council of High River, home town of Alberta sage W. O. Mitchell, passed a resolution against export under any circumstances, until all the farms and small villages of the provinces still without gas had been supplied. It was of little concern to them that such individual supply to isolated consumers, far from major gas lines or wells, was wildly uneconomical. It would have been far cheaper to hand out more Social Credit payments all round on the profits of exported gas.

On top of all this, something of the depression mentality still lingered on: the Canadian west was hit harder than any other place in the world during the dirty thirties. Furthermore, there were plenty of powerful rivals to the pipeline promoters who would be happy to see any scheme for moving a rival fuel by rival means of transport stopped dead. The Western Canadian Coal Operators Association, for example, claimed that some two thousand miners would be thrown out of work. It was estimated that Canadian railways would lose seven million dollars a year in freight revenue. Various experts were brought in with dire warnings about Alberta losing a new chemical industry if its precious fuel were allowed to be exported to the United States or to other parts of Canada. This last argument ignored one of the petroleum companies' strongest pleas: that it was precisely a market for dry gas that was needed in order to justify the removal of the sulphur from sour gas and establish chemical plants in Alberta.

As it turned out, there was something to be said for the extreme caution of the Conservation Board's estimates. In the early fifties the greatest gas field was considered to be Pincher Creek, owned by the Gulf Oil Company. Gulf was one of those who protested most bitterly when the chance to sell Pincher Creek gas to the American northwest was denied in 1951 and the company threatened to abandon its plans to spend over a third of a billion dollars in Alberta during the next decade. Pincher Creek has not been found to have the vast reserves that were once considered proven. Nevertheless, the Conservation Board's estimates of the province's total reserves did turn out to be far more cautious than even their most extravagant critics thought possible in 1951. Within a decade and a half proven reserves were ten times the 1951 estimate.

If there was pressure on the Alberta government to go slow on the export of gas, for fear of offending the home consumer, there was also pressure for immediate action from other sources besides the interested promoters and petroleum companies. On September 16, 1950, some two months after the outbreak of the Korean War, the Minister of Trade and Commerce, C. D. Howe, wrote to Eldon Tanner, Alberta's Minister of Mines and Resources, "The U.S. Munitions Board is very concerned at the lack of fuel in the Pacific North West because of the wartime industrial growth in that region and the diversion of oil to the Far East." Howe went on to point out that if Alberta gas was not made available, the American government would see to it that the Pacific Northwest was supplied from Texas. In fact, an application for a pipeline from there had already been filed with the Federal Power Commission. "I see little prospect of an Alberta line to Vancouver unless the Canadian line is extended into the United States. There is great urgency for a decision. I hope you will decide soon. I will see to it that the Board of Transport Commissioners settles on an application for export quickly. Time is of the essence." Unless there was action soon the most obvious market for Alberta gas could be permanently lost.

Tanner passed Howe's letter along to the head of the Alberta Conservation Board, Ian McKinnon. "The attached letter from C. D. Howe is self-explanatory," he wrote. "The Executive Council has directed me to ask your board to do everything possible to determine proven reserves and advise whether a surplus is available for export. I have told Mr. Howe this and explained to him this government's policy." Tanner then quoted from Premier Manning's budget address in which he said that it was provincial policy to "serve the needs of Alberta first and then to treat each application on its merits, Canadian requirements being given the next priority."

The Conservation Board's 1952 report estimated that by the end of 1951 the gas reserves of Alberta had increased to 6.8 trillion cubic feet from the 4.7 of its interim report in the previous year. The government decided that while there was still not enough gas in the fields near Edmonton and Calgary to guarantee a future thirty-year supply, there was a surplus in the Peace River district.

The first important gas export permit was therefore granted to Frank McMahon and his Westcoast Transmission to pipe gas from northern Alberta down to Vancouver and the U.S. border. The other applicants were invited to apply again. McMahon's two American rivals were dealt a decisive blow by this decision, since they had proposed to bring gas into the Pacific Northwest from southern rather than northern Alberta. McMahon still had to win permission from the U.S. Federal Power Commission, however, in order to bring gas across the border into the United States and so make his line to Vancouver economically feasible. There is some indication of the future hazards Trans-Canada was to encounter with the American authorities in the fact that McMahon, after receiving the Alberta permit, followed by an export licence from Ottawa, had only just begun a two-year struggle in Washington, at the end of which his application was refused. The FPC approved instead an application by Ray Fish to build a line all the way from Texas to Seattle. It was 1957 — six years after the original application — before Westcoast Transmission moved its first gas to Vancouver and thence into the United States. Even then it was only possible because McMahon and his American rival had arranged to co-operate on a deal by which a network of north-south pipelines was established for the Pacific coast.

After 1952 the main conflict in Alberta lay between the two rivals competing for a licence to move even larger quantities of gas east to Toronto and Montreal or to the American mid-west. The struggle was bitter and the barriers they encountered more formidable than either of them had expected.

Already, as it turned out, Alberta's failure to act more positively and promptly on export eastwards had left its mark on the future. It meant that pipeline construction was to be postponed beyond the days of low cost labour and material, and cheap interest rates. It may have meant that the last chance to finance an all-Canadian line without government help and public controversy had already vanished.

Chapter 3 The Sleeping Dragon

Older many times over than the swarm of primitive animal life whose buried remains have been transformed into the natural gas laid down under the prairies and the foothills of the younger mountains, the world's most ancient rock divides Canada in two. The fertile, populated regions of Canada are sundered by the enormous barrier of the Laurentian Shield. The breadth of this barren wilderness has always defied Canadians to make a single country of east and west. Northern Ontario is over twenty-four hours journey across by fast train, the distance of five inland seas themselves as unique on the earth's face as the vast Shield that touches their northern rim. The bridging of the Shield's wilderness has been one of the central recurring themes of Canadian history: the hard portages of the Nor'-westers bringing their fur-laden canoes east to Montreal; Wolseley's rabidly loyal Ontario volunteers trekking through the long summer of 1870 to put down the Riel rebellion; the heroic drive of Van Horne and the Canadian Pacific construction crews – the muskeg swallowing locomotives, the nitro-glycerine mutilating men's bodies (in those days before the safety of dynamite) as they blasted their way through the solid rock. There are railway travellers who can still recall seeing bleak clusters of white crosses near Marathon and Jackfish Bay: that roadbed along parts of the Superior shore cost more than one dead man per mile.

The finest business history written in Canada, as well as one of the few great narrative poems of the twentieth century, is E. J. Pratt's epic about the CPR, *Towards the Last Spike*. Pratt sees the Shield as a mythical monster: "On the North Shore a reptile lay asleep – . . . /Whose tail covered Labrador and swished/Atlantic tides, whose body coiled itself/Around Hudson Bay . . . /The neck went past Great Bear Lake until/Its head was hidden in the Arctic Seas. . . ./Her back grown stronger every million years. . ." "She was too old for death, too old for life/For as if jealous of all living forms/She had lain there before bivalves began/To catacomb their shells on western mountains." Pratt's epic heroes are not merely the men who risk their lives to claw their way across the monster's back, but those who conceive the possibility of defeating its challenge to human possibility, and who, against all odds, derision, sense and profit, persist until they have won, and out of their victory built a nation.

By mid-twentieth century the Shield had lost some of its terrors. Thanks to the railways and the mining boom, hydro-electric power and spread of forest industries, isolated pockets of northern Ontario were populated and productive. But the vast extent of it was still a wilderness – "all those damn Christmas trees and black flies." It was still rugged terrain for any mode of transport except non-stop airplane. For the new bulk carrier of the post-modern age, the pipeline, it was the worst territory in the world. Its myriad lakes and muskeg and rock presented a problem far tougher to a pipeline construction crew than the highest passes of the Rockies. Canada's first oil pipeline to the east from Alberta avoided the problem by cutting south of the Great Lakes through Michigan to Sarnia.

In one sense, an oil pipeline is different – rather more like an endless series of railway tank cars than like a pipeline for natural gas. If necessary it can be moved in sections and used again elsewhere, as was Canol's line from Norman Wells, N.W.T., after World War II. The commitment of gas to a certain route, however, is, because the attached consumer market depends upon it, similar to the commitment of hydro-electric power, and hence permanent. Its export has long been treated similarly by Canadian law.

Northern Ontario presented another serious problem for natural gas besides rough terrain, namely, the sparseness of population and industry over hundreds of miles of its route. The quantity of consumers who could be counted to make an American pipeline economically feasible by purchasing gas along the way simply did not exist in that part of Canada. To add to these difficulties the Trans-Canada Highway was still just a gravel road in places, and the service roads from the highway to any prospective pipeline route would almost all have to be carved out of the virgin wilderness.

During the early 1950s, amid the surrounding rhetoric of stormy controversy, and at the hurricane's eye – the mind of Clarence Decatur Howe – the idea of building an all-Canadian natural gas pipeline became associated with the precedent of the Canadian Pacific Railway. In some minds, the line was a means as vital for the building up of this east-west continental nation in the twentieth century as the Pacific railway had been in the nineteenth; and it was equally important that it be built entirely on Canadian soil. For many reasons — such as the history of North American western settlement; the relative power of the British Empire and its navy *vis-à-vis* the United States; the direct military value of a railway as opposed to a pipeline; and Canada's stage of economic development in the 1950s as opposed to the 1880s — the analogy is not really a sound one.

And yet the parallels are still remarkable. There are still some ways in which history does seem to repeat itself. The pipeline, like the railroad, was the great new means of transport of its day. It did promise to link the raw materials of the west with the consumers and manufacturers of the east. It could only in the end be financed with government assistance, because northern Ontario presented such a great physical and financial obstacle. The capitalists who went into the enterprise to make money ended up with an operation which most wise men predicted would never pay – "a pipedream not a pipe line," as one critic put it. In the end the pipeline became for its backers a matter of pride and honour beyond all rational economic sense: a test of their own willingness to survive an ordeal, a symbol of their ability to triumph over doubts and difficulties, an act of faith in progress or Canada or whatever sub-deity lured them on.

I doubt if anyone will try to celebrate the Texas geologist Frank Schultz or the Montreal financier Deane Nesbitt and their associates the way Ned Pratt wrote of the Montreal banker George Stephen or the American railroader William Van Horne – despite the fact that their skill and tenacity in Trans-Canada's enterprise never made them rich or honoured as the CPR eventually made its builders. But their situations do invite a comparison – just as it is possible to argue that without the personal commitment of two stubborn politicians, John A. Macdonald and C. D. Howe, in the face of heartbreaking difficulties and delays, the two great enterprises would never have been completed at all. Finally, there is an interesting analogy in parliamentary history. Just as there was a storm in Parliament over the first attempt at the Pacific railroad in 1873, followed by defeat of the government, so too there came another storm in 1956 and a government defeat the year after the great pipeline debate.

The first business man to take seriously the idea of a pipeline to bring Alberta natural gas to the industrial markets of the Canadian east was L. D. M. Baxter, president of the leading Winnipeg financial firm, Osler, Hammond and Nanton, a western outgrowth of that family whose many famous members have played such a large role in Canadian history. The Leduc oil discoveries in 1947 made it clear that there was also a tremendous potential supply of natural gas in Alberta even if reserves could not immediately be proven and established.

Baxter however had not long examined the proposition of an Alberta-to-Montreal pipeline before deciding that the Laurentian Shield would make it impossible to finance. Accordingly he settled for a more immediately viable project, that of bringing the new energy source to Winnipeg and intervening points on the prairies, and then running a line south from Winnipeg to the American border, from where gas sales could be made to Minnesota and markets nearby. Since even this project was far beyond the financial scope of the Osler firm, Baxter approached the heads of two large eastern investment firms, Wood, Gundy of Toronto and Nesbitt, Thomson of Montreal. For advice and influence in Alberta he naturally turned to his friend and fellow director of Osler, Hammond, H. R. Milner of Edmonton, who was president of the gas utility firms in Edmonton and Calgary. These four interests formed a company called Western Pipe Lines Limited, which was incorporated on April 30, 1949, by an Act of Parliament under the new federal pipeline legislation. The Osler firm was named manager of the pipeline project. To explore the feasibility of their scheme, Baxter entered into negotiations with the Winnipeg distributor of manufactured gas, along with similar utilities in other smaller cities along the route from Alberta, and with John Merriam, president of Northern Natural Gas of Omaha, one of the major American gas companies in the mid-west. They engaged the services of the leading American engineering firm, Stone and Webster, to study potential markets along the Western Pipe Lines route.

In February 1950 they made formal application to the Alberta Conservation Board for the right to export gas for a thirty-year period from southern Alberta to Winnipeg and from there down to Emerson at the United States border, with certain spur lines along the route. Hearings were not finally concluded until November, and the board's interim report of January 1951, as we have seen, concluded that there was not yet enough proven reserves in the province to meet Alberta's future need, although the board invited Western Pipe Lines and its rivals to apply again.

In the meantime the last of the important applicants seeking to export Alberta gas had arrived on the scene in the person of Clint Murchison of Texas. His branch company, Canadian Delhi, was incorporated in August 1950 and its subsidiary, Trans-Canada Pipe Lines, in April 1951. Murchison immediately became a fierce competitor of the Canadian group who were behind Western Pipe Lines. Canadian Delhi was the first company in Canada which actually sought to explore for natural gas rather than for oil. It had already a considerable history of natural gas exploration in the United States. Its executive vice-president was Frank Schultz, another Texan, with a graduate degree and great experience in oil and gas geology. The most unusual feature of Canadian Delhi and Trans-Canada, however, was that they were the first group that seriously proposed to build an all-Canadian pipeline from Alberta across northern Ontario to Toronto and Montreal.

It seemed obvious at the time that there would be enough surplus reserves in southern Alberta for only one company to export from the province. It would certainly be uneconomic, in any case, to have two parallel pipelines across the Canadian prairies to Winnipeg. On one of Clint Murchison's first trips to Calgary in the late 1940s he had met Ross Tolmie of the Ottawa law firm headed by the Rt. Hon. R. B. Bennett's brother-in-law, W. D. Herridge, which already represented several Calgary oil companies. Murchison proposed the idea of an all-Canadian line to Tolmie and Tolmie suggested that he should talk to C. D. Howe about it. After a meeting was arranged and Murchison had outlined his scheme, Howe remained sceptical.

"Mr. Murchison," he asked, "have you ever travelled over the Canadian shield? I come from there. It is a little more rugged and a lot colder than Texas." Murchison said that the severe climate would be no problem, and since dry gas was not seriously affected by cold, the pipeline could be laid on the surface of the rock. As it turned out later, in fact, the line was buried for protection from surface damage, but it did not have to be insulated.

Howe and Murchison had met briefly and formally at the opening of LaGuardia Field, New York, in 1939, when Murchison was a director of American Airlines and Howe Canada's Minister of Transport. On this later occasion they took an instant liking to each other and their friendship became a major factor in the history of the all-Canadian route from that time on. Murchison's decision to promote an all-Canadian line, without any reliance on export to the United States, was motivated by a desire to do something larger and more difficult than he or anyone else had attempted before, along with a canny sense of what the Canadian political climate was likely to be. He was conscious that as an American his best chance to win the licence for building the line would be to outdo his Canadian rivals, who had been first in the field, in the national and patriotic character of their enterprise. Above all he had a firmer conviction about the future of the new energy source than almost anybody else – especially in Canada. "You Canadians don't know the value of gas," he told Tolmie. "When you do, you won't want to be on the far end of a line from Texas."

Trans-Canada's rival reacted quickly to the threat posed by Murchison's all-Canadian line. Baxter realized that his own more immediately profitable scheme would require not only Alberta permission to export gas from the province but also, to make it financially feasible, federal permission to export gas beyond Alberta and into the United States. He kept western Members of Parliament well informed of Western Pipe Lines' plans. In a form letter to them late in 1951, he mentioned that his firm had concluded a contract with Northern Natural of Omaha, to supply their market area with Canadian gas. And he went on to attack his opposition: "You have no doubt heard of the Trans-Canada pipeline scheme. The objective of this American-sponsored line is an all-Canadian route to the east. But gas delivered to Winnipeg city gates on Western Pipe Lines' calculation averages 27.8¢ per mfc., while the projected price of Trans-Canada's gas is 50¢ per mcf." As they prepared for the bitter struggle to obtain permits from provincial and federal governments that would put one or other of them in business, the two rivals were both confident that their own advantages would win the day.

Western Pipe Lines had been first in the field. Its sponsors were Canadian, including three of the largest investment firms of Toronto, Montreal and Winnipeg. They had in Ray Milner a man who had been involved in the gas business in Alberta since 1911 and whose utility firms supplied the gas for both Calgary and Edmonton. There was clearly an advantage from Alberta's point of view in the more limited and realistic approach of this group. It would likely get a higher price for the Alberta producer and would not saddle him with the forbidding cost of building a line across the Laurentian Shield. On top of this, its contract with the American firm, Northern Natural Gas, looked like the only way to inspire solid confidence in public financing of the pipeline. There was doubt that Canadian sales alone could make the line pay its own way, even as far as Winnipeg.

On the other hand, Trans-Canada's advantages included American contacts and experience in natural gas exploration and pipelining. They were the first group to explore exclusively for gas in western Canada, and besides this expenditure by its parent, Canadian Delhi, Trans-Canada had by 1953 spent over twice as much money as Western Pipe Lines in feasibility studies – on potential markets and on the costs of buying right-of-way and of construction. Their scheme, unlike Western's, did not depend on approval from the Federal Power Commission in Washington for import into the United States. The prospect of submitting to the delays of American lobbies was not one that Canadians could look forward to. Nor did the Canadian experience with the St. Lawrence Seaway – blocked by powerful sectional interests for twenty years in the American Congress – augur well for any agreement that depended on American approval. During and after World War II the province of Ontario had experienced a critical fuel shortage and found it could not rely on an uninterrupted American supply of gas when it was needed inside the United States. By 1952 Premier Leslie Frost had become convinced by the Murchison group that it would be better for Ontario to have a supply of Canadian gas.

Over against this, the Consumers' Gas Company of Toronto, who had links with the Western Pipe Lines' advisory firm, Stone and Webster, were working against an all-Canadian route. They were well aware of the increasingly critical problem of supplying their customers and were planning to support an application before the FPC to bring American gas into Toronto. It would obviously be quicker to build a line from Niagara, eighty miles away, than a line two thousand miles long from Alberta. The institutional investors that largely owned Consumers' were also much happier at the idea of a small addition to an already established line than with the prospect of being dependent on the longest pipeline in the world across unpopulated territory. They were afraid that if Consumers' became dependent on this source it would end up owning the line itself, a potential white elephant. It could be stuck with fuel rates that could not compete with oil, coal and hydro power.

Political sentiment in favour of an all-Canadian pipeline was growing, however. This feeling more and more seemed to be the trump card held by Murchison and Trans-Canada. As early as 1950 certain western Conservatives in the House of Commons, such as Douglas Harkness of Calgary and Howard Green of Vancouver and several members of the CCF party, were speaking out against private bills to incorporate pipeline companies who proposed to build lines through American territory. In April 1950 during the brief periods reserved for private members' bills, there were filibusters to prevent such charters from coming to a vote. In 1950 when a pipeline bill was being presented, Howard Green moved that the Alberta Natural Gas Company be permitted to export gas and oil only in excess of the amount required by consumers in Canada.

Such amendments, if they were voted on, were regularly defeated by the government majority. But in 1951, when Canadian Delhi's subsidiary, Trans-Canada Pipe Lines, was first incorporated, Green tacked a rider onto the bill stating that "the main pipe line or lines shall be located entirely within Canada." The committee could accept this unanimously. The company had never proposed anything else: it was the essence of their policy. This proviso was included in later pipeline bills considered by the committee.

In 1952 Premier Leslie Frost of Ontario used the occasion of the opening of a new oil refinery at Sarnia to introduce the Premier of

Alberta to the federal Minister of Trade and Commerce. Such was the nature of dominion-provincial relations in those days that Manning and Howe had never met, though they had both been important members of their respective governments for seventeen years. Frost was interested in bringing federal pressure and involvement to bear on any project that could move Alberta gas east as quickly as possible to answer Ontario's rising need for new sources of energy.

One may speculate on what the response of Mackenzie King's government might have been to any such concern expressed by an Ontario premier. Frost was in effect seeking federal intervention and arbitration between western producer and eastern consumer, an act which would inevitably risk the anger of either or both parties if the project and its costs did not work out to their satisfaction. Mr. King, the argument runs, would have smelled political dynamite, and politely told the two provincial premiers to negotiate it between themselves with his blessing – just like the medieval king of France, who, when being asked for an urgent supply of troops and money by a Bishop whose castle was besieged by one of the king's barons, replied, "My Lord, you have always aided me with your fervent prayers, I assure you that I shall help you in the same fashion."

But then C. D. Howe was a different sort of politician than Mackenzie King.

Chapter 4 "Our Sort of Folks"

From the vantage point of 1970 it is not easy to recover or even understand the atmosphere of Canadian politics in the long dead past of the early 1950s. The outward calm of prosperity prevailed – the first solid prosperity that most Canadians had ever known. By 1950 the wartime upsurge of political radicalism and militant trade unions was over. The universities were hotbeds of quietism. There were no peace marches and social protesters making headlines. Such rebel clergymen as remained in Canadian politics from the depression had long been safely locked within the bosom of the CCF party, which was itself now a venerable institution on the Canadian scene.

After a quarter century of depression and war and post-war readjustment, Canada was experiencing by far the greatest boom in her history. Neither the dislocation of the Korean War nor the armistice that followed were able to interrupt the upward curve of the Canadian economy as it headed towards the dizzy heights of 1956. Most people seemed to be satisfied with what they had, living in expectation of more of the same, and fearful lest anyone upset the *status quo* and plunge them once again into the nightmares and grim struggles they had lived through in the recent past. Prime Minister St. Laurent seemed somehow more like an elected sovereign than a partisan politician. The government appeared to be not so much large-L Liberal or small-c conservative as simply governmental. It almost looked like Canada had outgrown politics.

As the prospect of the 1953 general election appeared on the horizon, it struck no terror in Liberal hearts. Party leaders were confident that they could, as in the past, override any conceivable combination that opposed them. The Liberal party was firmly ensconced at dead centre of the political spectrum between the extremes of left and right, between the socialists of Saskatchewan and the Social Crediters of Alberta, between the Progressive Conservatives of the prairies in the tradition of Bracken and Diefenbaker and the Tories of Bay Street and small town Ontario led by George Drew. There was a kind of hopelessness and futility about the whole operation of opposing this government in Parliament. Parliament was not the place where things happened. Little had taken place there of great dramatic import to the nation since the constitutional crisis of 1926, when Arthur Meighen and Mackenzie King, like the lion and the unicorn, were battling over the Canadian version of the Crown. Except for persons whose hobby or profession involved watching or participating in its business, there was apparently nothing of compelling interest in the activities of the House of Commons.

In spite of these handicaps the opposition, particularly a few western members of the Conservative and CCF parties, did an effective job of keeping alive the function of constructive opposition to the government. There is a good example in the work of Howard Green and Bert Herridge and their colleagues in the 1952 debate on a private bill to charter the Boundary Pipeline Corporation. The episode was something of a rehearsal for the parliamentary drama of 1956.

The ultimate objective of this corporation was to move southern Alberta gas across the border into lucrative American markets. But since, during the 1951 discussion of Trans-Canada Pipe Lines, the opposition had already attached the precedent-setting clause that required the main route of the newly incorporated pipeline to be located within Canada, Boundary's backers proposed a Canadian line to Winnipeg first. They were given a severe grilling in the House Committee on Railways, Canals and Telegraph Lines, during which serious doubts were expressed about the economic feasibility and the service to Canadians of their proposed line. But two Liberal MP's on the committee simply moved in favour of the incorporation, and the motion was passed against the votes of opposition members.

In the debate which followed Howard Green pointed out that

"the applicants for this present charter have done practically no development work whatever. They are trying to cash in on the efforts of the other companies [Trans-Canada and Western] who have spent several million dollars making surveys of the prospective routes and the centres that would be served and also of the reserves of gas in the province of Alberta. It was admitted, in effect, that all these people were trying to do was to get their toe in the door in Alberta, get permission to put in this small pipe line and in that way be in a preferred position. They admit they plan eventually to pipe gas to the United States and that they have no intention whatever of moving into Ontario and Quebec. Mr. Chairman, there will be only one gas line to the east. If the plans of this Boundary Pipeline Corporation are approved, Ontario and Quebec will get no – and I repeat, No – Canadian gas. They will have to go hat in hand to the United States for gas from Texas.

"Now there has been a tremendous demand for Texas gas in all parts of the United States. Some of their largest cities are not yet served. I have here a judgment of the Federal Power Commission which includes an application for permission to export gas to Canada dated August 31, 1951, which the FPC refused as being inconsistent with American public interest. They have been making similar rulings for some years. Is it any wonder that the governments of Quebec and Ontario want Canadian gas?"

Bert Herridge of the CCF put the case for national ownership of transport systems like the pipeline. But the heart of his speech was an appeal for Canadian gas to be brought east to serve the markets of central Canada as quickly as possible. He pointed out that one company had already received a charter from Parliament for that purpose and that "we would jeopardize the building of that pipeline to Montreal if we were to grant a charter in the bill before us." While the Boundary incorporation was a private bill and not government policy, Liberal members argued for it. Incorporation after all did not mean the right to build. Let all comers be allowed to exist and the best could be licensed when plans matured. The company's parliamentary agent incidentally was Duncan MacTavish, soon to be president of the National Liberal Federation. When it came to a vote, the bill passed the Committee of the Whole by 53 votes to 6. But in spite of being accused by Liberals and *The Financial Post* of indulging in a "ridiculous holdup" on the bill, when it came back to the House, its opponents talked it out, and so prevented it from becoming law in the 1952 session.

Their frustration in seeing Liberal majorities run roughshod over their arguments, without really answering them, helped build up the head of steam that eventually drove the great debate of 1956. It also encouraged the practice of filibuster. As early as 1950 the Prime Minister warned that the answer to "these talking-out tactics" might be the application of the long-neglected closure rule. Ironically, it was the opposition which was in effect putting the case for the Trans-Canada scheme at this time, while in 1956 the same groups called Trans-Canada Howe's "chosen instrument."

Howe on his part, though sympathetic to Clint Murchison and the Trans-Canada scheme, was not yet committed to any particular pipeline route nor had he publicly adopted a definite national policy on the use and export of natural gas. Nevertheless the arguments for Canadians' use of their own natural resources were having an effect on public opinion. Members of the Ontario and Quebec governments spoke out against the idea of being dependent on American supply. Ontario Mines Minister Gemmell said that the Trans-Canada scheme was in the national interest, and that its construction might have to be subsidized in order to ensure that it was built. Even Premier Duplessis said that though he had been approached by Texas gas operators, he preferred to support "a Canadian industry, not subject to a foreign authority."

By late 1952 Howe needed little persuading in favour of a pipeline to the east. The first move was not his, however. The Alberta government and its Conservation Board had yet to authorize the removal of any gas eastwards. And when they were ready to do so, they would have to face Alberta producers who were unhappy about tying themselves to the risks of crossing the Laurentian Shield. Most of them favoured Western Pipe Lines' scheme to export gas at Emerson. But export needed Ottawa's permission. The two governments thus held a veto over each other. There was obviously much political and economic advantage in using their powers jointly for a compromise to promote rapid development. In a letter to Premier Manning on January 2, 1953, Howe took up the argument he had begun at their first meeting:

"In our conversation at Sarnia when Prime Minister Frost was present, I said that the export of gas moving east or south of Alberta could not be authorized until arrangements are made to supply Canadian users in Ontario and Quebec. I am aware that a pipe line from Alberta to Minnesota would be preferable from the outset and that the owner of the pipe line could pay us a substantial price for gas in Alberta. Nevertheless I pointed out that government policy would not permit export unless prior provision is made for serving Ontario and Quebec.

"It seems to me that there may be a plan which would carry both projects while consumption in Canada is being built up. This plan would combine the two projects into one.

"In our telephone discussion this morning you suggested an independent committee to work out a reasonable combination. This would be satisfactory if the sponsors of the two projects agree on the personnel. While neither government would be bound by its findings, I am sure these would help us both. I am well aware that the government of Canada has no immediate concern with this problem but I hope that it will be helpful to you to have its views before a definite decision is taken in Alberta. We have worked in harmony to solve marketing problems associated with oil and gas up to the present and I hope we can continue to do so."

When Parliament met for its 1953 session, the government faced the prospect of more private pipeline bills coming before the House and more opposition filibusters, unless it adopted a definite position – and one that could accommodate the rising sentiment in favour of a Canada-first policy for the future use of Canadian gas. On March 13, 1953, having at least achieved common ground on basic principles with Manning, Howe made a statement to the House of Commons which became the cornerstone of government policy over the next four years.

"We are dealing," he said, "with energy similar in many ways to electrical energy, in that export under conditions that calls for investment in another country obligates Canada to maintain a continuous supply of that energy. Therefore the policy that has governed the export of electrical energy since 1907 must apply, within reason, to the export of natural gas. That policy has paid large dividends to the Canadian economy. Therefore the policy of the government of Canada is to refuse permits for moving natural gas by pipe line across an international boundary until such time as we are convinced that there can be no economic use, present or future, for that natural gas within Canada."

Howe explained that the permission already granted to West-coast Transmission to export gas across the border into the Pacific Northwest had only been given in order to make the pipeline from the Peace River to Vancouver economically feasible. He warned of the dangers of depending on the outcome of rulings by the U.S. Federal Power Commission. He was now convinced that "the only reliable supply of natural gas for the provinces of Ontario and Quebec must be from western Canada by means of an all-Canadian pipe line."

Howe's statement was received with approval, mingled with a note of triumph, as the opposition claimed to welcome him to the cause of Canadian nationalism. One senior Conservative, J. M. Mac-donnell, congratulated Howe and said "it was almost like the return of the Prodigal Son to hear him saying these things." Bert Herridge of the CCF reminded the House of what had been accomplished. "Some four years ago a few of us took a certain stand in connection with an all-Canadian route and at first there was very little interest in it. In fact, some people felt we were a bit dippy. Some of us spoke for hours and hours on private members' evenings much to the an-noyance of some. I am sure that this very small band of members in this group did have an effect on public opinion and government pol-icy out of all proportion to its numbers. I am interested to note that things we suggested at that time, and which were somewhat snickered at, are now of interest to the Canadian people as a whole and are receiving the support of the government."

Thus, apart from some Alberta members who warned against the risk of their province having to subsidize the high cost of a new national policy, "virtual unanimity," as Hugh Thorburn has said, "had been reached in the House on pipe line policy."

The group most immediately disturbed by Howe's statement was Trans-Canada's rival, Western Pipe Lines. Alan Williamson fired off a letter to Howe on March 19, enclosing a feasibility report on the Murchison project by Western's advisers, Stone and Webster. It showed why his group had decided against the attempt to build a line across Canada – at least for the time being. "My own view," he wrote, "is that the report demonstrates that though the Trans-Canada project cannot be financed in the ordinary way, it would not necessarily lose money if it could be built at all. We are anxious to do anything we can about negotiating along the lines you have enunciated from Ottawa, which policy I believe is approved in Ontario and Alberta."

In reply Howe thanked Williamson for the Stone and Webster report and hedged his bets by saying "whenever Alberta decides to release gas for transmission eastwards we will be able to get to grips with the Trans-Canada Pipe Line situation." As for the statement in the House of Commons, "I am hopeful it will stop a lot of waste motion and concentrate the efforts of us all in building a gas line across Canada."

The message was clear enough to Williamson and his group. Though they believed theirs was the only economic plan for moving Alberta gas east in the foreseeable future and though they had support for their view in Alberta, the government of Canada was now firmly committed to the all-Canadian route. Accordingly, to prepare for the next sitting of the Alberta Conservation Board, Western Pipe Lines began amending their scheme in order to plan to extend their main line from Winnipeg to the markets of Ontario and Quebec three years after the first delivery of gas to Manitoba and the American mid-west.

The Trans-Canada group was delighted with Howe's statement. Theirs was the only proposal that conformed in principle to it. Murchison wrote exultantly to a friend in New York who was inquiring about receiving a supply of gas from somewhere along the middle of the Trans-Canada line. He predicted success and estimated that "at some point along the line we might be able to supply you at 32¢."

Powerful confirmation for Murchison's position came through an independent study of an all-Canadian route made for the Imperial Oil Company in 1952 and submitted privately to Howe early the following April. In commissioning the study from the University of Western Ontario Business School and Stanford University Research Institute, Imperial Oil's only instructions were to be completely objective. The company's hope, however, was that some major pipeline project might be built soon in order to provide a source of gas sales and hence an incentive for their own expensive exploration programme. The study showed that an all-Canadian line was economically feasible. As Howe told Murchison, "according to them you can afford to pay Alberta to produce gas at 15¢ per mcf. This looks generous when you are dealing with present world prices and well-head prices in Alberta at 10¢ per mcf." It did prove to be exceedingly generous, since the first contracts eventually signed were at figures under 11¢. But the estimate was what counted at the time.

There were some people, however, who believed that with a general election in the offing in the summer of 1953 the announced policy of an all-Canadian route was still open to change. Perhaps it was only window dressing for the electorate, later to be removed from display and forgotten.

A new contestant who made some such assumption entered the Canadian battle over routes and pipelines. This was the most powerful of all American companies in the field, Tennessee Gas Transmission. Tennessee advanced an opposing scheme with the help and encouragement of a group in Toronto that included Mayor Lamport and Consumers' Gas who were still hoping to bring in American gas at Niagara.

This plan was naturally disturbing to those concerned to build a pipeline across Canada. On March 28, 1953, Howe wrote to Hume Wrong, the Canadian Ambassador in Washington, "I have been asked by Premier Frost to find out the facts as to the Tennessee project and to discourage it, for it would interfere with a satisfactory solution of the Ontario and Alberta problem." On March 30 Hume Wrong replied, "Tennessee Gas is trying to tie in its case with the Westcoast application [for export to Seattle] and it says that even if the Alberta and Ontario pipe line is possible this would preclude the use of Alberta reserves for the supply of the American Pacific Coast."

The danger for Canada lay in the possibility that Tennessee might exert enough pressure in Washington to have Westcoast's application for export dismissed if Tennessee's own request to export at Niagara were opposed in any way by the Canadian government. Murchison's group had already filed a motion asking the FPC to dismiss the Tennessee application on the grounds that Trans-Canada intended to construct a line to supply eastern Canada. Like Premier Frost, they hoped Howe would do what he could to support them. On April 17 the Canadian Ambassador advised Howe that "while we hope the Tennessee Gas application will be refused, since it will delay the Alberta-Toronto pipe line, I do not recommend intervention on your part. I agree with you it could be harmful to the application of Westcoast." On May 5, 1953, Howe told him: "If you can see your way clear informally to indicate to FPC members the Canadian attitude, it would be a helpful step. Mr. Schultz of Trans-Canada Pipe Lines will be in Washington and would like to explain his position to you. I hope you will grant him an interview."

During the spring and summer of 1953, Murchison kept Howe closely informed as to the state of Westcoast's application. On April 9 he told Howe that "the FPC has been sold on the idea that Westcoast's application should be refused because of certain technicalities in its license to export gas." In great agitation he asked Howe to "get your Federal and B.C. parliaments to enact laws guaranteeing a twenty years supply." In reply Howe pointed out the over-simplification in the argument on which both Murchison and the FPC had apparently been sold.

"My speech in the House of Commons was intended to convey to all concerned that Canada will guarantee gas export to the full term of our contract [concerning Westcoast]. A statement by a minister in the House of Commons is more effective in British law than contract, but evidently the FPC do not so regard it. Consequently I am amending federal government regulations and the Electricity and Fluid Exploration Act. A new licence will be admitted and a copy forwarded to the FPC via the Canadian embassy."

Howe went on to mention that he had some political advice of his own from other sources. "Last Friday I spoke from the same platform as George Humphrey [the U.S. Treasury Secretary] in Cleveland. George is an old friend of mine and he told me off the record that he intends to make one or two new appointments to the FPC. Anything you can do to delay a ruling on Westcoast's application until the situation can be reviewed by the new members will be very helpful."

In reply Murchison said that a new chairman, Jerome Kuykendall, was to be confirmed shortly and he went on to suggest that "you should write both him and President Eisenhower [and arrange to meet them together] because I know you can use your sagacity and turn on your personal charm and get any darn thing you want out of either of them. While I've not met Mr. Kuykendall personally, we have talked with him at length on various problems he has confronting him in his new job, and after checking carefully on him and his past operations, I have come to the firm conclusion that he is our sort of folks, and I know the President is."

Murchison was aware that Howe had other Canadian-American problems to cope with. Besides the tricky business of saving a market for Alberta gas in Ontario without losing export on the west coast, there was the St. Lawrence Seaway still hanging fire. He hoped the new Eisenhower administration could be persuaded to do something about it. In his letter, Murchison continued, "This Seaway situation is too complicated for me to try to work out politically just exactly what you want to do, but I feel sure that if you take it out of diplomatic channels and go see the President yourself you can get precisely what you want."

Murchison's letters to Howe usually strayed beyond the larger problems of government and business confronting them in Washington and Ottawa and ended up on a note of personal regard. Murchison kept wishing Howe would accompany him on a fishing holiday to one of his hideaways. At the end of his letter on April 16, he said "I hope you have a good time in London. [Howe was going to a Commonwealth meeting and trade mission at the time and had declined the latest invitation.] I know darn well I could show you a better time in Mexico, but I guess duty is duty."

In spite of his own penchant for direct personal dealings with old friends in Washington, and an often naïve estimate of their value, even Howe recognized the limits of Murchison's neighbourly approach to foreign policy. Amid the rumours and counter-rumours of what might happen to Canadian and American energy policy during the summer of 1953, Howe kept hammering away at one single point. He would stick by his statement in the House of Commons. At the start of the federal election campaign early in July, a press release was issued to affirm the government's commitment to an all-Canadian pipeline.

Late in August, after another overwhelming Liberal victory at the polls, Murchison's efforts in Washington received a serious setback. The FPC decided to allow Tennessee Gas Transmission a permit to pipe sixty million cubic feet of gas a day across the Niagara border into Canada. Howe was on holiday in St. Andrew's, New Brunswick. Murchison wired to tell him the news. He said that the FPC had not received Howe's latest letter. It was "buried somewhere in [the] State Department. We are attempting to get this decision rescinded. Please wire me your phone number if you will let me keep you informed."

In the meantime, during the summer of 1953, Howe's old friends Williamson and Milner of Western Pipe Lines were attempting to persuade him of the merits of their scheme, now amended to conform with his March 13 policy statement. At the very least they asked that he give a clear signal as to his intentions. "There are rumours about to the effect that the federal government would give assistance in building the all-Canada line," Milner wrote. Could these be confirmed or denied? His company's amended scheme was really no different from Trans-Canada's now, except that he proposed to build eastward in two jumps instead of one. Until markets were adequately built up, it would be impossible to finance the line privately. On the other hand if the government was prepared to shoulder some of the cost, then the "complexion of the entire project changes. So in all fairness I urge you to take us into your confidence."

Western Pipe Lines also saw hope for their scheme in the FPC decision. They moved quickly to take advantage of it. On September 2 Williamson wrote Howe, "We believe that we can work out an arrangement with Tennessee whereby Western Pipe Lines would build a big enough line to Winnipeg to ultimately look after the Ontario market. Tennessee can give Ontario enough fuel right away and so build up a market for gas. At the same time if our application is approved, we can provide an immediate market for all the gas that Alberta will let out. I will keep you informed."

"Dear Alan," Howe replied, "There is no enthusiasm here for a pipe line from Buffalo, though no one wished to take action that would interfere with [the FPC application from] Westcoast Transmission." He added, somewhat ingenuously, that everyone seemed to have a different view of what should be done and that his government would have to wait until Alberta decided to allow gas out of the province and Tennessee made a concrete proposal. In the meantime, through the late summer and fall of 1953, there was a propaganda battle raging between the city of Toronto, through Mayor Allan Lamport and Consumers' Gas Company, who published full page newspaper ads in favour of American import, and the many other Ontario municipalities demanding that the federal government require a pipeline across Northern Ontario.

The trouble was that Ottawa could do little under existing law to stop the import of gas into Canada. The old legislation only gave it power to license export. Once there was gas available for import at the border it appeared both legally and politically difficult to prevent it reaching the biggest closest market in Canada. This in turn would finish off any prospects of financing the Trans-Canada line in the foreseeable future.

Trade and Commerce lawyers cast about desperately for some means of stopping Tennessee at the Niagara River. It was Ross Tolmie of Trans-Canada who came up with the answer. Apply the Navigable Waters Protection Act – though the only ship that sailed anywhere near there was the Maid of the Mist. To their amazement and fury, Consumers' Gas and Tennessee were duly told that the boiling rapids below Niagara Falls were to be protected for navigation. And for the next session of Parliament, legislation was hurriedly prepared to require a federal licence for natural gas imports in the future.

Through the summer and fall of 1953, Trans-Canada and Western Pipe Lines battled away on several fronts. Before the Alberta Conservation Board, Trans-Canada claimed that Western's new plan to bring gas east from Winnipeg was not an amendment but a new application: It should be sent back to square one to begin all over again. The board did not agree, and allowed Western to proceed with their case. Then Western counter-attacked with figures to show that the eastern market could not possibly absorb as much gas as soon as Trans-Canada required if it was to finance its line. Long and bitter arguments from both sides ensued.

Prodded by Howe, both groups made abortive attempts to merge, as Howe and Manning had earlier agreed they should before any final licensing decisions by either government. At one point in November, one side believed its representatives had shaken hands on a definite commitment with their rivals, only to be met a few days later with refusal to proceed. The shifting sands of opinion and politics in four capitals, several financial circles, and within every public and private body involved, made any agreement to merge difficult. The two groups of contestants did not grow any fonder of each other personally in the process.

Finally on November 27 Louis St. Laurent and Ernest Manning met in Ottawa. Manning agreed to allow delivery of enough gas to supply the eastern Canadian market and a spur line to the American mid-west to a single company made up of the two competitors. Howe was to be given the job of driving them together and enlisting the active support of Premier Frost of Ontario.

On December 14 Howe wrote Frost, "As you know the pipe line project is opening up. Mr. Manning has dedicated sufficient gas and has asked our prime minister to work out a single application. The prime minister has assigned this job to me. The project seems to break into three parts:

(1) Supply: Manning will gather and deliver the gas in Alberta.

(2) The pipe line from this point to Toronto.

(3) Marketing the gas throughout Ontario.

"I suggest that you are the logical person to accept responsibility for number three. You have in the Ontario Hydro Electric Power Commission an organization capable of handling this marketing problem efficiently and in the best interests of your province. I am asking the two parties concerned to come to Ottawa about January 5. Our ability to work out the problem will depend largely on the volume of gas that can be sold and its price."

The difficulties with Howe's suggestion in Frost's view was that Ontario Hydro dealt in a competing source of energy and that its financial position was not strong enough to risk borrowing the enormous amount in bonds required to support a marketing organization for gas in Ontario. There were also the private gas utilities to be considered.

Howe pressed ahead immediately, however, inviting the representatives of the two rival groups to meet him in his office during the first week of January 1954. After their agreement in principle, the two parties continued to meet until financial and legal details were settled. A board of fourteen directors was chosen. It was made up in the manner of a Canadian federal cabinet, with members from every major interest and region. Western Pipe Lines was represented by nominees of its four chief sponsors: Deane Nesbitt of Nesbitt, Thomson in Montreal; Alan Williamson of the Toronto firm of Wood, Gundy; Gordon Osler of the Winnipeg firm that originally proposed the Western scheme; and Ray Milner of Edmonton. The Trans-Canada group was also represented by four members: Clint Murchison and Frank Schultz of Canadian Delhi and its subsidiary, the original Trans-Canada Company; John Fell of Lehman Brothers, the New York merchant bankers; and Ross Tolmie of the Ottawa law firm of Herridge, Tolmie. To these eight were added Premier Duplessis's personal lawyer Edouard Asselin, government leader in Quebec's Legislative Council; Jules Timmins, the Montreal mining tycoon; the corporation lawyer Senator Peter Campbell, a prominent Liberal; the broker Edward Bickle of Toronto, a Conservative who was close to Premier Frost; and from Saskatchewan, Murdoch Mac-Pherson, onetime candidate for leadership of the Progressive Conservative party and successful defender of Premier Douglas in a libel suit brought by the provincial opposition leader. All the provinces on the route from Alberta to Quebec, along with the most relevant Canadian and American business interests, were thus present on Trans-Canada's board.

The board's first task was to agree on a fourteenth member to be its chairman and chief executive officer of the new company. The man they chose was a former cabinet colleague of Premier Manning. His name was Tanner, and his biography is one of the strangest stories in the history of Canadian business.

Chapter 5 A Strange Story

Let us begin with a skill-testing question. What Canadian born in humble circumstances, a teacher by profession who rose to be a Bishop, became head of one of the most important organizations in the country then retired from his position to become a foreign missionary, and finally was chosen to be operating head of a world-wide church? Conceivably, one answer to this question might be Paul-Emile Cardinal Léger. He left his teaching post in Rome to run the great archdiocese of Montreal, which he in turn gave up for an African leper colony. He could become the first Canadian Pope. But if he does, he will not be the first but rather the second man to answer the description. The correct reply to the question is in fact Nathan Eldon Tanner of the Church of Jesus Christ of Latter Day Saints, an Alberta schoolteacher and Mormon bishop who became first chief executive of Trans-Canada Pipe Lines, left in his prime to become a Mormon missionary full time, and in 1965 became Counsellor to the ninety-five-year-old formal head of the Mormon Church, President David O. McKay, Prophet, Seer, Revelator and Trustee-in-Trust, lineal successor to Brigham Young, and in Mormon belief capable of receiving direct revelations from God.

We shall look in some detail at the personal life of Eldon Tanner, not only because of Tanner's position as head of the new company but because his biography is in itself a remarkable chapter in Canadian social history.

The Mormon Church, into which Tanner was born, is with the

exception of Christian Science the only significant new religion native to modern North America. It is founded on the assumption that it is the only pure church of Jesus Christ and that its founder, Joseph Smith, was the recipient of prophetic revelation from an angel of God who guided him to a hillside near Palmyra, New York, where he found buried under a stone golden plates brought in ancient times from the Middle East by the Indians of North America. By divine inspiration Smith translated these into what are now, along with the Bible, the sacred scriptures of Mormonism.

Perhaps the most remarkable thing about modern Mormons is the zeal, likened by many to that of the early Christians, with which they preach and practise their faith. Their unpaid lay ministry comprises one-sixth of their total world membership of three million. Thanks in part to their strict adherence to the Biblical practice of tithing – giving a tenth of their income to the church – the Mormons have reputedly become the richest church *per capita* in the world. Whether this is true or not, their business ventures now include the owning and operating of a life insurance company, a large university, a welfare programme providing for one hundred thousand cases a year, a vast real estate subsidiary called Zion's Securities Corporation, a multitude of manufacturing and agricultural enterprises, and what may have been the world's first genuine department store, Zion's Co-operative Mercantile Institution of Salt Lake City founded by Brigham Young in 1868, the year before Timothy Eaton opened his dry goods shop on Yonge Street in Toronto.

The Mormons are not only famous for their early practice of polygamy, and for one of the great folk heroes of western settlement, Brigham Young, but in later times for producing a fine choir and such prominent Americans as Agriculture Secretary Ezra Taft Benson and Governor George Romney of Michigan. But perhaps no Mormon has ever had a more varied career than Eldon Tanner.

A little time after the American frontier was officially declared closed by the Department of the Interior in 1891, signifying that the last vast stretches of free land in the west could no longer be demarcated by a line, Tanner's parents, like so many thousands of other Americans, moved north to the virgin lands of the Canadian west. They arrived in southern Alberta from Utah by covered wagon in 1897, and made a homestead against the side of a hill. The roof was of sod, the floor was the earth, one of its three walls was, literally, the hill, and the other three sides were of logs. It was a habitation more primitive than the proverbial log cabin in which western pioneers were born, and it conjures up images not only of Loyola's cave of Manresa and other caverns where great revelations have taken place, but also the hillside named Cumorah where the young Joseph Smith first discovered the golden plates of ancient scripture.

Eldon Tanner was born in 1898, during a return to the ancestral home in Salt Lake City, but he spent his first several months in Alberta in the primitive homestead until a two-room house could be built. Before he was twelve he drove a four-horse team and was sometimes put in charge of his younger brothers and sisters. Besides his tasks at home he earned his way through the lower grades of school by working parttime in a slaughter house. He then financed a year's teacher training by means of a $400 bank loan which he received on the only security he could offer: his father's integrity. At the age of twenty, on leaving normal school, he became principal of a three-room rural school at Hill Spring, Alberta. When his oldest class reached the top grade in the school, Tanner added a year at a time to the curriculum until they reached his own level of training, Grade XI. Then he and his class studied their Grade XII together, after which they all wrote and passed the provincial examinations.

In Hill Spring, Tanner also served as health officer, constable and local scout master; he trained cadets, ran school sports and acted as dance director. (The Mormons used to dance beneath the stars on their trek westwards, and have always been enthusiastic about Biblical injunctions to dance and make joyful noise before the Lord.) Since the school board often had to pay him in promissory notes or in kind rather than cash, he operated a small farm to help feed himself and his growing family of five girls, and set up a general store by making a down payment with the family's only tangible property, a Ford car. He supplied his store at night by freighting his own goods from a nearby railroad centre. The store became so successful that he added a post office to it and temporarily gave up teaching. He then sold out in 1929 in order to go to university and study law. But the beginning of the great depression and the need to support his family ended that hope. In 1930 he became principal of a larger school in Cardston, Alberta, where he remained until 1935, supplementing his salary by selling insurance and men's clothing, and also acting as the newly elected Bishop of his Ward. When "Bible Bill" Aberhart decided to take his Sunday School movement from the religious and social sphere directly into politics, he toured the province looking for Social Credit candidates to run in the 1935 provincial elections. Tanner's first reaction to Social Credit doctrine was scepticism, but when the crusade came to Cardston, he agreed to act as chairman of the local study group with the intention of exploring the doctrine thoroughly in order to prove it wrong. Before it was over he had become a convert. Aberhart personally selected him, much to his surprise, and for a time much against his will, as the local Social Credit candidate in the 1935 election. In the event, all the other candidates lost their deposits.

When the newly elected Social Credit caucus met in Edmonton, Tanner campaigned for the election of his friend Solon Low (later to be national leader of the party) as Speaker of the Legislative Assembly. Election was by write-in secret ballot, however, and Tanner had so impressed the other members in his advocacy of Low that when the votes were counted, his own name was at the top of the list. He was duly sworn in as presiding officer of the world's first Social Credit legislature. In 1936 Aberhart asked him to become his Minister of Lands and Mines, in spite of his protest that he didn't know an oil well from a water well. The ministry was later split into two departments with two deputy ministers, and in this double capacity Tanner served until 1952, when he retired from politics to go into business. In the course of his seventeen-year political career he became chairman of the Alberta Research Council and a founder of the Eastern Rockies Forest Conservation Board. As provincial Scout Commissioner, he dined with King George VI and Queen Elizabeth on their visit to Edmonton during the royal tour of 1939.

As mines minister Tanner was for sixteen years responsible for the province's oil and gas conservation programme policy. After 1949 he had disagreed with Manning, though not publicly, over the caution of the Premier and the Conservation Board in their estimates of gas reserves in Alberta and their unwillingness to dedicate gas for export. One of his last political activities had been a recommendation to force a large American petroleum company to pay higher rental on non-producing oil land – in other words, to produce, get out, or resell to Canadians. But the company convinced Manning that they could not or would not carry on under these regulations and Tanner's advice was not accepted.

During a stay with the Governor of the Barbados in 1949, to whom he was loaned briefly as an adviser, he met Charles Merrill, the head of the New York brokerage firm of Merrill, Lynch. Merrill had recently finished putting together the Safeway grocery chain, and had turned to an interest in oil promotion. He was impressed with Tanner and his position of political influence in Alberta. He proposed to put up money for a petroleum company if Tanner would agree to act as its president.

Tanner's new career in Calgary was less than two years old when he received a visit from a delegation of the board of Trans-Canada Pipe Lines in February of 1954. On Ernest Manning's recommendation they had selected him as their first choice for president of the newly amalgamated company. Tanner had the good will of the government of Alberta, long experience in dealing with petroleum companies, and he was known as a judicious person, well able to temper the latent conflict between the newly joined rivals. As it turned out, Tanner probably did not play as important a role in Trans-Canada's survival and ultimate success as half a dozen of the original sponsors on the board. Nor did his ability or style ever qualify him to be a member of the power *élite* of Canadian business and public life. But his quiet diplomacy was to be important both for the morale of employees and for relations with a great range of persons outside the company. Tanner's lean, carved countenance, dark complexion, deliberate speech and long silences suggested the presence of an Indian sachem – or some archetypal prairie farmer.

When the Trans-Canada directors invited Tanner to be president, he told them he was not interested. His chief concerns at the time were first, the Mormon Church, and second, after his long career in public life on a small salary, a chance to find obscurity and make some money. He thought perhaps that his first objection would be decisive. He asked his visitors where the head office of the company would be. They told him Toronto, a logical choice in view of the fact that matters of financing and marketing would be critical for the company's success. He told them he would not go to Toronto; he had just been appointed President of the Calgary Stake, the local division of his church. Both parties agreed to think it over for a few days.

In the meantime, Tanner got phone calls from C. D. Howe and Ernest Manning. Howe told him he was the one man in whom both sides had complete confidence, and Manning pleaded with him to take the job as his patriotic and religious duty. Manning, busy with his weekly Bible broadcasts, was also like Tanner a dedicated fundamentalist layman.

The directors returned to say that they would agree to the head office remaining in Calgary; they offered Tanner $35,000 a year, a salary equivalent to the one he was receiving at Merrill Petroleum: a guaranteed retirement allowance of $15,000 for five years in case Trans-Canada should fail; and future stock options at $8 a share, the same price at which sponsors were drawing down stock in return for the money they put up to meet company expenditures. Since Tanner could not afford much stock they offered him a block of their own, for which they had paid $8, at $1 a share. Although these terms were extremely attractive, the offer in fact amounted to far less than American executives in safely established major transmission companies were receiving. Tanner in the end accepted the call back to what proved to be a stormier career in public life than his last one.

No one in March 1954 had any notion of how low the company's prospects would sink during the next twelve months. March 1955, a year from Tanner's appointment, marked the nadir of its fortunes and its sponsors' hopes.

Things began well enough. On March 9, 1954, a private bill to authorize the incorporation of a company called Niagara Gas Transmission for the purpose of building a pipeline from the American border at Niagara Falls into the Consumers' Gas marketing area in Toronto came up for second reading before the House of Commons. As we have seen, Consumers' Gas for over a year previously had been anxious to acquire gas at Niagara Falls through the Tennessee system. Much to the concern of Trans-Canada's sponsors and of the governments of Ontario and Canada, the Federal Power Commission in Washington had given Tennessee a licence to export the gas. The fuel shortage in the Toronto area was becoming critical, however, and this problem was now linked with the need to build up a market for natural gas until the pipeline could be built from Alberta. C. D. Howe suggested in the House, after an interview with the general manager of Consumers' Gas, Oakah Jones, that the private bill might be satisfactory to all parties and fulfil the conditions of his 1953 policy statement if an extra clause were added. Let the bill come into force "at such time as a mutually satisfactory agreement between Trans-Canada Pipe Lines Limited and Consumers' Gas Company could be deposited with the Board of Transport Commissioners. I believe this procedure would allow us to receive the benefit that would be incidental from the building of this pipe line from Buffalo and at the same time protect both the financial and the sales position of Trans-Canada Pipe Lines.

"That is only my suggestion. There may be others. But I do think that to meet the requirements laid down by the Leader of the Opposition – that the government should assure the House that the interests of the larger project would be protected – this may be as good a means as any for bringing about the protection asked for."

Howe also proposed that discussion of the pipeline "should be entirely removed from politics. If it were not, I would be tempted to congratulate the Leader of the Opposition for adopting Liberal policies with reference to gas pipe lines. Since we are not talking politics, I shall refrain from doing so."

Davie Fulton interrupted, "You know just the opposite is true. You have adopted ours." And Stanley Knowles of the CCF asked, "Who taught the both of you?" Howe ignored this shot and proceeded grandly on his way, conjuring up a vision of "the greatest pipe line project ever undertaken anywhere in the world." Although the line itself might only cost around $300 million, if the costs of the gathering lines and the chemical plants and the distribution system were added in, the new amalgamated company represented a project running to around "one billion dollars, all of which is to be spent before the year 1960."

Another phrase also reminded members of his famous question "What's a million?" and his liking for large round numbers. He spoke of the exportable surplus of gas from Alberta and its growth "at the rate of .75 trillion cubic feet per annum over the next five or

ten years." One member gasped in disbelief: "Trillion?" Trillion!"
said Howe firmly. But even Howe's estimate, like Manning's, proved
to be far too conservative.

Stanley Knowles expressed the hope that there would be some
conversions among Liberal Members of Parliament in the matter of
public ownership of the pipeline, just as there had been a conversion to the policy of an all-Canadian route. However, he seemed to
accept with resignation that public ownership was out of the question for Howe, and he asked that every effort be made to ensure that
"the interests of the consumers of Canada would be protected, as
well as they can be protected under a policy of private ownership."

The only negative note was struck by the member for Cape Breton South, Clarence Gillis, who commented rather mournfully:
"The thing that irks me is this. Every time a member gets to his feet in
the House he figures that if you serve Quebec and Ontario from the
western provinces, that is a national project." He reminded the House
that there were four other provinces in Canada. Western gas might
replace Cape Breton coal on the Quebec market. "Only last evening
the Minister of Mines had a delegation from Nova Scotia wait on
him in reference to a mine closing for lack of markets."

On March 30, 1954, another private member's bill to amend the
Trans-Canada Pipe Lines Act was moved for second reading. Its
sponsor, John Decore, Liberal member for Vegreville, Alberta, commented, "I am sure the House will be pleased to hear that the apparent conflict between the Trans-Canada project and the proposal to
bring gas from Louisiana to Toronto has now been resolved. Under
an agreement concluded last week, the line from Niagara to Toronto
will be built by the Trans-Canada Company and leased to the Niagara Gas Transmission Company until the Trans-Canada line is
built to Toronto." The latter company, a subsidiary of Consumers'
Gas, along with Consumers' itself also agreed to cease taking American gas as soon as the Trans-Canada line was built. The purpose of
the amendment to the Trans-Canada Pipe Lines incorporation was
twofold: first, to enlarge its capital structure in order to build the
pipeline from Niagara to Toronto; and second, to enable it to take
over its former rival, Western Pipe Lines, as a wholly owned subsidiary, and thus effect the merger agreed to in Howe's office in
January.

In the meantime Trans-Canada asked the Alberta Conservation Board's permission to include in its plans the old Western scheme for exporting Alberta gas to the United States at Emerson, Manitoba. On May 14 a permit was issued by the province with the provisos that Trans-Canada submit evidence before the end of the year that it could finance the project, that construction would start by June 1, 1955, and that the first removal of gas from the province would begin by December 31, 1955.

Company officers also appeared before the Board of Transport Commissioners in Ottawa, seeking leave to construct a 20-inch pipeline from the middle of the Niagara River to a point outside Toronto where it would connect with the distribution system of Consumers' Gas. In the light of the critical energy shortage, the chief commissioner took the unusual step of delivering a judgment directly from the bench at the end of the first day of hearings, April 27. He granted the request and suggested a completion date of December 31, 1954, for the Niagara line.

The company still had to win the board's authorization for their main line from Alberta to Montreal, with branches south from Winnipeg to the border, north from Morrisburg to Ottawa, and west from the Toronto junction to Oakville to hook up with the Niagara line. The chief intervenor was one Cyril Young who appeared on behalf of the Chambers of Commerce of towns in the northern Ontario clay belt such as Geraldton, Kapuskasing and Haileybury. He argued that a more northerly route, while slightly longer, would provide an easier path for construction and also a better market for gas along the way than the old CPR route touching Lake Superior proposed by the company.

Young was a huge, loud prospector who had known C. D. Howe for a long time. A famous character in Ontario mining country, he was generally regarded as a nuisance by civil servants around Ottawa. Howe asked his departmental energy expert, Jack Davis, to investigate the feasibility of the clay belt route through the north country before the Board of Transport Commissioners hearings began. They did so, and found they agreed with him. Consequently, when Young appeared in June of 1954 he had a well-documented case prepared for him by the Department of Trade and Commerce. The company on the other hand had assumed that there was no significant market for gas in northern Ontario between Fort William and Sudbury and had not made a thorough investigation of sales along possible alternative routes. Young was able to show the board that the pulp and paper industries along the clay belt route (provided there were subsidiary lines shooting off to Timmins and the great refineries of Sudbury) would provide an excellent market for gas. These were all very high-cost areas as far as their present fuels, oil and coal, were concerned. So natural gas could easily compete. This industrial use of gas would help make the whole Trans-Canada project more feasible financially. Accordingly the board asked the company to reconsider its route through northern Ontario.

On the crucial question of the company's financeability, the commissioners questioned witnesses closely. In the end, however, they agreed with Trans-Canada's counsel, Ross Tolmie, that it would be unwise for the company to approach institutional investors until some major sales contracts had been signed. Tolmie pointed out that obtaining such contracts would not be easy. He felt the Board of Transport Commissioners would understand, as did the Alberta Conservation Board, that in Canada where natural gas was a new feature of the economy, it would be almost impossible to obtain contracts in the absence of any kind of approval from the board. His witnesses established that the engineering of the line was feasible and that construction costs were such that the total project would make gas a competitive energy source in eastern Canada once the line was constructed. He suggested that the board grant an interlocutory order timing its requirements according to the schedule already adopted by Alberta. The chief commissioner congratulated Tolmie on his presentation, and on July 26, 1954, the board issued an order granting Trans-Canada the right to construct a line, subject to reconsideration of the northern Ontario route and the completion of financing arrangements by December 31, 1954.

In addition to securing a president, Trans-Canada's executive committee decided to appoint an executive vice-president with experience in natural gas pipelining. Frank Schultz approached and was turned down by three experienced officers of large American transmission companies, each of whom, as it happened, became his company's chief executive shortly afterwards. Then he decided to try a Texas engineer named Charles Coates who was executive vice-president of the world's largest company in the field, Tennessee Gas Transmission. President Tanner and other board members had already been impressed with Coates when they saw him giving expert testimony at hearings in Ottawa.

When the president of Tennessee, Gardiner Symonds, was asked about Coates he told Tanner "If you can get him, take him." Symonds was convinced that anything Trans-Canada could offer, he could easily counter. To the surprise of both Symonds and Tanner, Coates accepted Trans-Canada's offer. It was a challenge to move from an established and powerful position into the risk and opportunity of the unknown and the untried, in a company with an uncertain future. On August 11, 1954, Coates was appointed executive vice-president of Trans-Canada Pipe Lines. He was given stock options similar to those of Tanner, and $10,000 more in salary —$45,000 a year. While his immediate assignment was to line up supply contracts with the gas producers of Alberta, he was also to be the key man in the construction of the Trans-Canada line. At the same time another vice-president, A. P. Craig, who had been with Canadian Westinghouse and had joined C. D. Howe's staff as a dollar a year man during the Korean War, was taken on as vice-president and given responsibility for negotiating sales contracts with the various gas distributors along the route.

The new executives of Trans-Canada soon found themselves trapped in an impasse. The potential gas purchasers did not consider the Trans-Canada project financially feasible. Consumers' Gas of Toronto was particularly interested in sticking with its immediate source of supply across the Niagara border. Gas distributors did not want to tie themselves to a company which might never get off the ground, or which if it did, might put them in deep financial trouble. The Alberta gas suppliers had even stronger reasons for hoping that the Trans-Canada project would in the end fail. It was obvious that there would be a profitable market in the central and western regions of the United States for Alberta gas, but it was not at all obvious that they could get an adequate price for their product if it had to be transported across northern Ontario.

Trans-Canada Pipe Lines could not possibly approach financial institutions without some supply and sales contracts in hand. And yet without proof of real interest on the part of investing companies, neither suppliers or distributors were prepared to sign the essential long term contracts. A further difficulty appeared on the horizon when the province of Alberta formed a provincial gas-gathering system, Alberta Gas Trunk Lines. Its voting shares were almost entirely limited to producers and distributors of gas in the province of Alberta and membership on its board to directors voted in by these two classes of shareholders, along with two directors chosen by the provincial government and one by the gas exporters. By forming this organization Premier Manning avoided the distasteful prospect of using a government department or crown corporation to control the direction and price of Alberta gas, while at the same time he effectively achieved the same thing by keeping jurisdiction over gas-gathering pipelines within Alberta.

In the fall of 1954 Alberta Gas Trunk Lines was unable to supply a schedule of tariffs for Trans-Canada. This fact alone made it impossible for Trans-Canada to arrange purchase contracts at that time with the major petroleum companies.

When the executive committee of the board met in Toronto on October 20, 1954, they agreed that there had been such little progress that C. D. Howe would have to be told immediately and asked for some form of federal assistance if the December 31 deadline was to be met.

There had always been a certain division of opinion on the board about government aid. Certain of the financial people, notably Deane Nesbitt, favoured a strictly private enterprise, whereas Murchison and Alan Williamson were counting on some form of government aid or assistance in order to initiate what was national policy in the building of an all-Canadian line. The executive committee now agreed that there was no other way but to approach the government. There were indications that the response would be favourable.

Alan Williamson had earlier sent his old friend Howe a handwritten note in order to report progress. He mentioned the acquisition of first-rate personnel, commenting in particular on Tanner, Coates and "Craig from your Department and Douglas Simpson from deHavilland." Bechtel-Mannix-Hester, a company created specifically for the Trans-Canada project by three international design engineering firms, was already hard at work on specifications.

Then he came to the problem. "We can't wait much longer if we are to build the line to Winnipeg in 1955 and commit ourselves to the expenditure of over one hundred million dollars in the next sixty days. I have quite a responsibility to all these fine people who have come with Trans-Canada and have given up fine positions elsewhere. Also to the many who are pouring in money on a no-profit basis, purely on my say-so that this is a national project greatly in the interest of this country and supported by the government and all other parties except the CCF. If I weren't dealing with you I might be really worried."

Howe replied on October 12 that he would be glad to see company officers on any convenient date. He also remarked that he had met Tanner along with some officers of the Union Gas Company the previous week and tried to give them all some help in agreeing on a contract. "They were to continue the meeting after I left and I hope they worked out something convenient. I am glad about your working organization. I can assure you the government is counting heavily on this program and prepared to do what it can to give you support at the crucial stages."

At the full meeting of Trans-Canada's Board of Directors on October 21 the executive committee was able to report on a visit to Howe that same morning. He had shown great sympathy for the company's position and expressed the view that sales tax and duty could probably be recovered by the company. The question of additional government support was not explored in any precise way.

When the executive committee met five weeks later in Calgary there were no further signs of progress in any direction and new difficulties had appeared. Trouble over the uncertainty about gathering facilities and other matters in Alberta arose during hearings before the Alberta Conservation Board. While it was hoped that this could be straightened out by meeting Premier Manning and the Conservation Board on December 2, there was a much more serious difficulty over the export of gas at Emerson to their prospective American customer, Northern Natural Gas of Omaha. Hearings before the Federal Power Commission in Washington were going very badly. Because no Trans-Canada contracts were yet signed with Alberta producers, Northern Natural could not assure the FPC of a committed supply of Canadian gas.

Tanner reported that the FPC had postponed its hearings to January 4, 1955, and that Trans-Canada would have to supply precise information about natural gas purchase contracts if there was to be any hope of American export. Financial institutions in Canada and the U.S. regarded this permission as essential before they could attempt to raise the money to build the pipeline.

It was also essential for Trans-Canada to have a contract to supply gas in the Montreal area. Here again there was trouble. As early as 1951 Frank Schultz and Ross Tolmie journeyed to Quebec City on behalf of Canadian Delhi to sound out Premier Duplessis on bringing natural gas into the province. Duplessis told them of the failure of the natural gas company in Three Rivers in his youth and of the many local residents who lost money on it. He also expressed scepticism about the economics of bringing gas all the way from Alberta. Nevertheless, since Quebec would soon be facing a severe power shortage, he would listen to any proposition they might make.

Before leaving, Frank Schultz asked, "Would it be presumptuous of us, Mr. Prime Minister, to ask who should be our lawyer in Quebec?" Duplessis laughed uproariously, "No, Monsieur Schultz, it would not be. It would be goddam wise! I think you ought to have my personal attorney, Edouard Asselin." Schultz and Tolmie flew to Montreal that afternoon and called Asselin's office for an appointment. They discovered that Duplessis had already been in touch with him. Within ten minutes they had arranged for him to represent their company. After the merger of early 1954, when Trans-Canada's new Board of Directors was being formed, Asselin was made a member. He remained until 1960, when he resigned because of his position on the board of Trans-Canada's customer, Quebec Natural Gas.

There already existed a manufactured gas system in Montreal, completely owned by Quebec Hydro. The prospect of having a major customer that was backed by the credit of a provincial government was particularly important for Trans-Canada's demonstration of financeability, since none of its other prospective customers except Saskatchewan Power were in that position. During most of 1954 Duplessis appeared to favour distribution of natural gas through Quebec Hydro converting and operating the old Montreal gas system. Towards the end of the year, however, Asselin phoned

Ross Tolmie from Quebec City with bad news. Quebec Hydro would not go into the natural gas business. It would cost too much. Worse still, such a risky venture might put the whole credit of the province in jeopardy or at least raise the cost of its borrowing money on the bond markets.

Tolmie called Frank Schultz in Dallas. "Maybe they'd sell it," Schultz suggested. Tolmie went immediately to Quebec City and Asselin took him in to see the Chief. Duplessis expressed an interest in selling the Montreal system to someone who would convert it to natural gas, then looked at the ceiling and told Tolmie, "But of course you will have to pay the full depreciated cost." Its book assets included such items as $6 million worth of ancient ships once used to carry coal from Nova Scotia to Montreal, useless now for anything except scrap, and a coke plant for turning the coal into manufactured gas. It was obvious that there would be long, hard bargaining ahead and a great deal of complicated legal manœuvring before a customer for Trans-Canada's gas could be created in the province of Quebec. One of the largest potential customers, and the most credit worthy, thus vanished. The best that could be hoped for was that some time in the future a viable company could be set up to make the purchase from Quebec Hydro and in turn sign a contract with Trans-Canada.

With the date for proof of financeability only a month away, the company desperately needed to pull off some bold coup that would change the highly sceptical view of potential investors, consumers and producers, as well as the Federal Power Commission. They, therefore, decided to approach the consulting engineers, Stone and Webster, who were employed originally by Western Pipe Lines, and currently by Consumers' Gas of Toronto. Perhaps this conservative and widely respected firm would be prepared to make another survey of the natural gas market in Canada that might lead them to alter their original pessimistic conclusions. These conclusions had been part of the reason why Western Pipe Lines back in 1949-50 decided not to supply the eastern Canadian market at all, but rather to export into the American mid-west. Stone and Webster, in spite of every inducement and Trans-Canada's willingness to take the risk of an adverse report, simply said they were not interested in conducting another survey; the markets for natural gas in Canada could not have grown sufficiently to alter their original conclusions. There was, after this, no hope of success by December 31. On December 6 Trans-Canada officials resigned themselves to the embarrassment of seeking an extension of their deadline for proof of financeability to April 30, 1955, and an extension of their start-of-construction date from June 1 to June 30, 1955.

More bad news appeared on the horizon as the new year began. The major Alberta petroleum companies were still refusing to tie themselves down to purchase contracts with such a doubtful risk as Trans-Canada. The sales contracts that Trans-Canada had been counting on in the prairies, particularly from the Saskatchewan Power Commission, were not yet signed, and the most important Western customer, the Winnipeg and Central Gas Company, was in serious financial difficulties as a result of heavy bank borrowings made to tide it over until the arrival of natural gas. Trans-Canada believed they had an agreement with Consumers' Gas, but when this was pressed for formal closing, Consumers' refused to honour it and demanded conditions which would put Trans-Canada in an impossible position *vis-à-vis* potential investors. Negotiations with Quebec Hydro for the acquisition by a new private company of the Montreal distribution system had begun, but there was little progress to report.

The only marketing area that showed promise was that of the Union Gas Company in southwestern Ontario. This company had the advantage of possessing huge storage fields, emptied by the withdrawal of natural gas from them over the past half century. There was a greater inducement for them to take Alberta gas since they could ration out peak loads more easily than other companies in Ontario.

Trans-Canada executives kept Howe closely informed of their difficulties throughout December. They now decided to meet him with a proposal by which the federal government might help the company get launched.

The investment dealers on Trans-Canada's board agreed that the best way to involve the federal government for a minimum amount of aid would be to ask for an undertaking to meet any payments due for the first few years on the first mortgage bonds that the company was unable to provide out of its depreciation and net earnings. Such a proposal would make the project readily financeable by breaking the deadlock in negotiations between the company and the producers and distributors. Even under the worst circumstances envisaged by feasibility studies, it would not involve the federal government in paying out more than $25 million (against the pipeline's estimated cost of $350 million). This $25 million or less the government would be repaid with interest, subject only to amortization of the first mortgage bonds and ahead of any payments to other security holders.

When Alan Williamson presented the idea on January 6, 1955, Howe expressed his complete satisfaction with the proposal. He advised Williamson that he would put the matter before cabinet and that he expected full endorsement at an early date.

Howe was in for a rude surprise.

When the Minister of Finance, Walter Harris, received a copy of President Tanner's letter outlining the proposal, he interpreted it as a request for a guarantee on the bond issue. He took the matter up with his senior advisers, Kenneth Taylor and John Deutsch, and with the Governor of the Bank of Canada, James Coyne. They in turn discussed it with Howe's senior energy expert, Jack Davis, as well as with the two financial negotiators for Trans-Canada, Deane Nesbitt and Alan Williamson. In two letters to Howe, dated January 12 and 13, Harris summed up the results of these discussions:

"The request for a guarantee raises awkward problems of precedent and past practice. Apart from defence production, there are no recent precedents for direct guarantees on marketable securities to large-scale private industry. There are of course the railway construction precedents of an earlier generation, but I doubt if there has been a guarantee of this magnitude since about forty years ago."

Harris went on to point out that the post-war oil pipelines had been financed privately. A guarantee to Trans-Canada at this point would invite comparable requests from Westcoast Transmission. B.C. Electric too had been pressing annually for tax concessions to enable them to raise new capital more cheaply.

He raised the further difficulty that the interest rates on Trans-Canada bonds might undermine the price level of outstanding government bonds, and this could in turn hurt provincial, municipal and other corporate bonds. Some potential borrowers would postpone their plans to float new issues, and the effects could have a widespread influence on the whole Canadian economy. "Sharp adjustments would hurt our credit ratings in New York." In conclusion, Harris advised that "my officials are unable to recommend this course, partly on principle and partly because there has been insufficient time to explore all other alternatives. The proposals of the company are quite unsatisfactory."

In his reply Howe pleaded with Harris as a matter of urgency to try to devise a plan to break the deadlock in which the company found itself. "I think I can state that anything satisfactory to the government will be acceptable to the sponsors of Trans-Canada." The sponsors would not be allowed to dictate terms, nor did they have any wish to do so.

"One objection in your letter is greatly overstated, namely that the deficiency payments constitute a government guarantee of bonds, and if these sold at 4% in Canada and $3\frac{3}{4}\%$ in U.S., Canada will be the laughing stock of the financial fraternity." As for precedents, Howe cited the government-backed dry docks which under his own aegis in the late thirties had received a "far more liberal form of assistance" than what was now being proposed. The core of his argument centered around the fact that "for all pipe lines into new markets, a deficiency guarantee has always been required, and in the case of the two inter-provincial oil pipe lines in Canada, this was furnished by Imperial Oil Ltd. Unfortunately in Canada, no sponsorship other than the Canadian government exists which can assume the type of responsibility for so large a project as Trans-Canada Pipe Lines. This is no ordinary project, but the largest capacity and longest pipe line ever undertaken."

The rest of Howe's letter was largely taken up with its crucial importance to Canada. "One of your letters refers to the relative value of the project in terms of labour and Canadian materials. This is a very small part of the benefit to Canada. The principal expenditure will be for distributing lines and apparatus to use gas, practically all of which are of Canadian manufacture. Studies made in this department indicate the project involves an investment of one billion dollars over the next six or seven years.

"In my opinion the Government is committed to the hilt to seeing that natural gas is brought to eastern Canada. I am convinced that a guarantee in any form will cost the government nothing, as my studies indicate that the line can be made self-sustaining after the first year of operation. I am also of the opinion that a transcontinental pipe line wholly within Canada is a national project that warrants government assistance, and that the project is comparable in importance to our transcontinental railways. In my opinion if the project is allowed to collapse, the use of western gas in eastern Canada will be a dead issue for all time, and any natural gas used in eastern Canada will be supplied from the United States with no real gain in the direction of a Canadian fuel policy."

Howe concluded, rather optimistically, that most of the supply and marketing arrangements for the project were ready, and that all that was needed was something to break the deadlock. "The finalizing of all these projects depends on financing the pipe line. Time is not working in favour of the project. I have always envisaged government help for this project would be required."

Howe's arguments did not convince the younger members of the cabinet that there was any ground for giving a private corporation, even though it was acting in the national interest, a guarantee on its bonds. They also sensed a restlessness in the country. The charge of helping big business on the path to profit would be too good a political target for both leading opposition parties in the next federal election.

President Tanner of Trans-Canada had the first intimations that things were not going well when a promised phone call from Howe did not reach him in Washington. He was there waiting for the word to go ahead and meet members of the FPC to tell them that the Canadian government had just agreed to help Trans-Canada.

In Ottawa, when Alan Williamson and Deane Nesbitt presented themselves at Number One Temporary Building to receive the verdict, they were appalled at the first sight of Howe behind his desk. He had all the appearances of a man who had suffered a severe shock or illness. He listlessly advised them of his defeat in the cabinet. It was obvious that he felt his defeat had badly hurt the chances of the project ever being undertaken.

A possible solution suggested by the finance department was one distasteful and unsatisfactory to both Howe and Trans-Canada. Possibly the government could offer aid through the Industrial Development Bank; negotiations for a loan from the IDB should be carried out with the Bank of Canada, its parent body. At that time the IDB's financial structure was completely incapable of supporting a large venture such as Trans-Canada. It had been founded to support small companies, such as private airlines in the north, which might have difficulty raising money from the chartered banks. It was agreed however that if negotiations as to the form of aid were successful the federal government would authorize an increase in the IDB's capitalization. Howe instructed Williamson and Nesbitt to get in touch with Governor James Coyne of the Bank of Canada as soon as possible.

Over the next eight weeks these two men remained in Ottawa to wait upon the government and its officials, clinging to this last hope, just as George Stephen and his colleagues had waited there in the 1880s, with Macdonald's gloomy sympathy, as they pleaded for loans and subsidies to enable the Canadian Pacific Railway to survive.

Some comfort could be derived from four bits of progress made during January: a decision to accept the longer but easier and more productive route through the clay belt of northern Ontario; a reduction in total capital cost by the discovery that the size of the Alberta-to-Winnipeg line could safely be reduced from 36 to 34 inches in diameter; acceptance of a new plan for Trans-Canada to deal directly with Alberta gas producers and then pay the gathering system for transportation to the Saskatchewan border; and finally, the signing up of Trans-Canada's first important customer, Union Gas of southwestern Ontario.

As Deane Nesbitt noted at the time, however, these were bright spots in a dark picture. He and Williamson entered into negotiations with the Bank of Canada "with heavy hearts."

Chapter 6 Coyne's Bank

Governor James Coyne of the Bank of Canada was known as a man of high principles and fixed positions, both of which he was capable of defending with great vigour and tenacity. His views on American investment in Canada and on tight money during the recession of the late 1950s were to gain him the enmity of a great range of persons, all the way from John Diefenbaker to most of the academic economists in Canada. His stubborn resistance to the attempt to get rid of him as Governor in 1960 was, thanks to the forum of the Liberal-dominated Senate, the first successful defiance of the huge Conservative majority in the House of Commons. But Coyne's record at the Bank of Canada, like his later presidency of the ill-fated Bank of Western Canada, was not such as to earn him a reputation for subtlety and flexibility or to stir confidence in the hearts of Trans-Canada's negotiators as they prepared to meet him.

They were agreeably surprised by his initial approach. He told them that the bank's only object was a desire to play a constructive part in assisting "an undertaking of national interest, indeed of national pride, and promoting the economic use within Canada of Canadian resources."

Before their first negotiating session, Trans-Canada's representatives Alan Williamson and Deane Nesbitt had to decide what size of investment by the Industrial Development Bank, in what type of Trans-Canada security, would have the greatest influence in persuading other investors to buy the remaining securities. The formula for the projected financial structure of Trans-Canada, already adopted in principle by Trans-Canada's Board of Directors, was one based on the successful pattern for financing large gas pipelines used in the United States. The pattern there generally ran to a capitalization of about 85% debt, made up of 70% first mortgage bonds and 15% subordinated debentures, and about 15% equity in common stock. Because Trans-Canada's line was longer and was to be placed through far less fruitful territory for gas sales than any line yet built, the company seemed unlikely to achieve as good a dividend record as its American counterparts. Since there would be difficulty in placing large amounts of common stock, the board concluded that the balance of the formula should be weighted slightly towards debt rather than equity. Of the estimated capital requirement of $350 million, $240 million should be obtained by first mortgage bonds, $70 million by subordinated debentures and $40 million by common shares.

Nesbitt and Williamson decided that the best possible approach would be for the Industrial Development Bank to buy any first mortgage bonds that could not be sold to the public. This would give a strong lead to the large financial institutions which had responsibility for investing other people's money in safe securities. That in turn would make it possible to establish the most important sales and purchase contracts. Nesbitt felt that at the very most the bank would have to take $70 million worth of first mortgage bonds, or 20% of the company's total capital requirements.

The Trans-Canada negotiators outlined their proposal to Coyne and his deputy, Ralph McKibbin. They were staggered by the Governor's reply. He proposed a maximum investment on the part of the bank of 10% of the total capital. He said that it must be in the form of debentures which would carry first mortgage security but would at the bank's pleasure be convertible into common shares – when and if the shares acquired value and began paying a good dividend. The most dismaying part of Coyne's proposal, however, particularly in the light of the American experience of financing pipelines, was his requirement that the company's total equity capital be 30%, i.e. $105 million, comprised of the bank's $35 million worth of convertible debentures plus $70 million in common shares. He asked Nesbitt and Williamson to consider this proposal and in the meantime promised to discuss theirs with the Minister of Finance, Walter Harris.

The two negotiators retired and summoned to a meeting in Ottawa representatives from Lehman Brothers of New York and from the other two Canadian financial houses now involved, Osler, Hammond and Nanton of Winnipeg and McLeod, Young, and Weir of Toronto. This group quickly agreed that the high equity ratio proposed by the bank would make the common stock quite unsaleable to the public. They also attempted to find some means whereby an investment as small as the bank's proposed 10% could make the company financeable. They failed to do so. The group broke up on the understanding that each member would continue to consider the problem and keep in touch with the negotiators, who were to go back to the bank with whatever modification of their case they could manage.

Nesbitt and Williamson returned to try to convince the Governor of the impossibility of selling common shares with the poor earning prospect available on an equity proportion as high as his proposed 30%. They then made a new proposal: the bank should subscribe to half of the company's debentures and agree to underwrite the balance. If that were done they thought they could place on their own all the first mortgage bonds and all the common shares of the company, as well as the balance of the debentures underwritten by the bank.

The Governor was not impressed. He continued to insist on a minimum of $105 million equity. He said it was a principle of sound finance to keep down interest-bearing debt by means of a sizeable issue of common stock. Furthermore, the company and the bank had to be protected from any charge that Trans-Canada was earning an unduly large profit for the benefit of a small group of shareholders. The government was not going to make it possible, through the use of its credit, to benefit such a group. Coyne did concede, however, that once the company's bonds were sold, the bank should relinquish the first mortgage security behind its debentures.

Williamson and Nesbitt returned to the argument that the bank was offering to take debentures which would bring in a normal return on its money, and yet be convertible into common shares on its own option if the project was successful. The investing public would be asked to subscribe for two-thirds of the total equity – $70 million of common shares – without any hope of return for many years. But the Governor remained adamant.

During the protracted negotiations over the next few weeks meetings were held almost daily. Communications had to be kept open with Trans-Canada's widely scattered group of sponsors in Ottawa, Toronto, Montreal, Calgary, Edmonton, Winnipeg, New York and Dallas. The sponsors gave the two negotiators authority to offer further concessions to the bank subject to their approval of any final agreement.

While negotiations were proceeding between the bank and Trans-Canada, bits of news and gossip about the original company proposals for a government guarantee on its bond issue, and about the disagreement in cabinet between Howe and the younger ministers, began appearing in the press.

Michael Barkway expressed agreement in *The Financial Post* with unnamed political spokesmen who were quoted as having said that if the government was to be involved in the pipeline at all then the government should have control or ownership or both.

Much less friendly criticism came from two opposite extremes. The dominant view in Alberta was well expressed by a Calgary writer who said that "the Trans-Canada people had no business to allow themselves to be forced into the costlier scheme of taking gas via a thousand miles of nothing through northern Ontario." At the other extreme, the Alberta CCF leader, Elmer Roper, stated that the Canadian taxpayers' money should not be used to aid "an unsavoury promotial racket."

On January 28 during the House of Commons question period, the CCF member for Vancouver East, Harold Winch, asked C. D. Howe about a story published in *The Vancouver Sun* to the effect that common shareholders in the Trans-Canada Pipe Lines Company would stand to make from 20% to 40% profit annually, either under private or government-guaranteed financing. When Howe answered, "No – to all phases of the question," Winch went on to ask whether the minister was considering any policy for the protection of the Canadian people with regard to the pine line? "Is the answer to that question also No?" Howe replied sarcastically, "Mr. Speaker, the answer is that the minister spends nights and days considering the welfare of the people of Canada."

On February 4, Carl Nickle, the Progressive Conservative oil journalist and member for Calgary South asked Howe to explain why no gas purchase contracts had been signed between Trans-Canada and the gas producers. Howe replied, "My honourable friend has more information about the subject than I have. He evidently is in close touch with the people for whom he is asking the question and I suggest he seek the information there." And for the next six weeks the government kept silent.

Towards the middle of March, as journalists sensed that negotiations were coming to a head and a decision was imminent, the tide of comment and criticism mounted. That friend and scourge of Liberal governments, the *Winnipeg Free Press,* headed their lead editorial of March 11 HOWE DISPENSABLE? and went on to say, "more lobbying than thinking has been involved in the intense discussion in Ottawa this week. C. D. Howe is said to be sticking to the view that the company should have got the sort of help it asked for two months ago, that is, the federal government should guarantee its bonds. He may well have found ways of obtaining the acquiescence of his weaker colleagues. But Mr. Howe is not invincible; his beloved TCA monopoly, for example, was broken recently when the cabinet at last allowed Canadian Pacific Airlines to fly to Amsterdam." The *Free Press* attacked the requested bond guarantee as "irresponsible finance, bad economics and worse government. This should be clear in the mind of Mr. St. Laurent. One cannot help believing that it really is clear to Mr. Howe too. But if it is not, if he feels personally committed to a bond guarantee, then the final step by which Mr. St. Laurent should close the argument is also clear. In the last resort the Prime Minister should be compelled to require Mr. Howe's resignation." If he failed to do so, the *Free Press* invited any members of the cabinet who have "some political horse sense and a modicum of courage" to protest by resigning themselves.

The most scathing criticism of Trans-Canada came from one of the FPC commissioners in Washington, Lee Smith, and it was widely reprinted in Canada. On March 11 Smith stated that pipeline applications which come before the FPC were required to measure up to certain standards. Trans-Canada had not reached them. Its financial plans were not perfected after months of effort. "It is completely lacking in firm purchase contracts. It lacks firm market commitments in eastern Canada. . . . In the absence of pipe line experience over the route of the proposed line, or reliable cost estimates, the Commission is without knowledge whether the gas can be sold in competition with other fuels in Trans-Canada's potential markets. It is difficult to see how any project could more completely fail to meet the standards enunciated by us." He was in effect telling Trans-Canada they had no business coming to the FPC without all arrangements completed in Canada. This must have felt like particularly gratuitous advice to men who had been struggling for a year to sign any contracts at all.

Commissioner Smith went on to ask for proof that American consumers in the mid-west were not being asked to subsidize a pipeline across Ontario. He concluded by saying that he was strongly impelled to dismiss the application, but he was concurring in the decision of his more lenient colleagues on the FPC to keep the application alive a while longer in case, against all expectation, Trans-Canada were able to meet the requirements he had mentioned. "I deem it important that the gross deficiencies of their record to date be pointed out now, thus enabling the applicants to correct them if they can. There should be no complaint from any quarter that they have not been warned."

Perhaps Commissioner Smith, like the Alberta producers, was really complaining that anyone should be foolish enough to expect Canada to be an economic entity at all. Critics were on a stronger ground when they said that if there had to be a Canadian pipeline, Ontario consumers should be required to share the extra cost with the Alberta producers. Criticism of Trans-Canada on the grounds that it should be publicly owned was much more plausible and open to more complex investigation. For the moment, however, the government did not seriously entertain the idea of public ownership, although later it was accepted as a possible last resort.

In addition to the public criticism, the negotiators found themselves under great private pressure. Alan Williamson wrote Howe on February 15, during a brief respite he had taken from the Ottawa talks to meet commitments in Vancouver:

"Dear C.D., This is just a note to thank you for your continued attention to the problems of Trans-Canada. I judge from talks with several people that your task is not easy. The time being consumed in getting action must be trying to you as it is to us. I can hardly believe I submitted a letter outlining a suggested method of proceeding as long ago as January 6.

"Since the only chance of proceeding this year is to act as if there is no doubt of our being able to finance, I have as treasurer, continued to assure my associates that assistance will be worked out. I have to collect a further half million dollars for our March expenditures within the next two weeks. Putting up these very large amounts is quite an act of faith. I have checked with Deane Nesbitt who has been in regular touch with you and he tells me that you approve and appreciate our proceeding as outlined above. He informs me that every single bit of information requested has been made available.

"While the granting of assistance may cause difficulty with the rank and file of your group, [i.e. the cabinet, the party and the senior civil servants: some rank and file!] I feel sure that they would all favour it if they understood the tremendous advantages to the country and particularly if they understood the mess we would all be in if the well-established policy of an all-Canada line had to be abandoned.

"I hope, C.D., you will find these comments of some value. I feel we are in this together and so far I have been able to have all my associates support anything that I think is in line with your thinking.

Regards, Alan."

Howe replied by telephone to the effect that he was desperately sorry concerning the attitude of the Bank of Canada but for the time being the matter was out of his hands.

Whatever the justice or accuracy of the criticism levelled at Trans-Canada, it did incline the company's negotiators to accept conditions from the bank that they otherwise would have refused. They felt a personal and moral obligation to Howe. They were aware of his own delicate position in the cabinet and they suspected his support was the only hope their project had left of staying alive.

Two deadlines loomed ahead. They had been given until April 30 to show proof of financeability by the Alberta and federal boards from whom they held conditional permits. An agreement with the bank might enable them to avoid the embarrassment of returning for further public hearings on yet another extension of the deadline. More immediate still was the need to place a firm order for pipe with the United States Steel Corporation by March 15. Steel was in extremely short supply – no Canadian companies manufactured large-diameter pipe – and there was no hope of starting construction in 1955 if Trans-Canada failed to hold its place in U.S. Steel's production schedule. To do so, definite evidence that Trans-Canada could finance the pipeline and pay for the steel pipe was demanded.

In desperation Nesbitt and Williamson went back to the bank and said they were willing to attempt to finance the company with a capital structure of $80 million worth of equity, which was double the size of their original proposal of $40 million. The Governor insisted as before on the original magic figure of $105 million. Since he would not budge from it, they suggested that the balance of $25 million of equity be taken by the bank in convertible debentures, but that these not be converted until earnings per share reached $1.25 and that the bank then pay $2.50 above the original $10 price of common shares offered to the public.

To this proposal Coyne agreed. He also agreed to show the bank's confidence in the company's stock by taking $5 million worth of shares before they went on sale to the public. The bank's total commitment would thus be $60 million in convertible debentures and $5 million in common shares.

With the financial structure settled in principle, a final meeting for negotiation, prior to formal signing the next day, was called for Sunday evening March 13 in the board room of the Bank of Canada.

At that meeting Williamson and Nesbitt were joined by President Tanner as well as the two senior members of the original pipeline groups, Clint Murchison from Trans-Canada and Ray Milner from Western. The meeting reviewed a long list of the bank's conditions. No change in the capital structure or in the officers of the company could be made, for example, without the bank's consent.

None of these conditions presented a problem. There was, however, one new factor introduced which threatened to destroy the whole arrangement. This was the question of whether the government, through the bank's possession of a majority of shares, should control the company. During the ten weeks of bargaining the two junior negotiators, Deputy Governor Ralph McKibbin for the bank and Deane Nesbitt for Trans-Canada, had frequently been given the task of working out a formula to resolve the deadlocks that arose. On one occasion with McKibbin, Nesbitt expressed his concern about the potential control of Trans-Canada by the bank, because the major potential gas supplier, Gulf Oil, had long followed an international policy that it would not sell oil or gas to a company controlled by a government body. William Whiteford, former president of Canadian Gulf and now president of the parent company in Pittsburgh, had expressed his concern over government participation to Nesbitt during negotiations, but the more serious question of the government owning a majority of common shares had not arisen in the discussions with Gulf. To head off this difficulty in advance, Nesbitt suggested to McKibbin that if the bank was to convert its debentures into common shares these should remain non-voting until they were sold to the public, at which time they would have the same voting rights as other shares held by the public. This idea did not seem unreasonable to McKibbin, and on his part he said he was ready to accept it and recommend it to the Governor. Unknown to either of them, on January 26, 1955, Robert Bryce drew up a memo for the Prime Minister, based on all the information he had seen on Trans-Canada and on conversations with officials in Finance, Trade and Commerce, and the Bank of Canada. Bryce commented, "I would think that the Crown equity need not have voting rights or a voice in management as long as it is getting a reasonable return." He warned against the dangers of government providing some portion of the capital required as leading to government participation in other projects, "no matter how cleverly we distinguish this case." But he concluded that if the government were prepared to embark on "a policy of assisting in the finance of a program of national development, this consideration need not be an obstacle on the pipe line."

Governor Coyne, however, was not prepared to rule out government control. To the dismay of the Trans-Canada negotiators he informed them, for the first time, on that Sunday evening, that any shares held by the bank resulting from conversion would have to be voting shares. He also added a further condition that the Bank of Canada's agreement to the proposals would be dependent on the company having signed a purchase contract with Canadian Gulf for approximately one-third of its gas supply. These two conditions, as

Williamson and Nesbitt pointed out, made it almost certain that the project would fall through. However they said that Trans-Canada itself was prepared to accept, while warning that under such terms any agreement with Gulf, who had already balked at signing a purchase contract, might now be impossible. The meeting broke up about midnight and the Trans-Canada negotiators returned to their hotel in a depressed state.

Early the following morning they began phoning all over the continent to those partners in the project who were not present, urging them to accept the proposal. None of them liked it, but if they turned it down, as the negotiators pointed out, "the general public would feel that the company had not lived up to its obligations in taking advantage of the Bank's offer and getting this nationally important project under way." By Monday afternoon all the sponsors had given their consent.

Throughout the day Williamson tried to contact President Whiteford of Gulf by telephone. He finally tracked him down in a Vancouver hotel room. When Whiteford heard about the bank's shares giving it potential control of Trans-Canada, he categorically refused to sign a contract for gas supply. In spite of much pleading, Williamson was unable to budge him from this position. Late in the day, Williamson and Nesbitt returned to the bank board room to face the Governor. Coyne stated that Gulf's attitude was flagrant defiance of the government of Canada by a foreign company, and urged them to tell Whiteford that he had better change his mind. On Tuesday Williamson phoned Whiteford and reviewed the situation again, but was met once more with a flat refusal to tie himself up in a long term contract with a company that could be controlled by the government. He said that this had no specific relation to the government of Canada but was a matter of his company's international policy.

Before the final Sunday night meeting, it was assumed that an agreement would have been worked out in time to meet the United States Steel deadline of Tuesday, March 15. Williamson frantically contacted an officer of the corporation and requested an extension of the Tuesday midnight deadline. He said that they might possibly arrange to give Trans-Canada until Saturday night of the same week. At this point Williamson and Nesbitt decided to summon all board members to meet in Ottawa on Wednesday, so that in case everything fell apart, they could take immediate action.

As they each arrived in Ottawa on Wednesday morning after a night in planes and airports, they were greeted with the unpleasant news that U.S. Steel would not hold Trans-Canada's place in their schedule unless they received a commitment by midnight of that same day.

The board meeting had scarcely begun when there was a knock on the door and a member opened it to find awaiting them the Deputy Governor of the Bank of Canada, Ralph McKibbin, with a thick letter from Governor Coyne. The letter was read out immediately.

In it Coyne said that the two Trans-Canada negotiators had previously told him that Gulf would sign a supply contract by the end of March. "It was accordingly an astonishing development to learn on Monday, March 14, when papers would be completed for signing that afternoon, that Mr. Whiteford said he would not let the Canadian company sell gas to your company now or at any time in the future. . . . I am by no means convinced, on the one hand, that the Canadian Gulf Company cannot be brought back into the picture, nor on the other hand that co-operation of Mr. Whiteford is necessary for the successful operation of this enterprise in the long run. . . . You assured us you had no reason at any time for expecting Mr. Whiteford to adopt this attitude."

The board members were incensed over the tone of the letter and by what they considered its serious inaccuracies and false assumptions. But they decided it would be politic to draw up a brief and restrained reply for signature by President Tanner. The only attempt at a rebuttal took the form of two observations: "Gulf Oil did not tell us they would not sign a contract with us because they did not trust the Canadian government. Gulf Oil takes the position that they do not wish to tie up their gas in a long term contract to a company that can be controlled by a government or any agency thereof."

The board concluded that any attempt to build the pipeline during 1955 was now completely out of the question. They also informed Coyne of this and told him they would delay release of a press statement, which they had planned for that evening, until the following afternoon, so that the government might, if it wished, make a statement of its own first.

During Wednesday evening, Deane Nesbitt received a phone call from Governor Coyne who was at the home of the Minister of Finance, Walter Harris. Coyne asked if he would read out Trans-Canada's proposed press statement. This Nesbitt did and the Governor made no comment. Next day there was no government statement. At Trans-Canada's press conference Thursday afternoon the directors avoided any specific reference to Canadian Gulf or any potential supplier, since some other oil companies had also expressed similar views, and quite apart from trying to be fair, they had no wish to alienate their largest potential source of supply. The essence of Trans-Canada's position was summed up in three sentences: "To date the company has been unable to negotiate a type of financial assistance that does not result in an agency of the government of Canada being in position to control the company, and such an arrangement makes it impossible for the company to purchase its gas requirements. Under the circumstances the directors of Trans-Canada have most reluctantly reached the conclusion that there are no further steps within their power which can now be taken to arrange the financing to meet this year's construction program. Trans-Canada will continue its efforts to arrange the financing of its project from private capital sources."

It was evident at the press conference that several of the reporters had been tipped off about Canadian Gulf's role in the affair, and when the reports appeared they all included the reference to that company as being responsible for the breakdown.

In the House of Commons the next day, Howard Green noted Trans-Canada's press release and asked the Prime Minister for comment on whether there had been any change in government policy. St. Laurent expressed his disappointment that circumstances did not permit construction of an all-Canadian line in 1955, but added that there was no change of the policy expressed in Howe's statement of March 13, 1953. It was not until March 23, that the government, in response to a question put on the order paper by Stanley Knowles in January, finally announced it had turned down the Trans-Canada request for a bond guarantee. In response to further questioning by Knowles about whether the proposed all-Canadian pipeline should be owned by the government, Walter Harris replied that the question was not applicable because the company had announced that it was going to go ahead without government aid.

The leader of the CCF, M. J. Coldwell, attacked the postponement of construction: It showed "the power of American oil monopolists to stymie any economic development" and was a serious blow to a nation already facing a severe unemployment problem. *The Financial Post* of March 26 also put its finger on Gulf Oil as the chief culprit. After conceding that some credit was due the original sponsors for having "burned up a terrific amount of energy in efforts to line up the sundry parties involved," the *Post* concluded that, "the important thing now is to get going. If Trans-Canada can't perform, let somebody else have a crack at it. Although the Company is understood to be still talking hopefully, before renewing its authority on April 30, Ottawa should take the sharpest view of Trans-Canada's record of endeavour and look closely too at some alternate groups who want to step into the picture. Have all reasonable steps been taken? We doubt it. The two great national railways are in the transportation business, both of them with the problem of low and declining revenues. Finding a gas line deal won't be easy. But doing the far-sighted creative thing never is easy. This is not an enterprise for men of little faith."

The public debate continued during March. A Liberal MP picked up the idea of asking Canadian National Railways to do the job. It was not public knowledge at the time, but Howe had privately asked CN President Donald Gordon to consider the matter. Gordon took the view that his main priority was railways rather than public transport in general and that CN had enough troubles as it was without tackling more.

Howe was repeatedly criticized for attempting to give help to a private company. Satisfaction was expressed in many editorial columns at Howe's defeat in cabinet. But if he was blamed in some quarters for offering too much of the wrong kind of support in order to make an all-Canadian route possible, he was criticized elsewhere for precisely the opposite reasons. "Alberta has more gas than it knows what to do with," said *Myers Oil Quarterly*, "and the all-Canadian line will cost forty million dollars more than it would via a partial U.S. route. If Ottawa wants the line to go this way for the benefit of the nation, it should not saddle either western producers or pipe line builders with the extra burden. Either set them free or get in and pitch." Carl Nickle, the Calgary oil journalist and Conservative MP, returned to his programme for seeking sales first in the United States, and denounced Howe for putting "the shackles of political expediency on the piping of Alberta gas into eastern Canada." He nicknamed the pipeline "Howe's folly." Government insistence on an all-Canadian route was based "on denial of economic sense in favour of nationalism." He proposed that the government support freedom of the market and "yank down the barriers at the U.S. border."

Apart from those who proposed government ownership of the line, however, there was little certainty as to what precisely might be done. *The Financial Post* on April 2 summed up the general feeling of dismay. "The failure of Trans-Canada is certainly no cause for private enterprise pride. Here is a great national utility that has crumbled . . . an obvious need that is not being met. This project has suffered from apathy and pettiness of vision in quarters where it has deserved a very different reception. The shuffling mentality was not the one that built Canada or set it on its path to greatness. It takes more than talk or the mouthing of slogans to make private enterprise work."

It was not clear whether *The Financial Post* (and those in the Canadian business community who agreed with it) was really blaming senior civil servants in Ottawa or C. D. Howe or Trans-Canada or American oil companies, or whether its approach was any less shuffling or confused than theirs.

Once Trans-Canada's directors made their decision on Wednesday, March 16, that there was no possibility of building the line in 1955, it is fair to say that none of them had any idea of what their next step might be. They were faced with mounting expenses as engineering work on rights-of-way and construction planning was now in full swing. They instructed company management to cut costs to a minimum and to inform the board within six weeks what the continuing expenses would be.

At the end of the board meeting Alan Williamson, who had been badly shaken at the news of Howe's defeat in the cabinet and exhausted by the ten weeks of negotiations with the bank, announced that his doctor was insisting he retire. He submitted his resignation from the board. Another representative of Wood, Gundy, Jack Mc-Causland, was appointed in Williamson's place, and Deane Nesbitt was elected to succeed him on the management committee. Williamson never recovered his health, and he died in 1961.

On the following day, when the press conference was over, the directors returned home. They were all faced with the formidable and unpromising task of trying to find some new approach to the company's financing. Whether motivated by such personal ambitions as Clint Murchison's for building the last and biggest project of his life, or by more mundane considerations like salvaging some of the effort and money that they had put into the project, none were sanguine about the prospect ahead. Few of them expected that day that their five-year struggle could now come to anything at all.

Chapter 7 "Damn Rhodes Scholars"

Twice within ten weeks now the launching of Howe's great national project had been frustrated by his colleagues in the cabinet and the public service. It was perhaps the only time during his twenty-year career in government that he had been defeated on a major issue on which he was determined to get his way. With his encouragement the project's sponsors had invested months of time, risked millions of dollars, and exposed themselves to public attack without being free to defend their position. He felt angry and humiliated that he had failed them. The issue had a particularly personal character. For Howe the engineer Trans-Canada was to be the greatest engineering feat of his lifetime and the crowning point of his career. The thing had been undermined, in his view, by men with sophisticated minds but little practical experience and less vision. He told old friends that he was involved with "a government that has fallen into the hands of children."

C. D. Howe was not an easy man to work for in March of 1955. His departmental energy consultant, Jack Davis, came into his office one morning and found him hunched over the pile of papers on his desk with a look of thunderclouds on his face and a particularly ferocious growl in his voice.

"Mr. Howe, some of us have been talking with Ross Tolmie of Trans-Canada and I think we have an idea that will work." Howe was in no mood to talk about pipelines and bright ideas. "Oh you and all the other damn Rhodes Scholars! Get the hell out of here!"

Pipeline construction as far as the eye can see.

Top: Charles S. Coates, C. D. Howe and N. E. Tanner, in February 1957, when $50 million loan was repaid to the Crown Corporation.

Bottom: James W. Kerr with James A. Roberts, Deputy Minister of Trade & Commerce, on the occasion of the purchase of the Northern Ontario Section of the pipeline, May, 1963.

Right: Pipelining in the Cambrian Shield.

Top: Final weld on initial Trans-Canada Pipe Line system — near Kapuskasing, October 10, 1957.

Right: Pipeline patrol in North Western Ontario.

Bottom: The pipeline on the Prairies — protection from corrosion.

Bottom opposite page: Concrete weights and specially protected heavy wall pipe for water crossing.

Top left: Sideboom tractor in action on third line near Portage la Prairie.

Above: James W. Kerr, right, and Ralph T. McElvenny, Chairman of American Natural Gas Company, turning first sod at start of Great Lakes construction, July, 1967.

Above right: St. Clair River crossing — preparation to link up with Great Lakes Gas Transmission system.

Bottom left: Coat and wrap machine in action near Cabri, Saskatchewan.

Bottom right: Looping near Swift Current, Saskatchewan.

Top: Construction of main line for export at Emerson, Manitoba. This line supplies both the Midwestern and Great Lakes systems.

Right: Modern aircraft jet turbine and compressor used in operations. This is one of Trans-Canada's pioneering efforts in pipeline engineering.

There is little doubt as to who were the Rhodes Scholars-in-chief in Howe's mind: the ones in Finance and the Bank of Canada. A few minutes later, however, it occurred to him that Davis 'and Tolmie also fitted into that category. He slammed the buzzer to Davis's office and a penitent voice came over the intercom, "Jack, forget what I said. Come on in and tell me what your idea is."

For the moment nothing further came of the idea Davis sketched out, but its chief author, the man who from that point carried the project through to a successful solution, now appeared on the scene. This was the associate deputy minister of Trade and Commerce, appointed before he was forty and personally selected by Howe himself. Mitchell Sharp had the reputation in the department of being the only person who could cope with Howe in a real crisis. He could stand his ground until one of them was convinced that the other was right. He had been away in Europe on departmental business earlier in the year and when he returned he was told, "It's been awful around here. If only you had been back."

In later years Sharp has been called the very model of the Ottawa mandarin. He was actually more than a generation younger than the first members of the species like Clifford Clark of Finance and Norman Robertson of External Affairs, and in point of service he was more junior still. Sharp was one of the few senior civil servants before the 1960s to have sprung from a working class background. With his country western look and his Stan Laurel face (He was once described as "a sort of Prairie Gothic Junior, son of Jest Folks.") he did not quite look the part of the discreet professors from Queen's and Toronto who for so many years advised the ministers of Mackenzie King. But except for a disarming openness of attitude and an informal manner, which helped him to relate to businessmen – and Mr. Howe – more readily than most deputy ministers, Sharp was very much one of them.

Sharp had not been following the Trans-Canada situation during his absence but he was horrified to learn that Howe should have taken up the idea of a bond guarantee so readily, and committed himself to it without regard for the political consequences. At the same time he was concerned that a vital national project might either be forced to build through the United States, or fail completely. He told Howe he was sure there must be a solution and asked for a chance to find it.

Howe said Yes, he guessed he could try – things could hardly be worse.

In the meantime, after the failure of negotiations with the Bank of Canada, no one in Ottawa and no one in the company had any clear idea of what could be done next. An increasing number of Albertans, especially several of the impatient petroleum companies, were quietly satisfied that an end to the foolish scheme had come. Within a short time the laws of economics would take over, supplemented by local political pressure, and the government would have to let Alberta gas move south across the border into its natural market.

But Trans-Canada's sponsors tried to gain time and prevent the government from responding to various pressures that would kill the project completely. On March 22 Eldon Tanner wired Prime Minister St. Laurent, "In view of reports that you may be planning a statement on the Trans-Canada pipe line, I have been asked to assure the government of our intention to do everything possible to bring to fruition this national project through the medium of private financing. We hope soon to be able to report better progress."

Murchison wrote a personal letter to Howe the following day in which he compared his situation to that of Marshal Foch ("My center is giving way, my right wing is in retreat. Excellent! I shall attack.") In a characteristic burst of optimism scarcely justified by any objective view of the facts, he told Howe, "If I have the full co-operation of you and Mr. St. Laurent I do think I can put the deal over without any other governmental help except tax relief. I am going to work immediately to that end and I have nothing but sanguine hopes of a definite successful conclusion to the venture without government aid." He then suggested the germ of a plan, on which he and his fellow directors would begin to work in the next several weeks and which implied a drastic modification of the scheme proposed so far. As the old Western group had suggested when they were fighting Murchison, the line might be built in two stages. The first stage would involve building from Alberta to Winnipeg, along with the spur down to Emerson at the American border and the line from Toronto to Montreal. The latter would be supplied from the northern end of Tennessee Gas Transmission's system. The second stage from Winnipeg to Toronto, which had been the chief stumbling block to Trans-Canada's financing all along, would be constructed later, once markets had been built up in eastern Canada. Murchison made a personal plea to Howe:

"I know I have taxed your patience and tolerance, but I beg of you to be lenient because I have the completion of this pipe line as my definite goal of achievement before I retire to the sunny valleys of Mexico.

"In view of the rumours that we are going to make innumerable millions of dollars out of this project, it perhaps has never occurred to some critics that this is a venture that challenges the imagination of people and can only be accomplished by those who are willing to put their blood and sweat into the soil of Canada. The money in this particular instance happens to be a secondary consideration. [I have] not received one penny for my time or my efforts, nor [have] we of Trans-Canada received one share of promoter's stock. The only stock available to us has been purchased at $8 per share in an amount equal to the actual money which we have spent on this project. Our next commitment is to purchase stock at $10 per share, which is the same price at which it will be made available to the Canadian public.

"But I do consider it a rare honour to associate myself with those developers of a new frontier to the end that in my old age I can look back to the accomplishment as a great source of personal satisfaction. I shall be forever indebted to you for your fine and warm friendship and advice."

Howe replied: "I am glad to know you are determined to put through the line. I am determined to see you get all the help the government can give you to that end. While I felt badly let down about government financial assistance, I am prepared to re-enter the ring when the time comes."

In the meantime, the one Trans-Canada director resident in Ottawa, Ross Tolmie, had heard that some sort of cabinet decision was coming soon. He telephoned Deane Nesbitt and wrote Frank Schultz to tell them he thought they should come back to Ottawa and stay until the decision was made. "I have gathered from several quarters here that there is a general impression in government circles that nothing is being done by Trans-Canada, that we are not pushing things, that we are divided, disheartened and indifferent. There is great danger that in our absence the government might take the easy course and defer decision until fall, by which time our permits expire and the possibility of the government opening up the field to all applicants becomes very real. While the management committee might not even be permitted to see the cabinet ministers who will be making the decision, I think it only a wise precaution and sound strategy for them to be in Ottawa and offer themselves for frank discussions with whatever ministers they can see. At least Clint and you should come from Dallas, Eldon and Charlie from Calgary, and Deane from Montreal, early next week, and see Mr. Howe in the first instance and whatever other members wish to discuss the case with you, and indicate that the majority of your group will stay on in Ottawa until a decision has been reached. This in itself will help to force the case and prevent the matter from being postponed."

Schultz and Nesbitt arrived and met Howe on March 27. They suggested that either the company should be allowed to build the line south of the Great Lakes through the United States and thus save $40 to $50 million in capital cost or else that the government should provide this difference in cost to carry out the present national policy of the all-Canadian route. Howe said it would be impossible to change national policy and allow the route to go through the United States. As far as the subsidy was concerned, while he favoured it himself, he had grave doubts about his ability to persuade the cabinet. Schultz and Nesbitt then put forward the idea already mentioned in Murchison's letter, of building the Alberta-Manitoba and the Toronto-Montreal lines first. In the second year or whenever possible the line could be completed from Winnipeg to Toronto. While sympathetic, Howe insisted on assurances, which they could not yet give, that the line would be completed within the second year.

Following their meeting, Howe wrote Nesbitt to say that during his coming absence on a trade mission in Australia, Mitchell Sharp would be his stand-in and the government's representative in the matter. "I have explained to him my commitments to you and have asked him to take up your problems with the Prime Minister. I will have a talk with the Prime Minister before I leave Canada and I am confident you will obtain the support of the government if you are able to carry out the plan you outlined here." Howe also wrote Tanner urging him to do everything he could to get more Alberta gas producers signed up as quickly as possible. "As you know, the situation in Alberta was the principal cause of lack of progress in your negotiations with the government" – a reference to the objections raised by Canadian Gulf and others over possible government control of the company.

On March 28 the day after Schultz and Nesbitt met Howe in Ottawa, a meeting was held in Premier Manning's office attended by Eldon Tanner and Ray Milner of Trans-Canada, along with William Whiteford and E. D. Loughney of Canadian Gulf. Manning wondered aloud whether some scheme could be worked out under which all three governments, Alberta, Ontario and Canada, might give the company joint assistance. He said he would discuss the whole matter with Premier Frost of Ontario. But he also expressed the Alberta view that his province should not be asked to subsidize the least satisfactory market available for Alberta gas, namely, Ontario and Quebec. He asked the company if they could study the costs of building south of the Great Lakes and carrying the gas through the United States into eastern Canada in bond. Whiteford stated that Gulf would be prepared to invest in the Trans-Canada venture if the southern route were adopted but that he had always been concerned about the economic feasibility of the all-Canadian route.

As a means of budging Ottawa from its announced national policy, Manning suggested that Alberta issue a permit to Trans-Canada allowing the line to be built south of the Lakes and that the company could "throw the order in the face of the federal government."

As promised, Manning met members of the Ontario government on April 12 and following this meeting the newspapers reported that Trans-Canada had revised its plan and might be able to make a start in 1955.

Because of renewed speculation that the federal government might modify its declared national policy, the giant American company, Tennessee Gas Transmission, now moved in with a proposal for a north-south continental exchange. On April 25 Tennessee offered to buy gas from Trans-Canada at the American border south of Winnipeg in order to gain entrance into mid-western markets where they had not sold gas before. To balance this they proposed to sell to Trans-Canada the entire gas requirements of eastern Canada at the Niagara end of their system, so that the Winnipeg to Toronto section of the line would not have to be built at all.

Tennessee's arch rival Northern Natural Gas of Omaha learned of this, and its president, John Merriam, wired Prime Minister St. Laurent on May 17 to say that his company was working on a gas exchange plan which "will provide the maximum joint United States and Canadian benefit." At the same time Merriam took the offensive against Trans-Canada, which until April 30 had been under contract to supply his firm with Alberta gas. Before that date Trans-Canada made every effort to renew their contract, but Merriam showed little interest. He apparently regarded Trans-Canada as next thing to dead anyway, but if it revived, felt he could renegotiate for gas at a more favourable price. Once he heard of Tennessee's move, however, Merriam threatened Trans-Canada with "legal and other appropriate action" if it did not "live up to its obligation to offer gas to Northern Natural before offering it to anyone else." Since the contract with Northern Natural had expired and Merriam had resisted their efforts to extend it, the management committee of Trans-Canada decided to ignore the threat, and in fact nothing came of it. They were now inclined to try for some sort of arrangement with Tennessee so that they could at least get a large supply of gas temporarily into eastern Canada with permission of the federal government. Nevertheless, Tanner discussed possible renewal with Merriam and Merriam got in touch with Howe.

Whichever way Trans-Canada moved a ferocious battle would ensue before the Federal Power Commission in Washington. Howe tried one way out by going to the top. He discussed the matter with American Defence Secretary Charles Wilson on a fishing trip. But Wilson was pessimistic about the prospect of getting the Tennessee proposal rammed through on a national defence basis to eliminate the long FPC hearings, an approach that Howe was naturally inclined to. In any case, Tennessee's enemies might still apply to the U.S. Supreme Court and create serious delays through litigation. Wilson told Howe that Northern Natural would do everything they could to block the Tennessee proposal.

In the meantime at a cost of over $150,000 a month, Trans-Canada kept its engineering firm, Bechtel-Mannix-Hester, steadily pushing ahead with the design for the whole line, the surveying and the acquisition of options along the pipeline route. The company officers continued to negotiate, with some slight progress, for contracts to buy gas in Alberta and sell it in the other provinces. The most important step made during the spring of 1955 was towards the creation of a customer in Montreal. Premier Duplessis and Quebec Hydro agreed, under stiff terms, to an option to sell the Montreal distribution system and to grant a provincial charter to a company formed for the purpose of buying it. Some members of the two original groups behind Trans-Canada independently undertook sponsorship of this new company, to be called Quebec Natural Gas.

Deane Nesbitt then arranged for the Royal Bank of Canada, on condition that the sponsors put up $13.5 million in equity, to loan the new company $25.5 million at the time the money would be needed for actual purchase and modernization. Nesbitt also persuaded Trans-Canada's two bankers, the Royal and the Canadian Bank of Commerce, each to loan 50% of the estimated cost of the Toronto-Montreal pipeline when the time came for its construction. It was the first proof of financeability that Trans-Canada had been able to obtain for any major portion of the pipeline and a crucial move towards financing the whole system. Astonished at this coup, Frank Schultz remarked that American banks would never have taken on such a risk. He later commented that it was only this sort of support from their bankers that had enabled Trans-Canada to survive at all.

Throughout the spring of 1955 the public fortunes of Trans-Canada Pipe Lines continued to look bleak, however, and its original plan was now widely assumed to be defunct. Late in May Howe himself proposed in cabinet the acceptance of Tennessee's continental exchange plan, but did not press his case and was quickly turned down. After the meeting he remarked that now he had been over-ruled on a bad plan nobody could attack a good one when he brought it in.

Part of the story leaked to the press. On May 31, 1955, under the headlines ALL-CANADA LINE FADES and CONTINENTAL POLICY LIKELY FOR NATURAL GAS, *The Globe and Mail* speculated that the idea of an east-west pipeline to carry Alberta gas across northern Ontario would be abandoned. "Trade Minister Howe is reluctantly said to have come to the conclusion that the all-Canadian line of which he was hitherto the leading advocate is not an economic proposition under existing conditions. Of course the line could be built with government assistance, but as the cabinet found last March, Alberta's big supplier,

Canadian Gulf, will have no truck nor trade with any company financed with government help." Whiteford of Gulf wrote immediately to Howe to complain of *The Globe's* over-simplification of his company's position. Nevertheless, Alberta producers were generally happy at the prospect of a change in course. So were Toronto interests who still hoped to stay with their American gas supply.

But there were pressures from other sides too. Most opposition MP's were eager to attack the government for any shift away from their announced national policy. The president of the Northwestern Ontario Liberal Association wrote to Prime Minister St. Laurent: "There was enough criticism of the oil pipe line going through the United States. Any suggestion that the gas line would do the same would kill the prospect of ever electing another Liberal from Manitoba to Sudbury for a generation. This barren sea of rock has proved since Confederation to be the uniting link of east and west instead of an impenetrable barrier of separation. Surely we deserve better than this." By early July the mayors of northern Ontario were flooding their Members of Parliament with wires against delay or abandonment of the all-Canadian route. At a meeting of the Ontario Council of Mayors and Municipalities they persuaded many of their colleagues outside of Toronto to do the same thing.

For some weeks in the early summer the government was leaning towards the removal of a fixed time limit on building the northern Ontario link, and hence the tacit admission that the import of large volumes of American gas into eastern Canada might become a permanent fact of life. By mid-July, however, the outline of a better solution was taking shape.

Mitchell Sharp had convened, with Howe's blessing, a small interdepartmental committee to review the problem. At one point with Kenneth Taylor of Finance he was discussing the economics of transportation, one of Taylor's special fields before he left McMaster University for government service at the outbreak of World War II. Taylor commented that it was a pity the transcontinental railways could not have been built by the government and then leased to the railroad companies for operation. At that moment Sharp saw what they had been looking for.

It was one of those obvious ideas that had been staring them in the face all along. The government would build the pipeline through northern Ontario and then lease it for operation to the company. Sharp's image and phrase for the solution, as with most important discoveries, was clear and utterly simple. He called it "a bridge in time," a bridge that would enable the enterprise to happen now rather than much later or never. It need not guarantee high profits to a small group of private stockholders, but it would assume the insurmountable costs of an unfinanceable but nationally desirable policy.

To do so the government would use a crown corporation, an instrument central to Howe's own policy and thinking during his twenty-year career in government. A public enterprise run like a private business rather than part of the civil service, the crown corporation has been used to manage the nation's largest harbours and for the creation of a national broadcasting network, as well as for the proudest single achievement of Howe's career, a national airlines to reduce the vast distances of Canada to a more human scale. During the war Howe created twenty-eight crown corporations to cope with the demands of the emergency. The crown corporation is now used for a range of activities as disparate as the Canadian National Railways, the largest; the National Research Council, the oldest; and half a century later, the Company of Young Canadians. It has been a crucial instrument for Canada's growth and survival in the twentieth century.

After further discussions with his committee and with Jack Davis of Trade and Commerce and Ross Tolmie of Trans-Canada, Sharp's idea was put to Howe. Howe was reluctant to embark on yet another radical departure, as long as some hope remained for financing the line privately with the help of any minor amendments to national policy that could be devised. He was feeling particularly tender still over the failure of his attempts at government involvement earlier in the year. He called Sharp back very quickly, however. "I had a talk with Mr. St. Laurent about your idea. He says you're right." From that point things moved swiftly for the rest of the summer.

It was determined that the uneconomic portion of the line could be best defined as lying between the Manitoba border and Kapuskasing, Ontario, and that this would cost a little over one-third of the total sum needed for the whole enterprise. There was a good chance the rest of the line over the prairies and from central Ontario to

Montreal and Ottawa could be financed privately. This solution in turn did not need to run counter to the Trans-Canada-Tennessee exchange proposal. Immediate supply of Ontario and Quebec with American gas could be used as a means of building up markets rather than as a permanent excuse for not putting the line across Northern Ontario. Permission for import and for building the Toronto-Montreal line would be granted only on condition that Ontario and Quebec use Alberta gas after the northern Ontario section was built.

Early in August Trans-Canada's management committee agreed in principle to the idea of a crown corporation for the line through northern Ontario. They then signed a contract with Tennessee Gas Transmission in Houston. On August 15 Eldon Tanner wired all Trans-Canada directors: "The government of Canada has offered to arrange for a form of assistance which we feel would make the project possible. Trans-Canada has been asked to prepare detailed information as to what is necessary and how the project can be carried out. This report will be discussed with Mr. Howe and his associates about September 1. To this end Trans-Canada has completed a contract with Tennessee Gas Transmission to sell them 200 million cubic feet of gas daily at Emerson and to buy gas from Tennessee at Niagara to supply the markets of Toronto and Montreal until Alberta gas arrives. Tennessee also agrees to buy off peak gas at Niagara if offered by Trans-Canada when the Canadian line is completed. Good progress is being made on all fronts. We are happy to advise that the whole program looks more encouraging."

It was the best news the company had had since its formation. The meeting mentioned by Tanner was duly summoned for the Prime Minister's office on September 1, 1955, to review the whole situation and insure that no further major breakdowns developed like that which had taken place in negotiations with the Bank of Canada. Both Howe and Walter Harris were present, along with Mitchell Sharp and the Clerk of the Privy Council, Robert Bryce, who acted as secretary. The Alberta delegation was headed by Premier Manning and included the chairman of his Conservation Board, Ian MacKinnon, and the president of Alberta Gas Trunk Lines. Trans-Canada was represented by its two chief executives, Tanner and Coates. Representatives of the Canadian Petroleum Association and of Canadian Gulf, the chief potential supplier, were also present. Manning began by stating that the Alberta gas reserves now showed a huge surplus. He urged one last effort to arrange for western gas to be moved east with 1956 as the target year for the beginning of construction. Otherwise Alberta would begin looking to sell its gas in the western part of the continent.

Tanner reported that the company's engineering work was almost complete and that 90% of right-of-way had been acquired across the prairies and 75% of the Toronto-Montreal route. Among the main potential customers, only the largest, Consumers' Gas of Toronto, was still holding out. Off-the-record talks with several financial institutions about the possibility of government involvement in the northern Ontario section of the line, revealed no substantial problem with potential investors.

The most important party not represented at the meeting was the Ontario government, but they were already known to favour the idea of a government-built line. A series of three important meetings took place during the course of September for the purpose of establishing more precisely what Ontario's role might be: the first on September 13 between Prime Ministers St. Laurent and Frost; the second on September 22 between Ontario government officials and Trans-Canada; and finally a crucial meeting of civil servants on September 27, chaired by Mitchell Sharp, at which A. R. Crozier of the Ontario Department of Mines put his government's view. His chief concern was the further delay that waiting upon FPC approval might involve, since the successful financing of Trans-Canada still presupposed some U.S. sales. For this reason Ontario proposed that the whole pipeline be built by a crown corporation and leased for operation to the company until it could be purchased.

This idea was unacceptable to the gas producers and the government of Alberta as well as to Trans-Canada. Ontario had no plans for such a line, and the federal officials put their government's case for leaving as much of the job to private enterprise as possible. If it owned the whole line, the federal government would be subjected to opposing political pressure from both producers and consumers over the price charged for transporting gas. Financing part of the line would make the national policy possible, while leaving it to the company to work out the inherent east-west conflict. Government financing of the northern Ontario section was not a subsidy, but a means of bringing Alberta gas to central Canada sooner rather than later and through Canada rather than through the United States. "The aim is to provide the minimal assistance necessary and to achieve these ends through an otherwise privately-owned and operated line."

Both parties agreed that a crown corporation receiving its powers from Ottawa and Queen's Park would be the proper instrument for financing and administering the northern Ontario bridge, and that its capitalization would be best achieved by direct advances from the governments rather than by an issue of guaranteed bonds to the public.

The federal officials left the meeting with the promise that government ownership of the whole line would not be ruled out, at least until it was discussed at the October dominion-provincial conference. But as Premier Douglas of Saskatchewan later remarked in a letter to Prime Minister St. Laurent, "The federal government had really made up its mind long since." Neither he nor Premier Campbell of Manitoba were effectively consulted about the possibility of a multi-government crown corporation.

On September 21 the federal Board of Transport Commissioners issued an order granting Trans-Canada leave to construct the Toronto-Montreal line and again extending the date for proof of ability to finance, this time from October 31, 1955, to April 30, 1956. The Alberta Conservation Board followed suit. It was decided that the engineering and construction of the northern Ontario line would be undertaken by the firm responsible for the rest of the pipeline. Their estimate of the cost was slightly under $118 million. A major North American insurance company, Sun Life, advised that the government proposal would in their view make it possible for Trans-Canada to finance the balance of the line, provided that all necessary regulatory bodies and governments gave their approval in time.

Asked by Trade and Commerce when it might be able to pay the government and take title to the northern Ontario section of the line, the company replied that it hoped to do so once annual sales reached about 235 billion cubic feet. Trans-Canada estimated that this should happen during the fifth year of full operation from west to east. That figure was in fact reached during the fourth year of full operation, 1962.

At the fall board meeting on October 7, President Tanner had to

report, along with the good news, that at least four areas of serious
difficulty remained. Consumer's Gas of Toronto would still not sign
a contract and were now raising difficulties about letting Trans-
Canada use the facilities of the Niagara-Toronto line in order to
supply Montreal. (The C. D. Howe papers contain cheerful letters
about expanding gas sales in Toronto area from Oakah Jones of
Consumers' Gas, to which Howe replied cheerfully in kind, but also
with the pointed question, "Why don't you sign a contract with
Trans-Canada?") In Alberta the Conservation Board was in effect
making requirements that amounted to direction of the Trans-Canada
project. As far as gas buyers were concerned, now that there was a
possibility of federal assistance to Trans-Canada, Canadian Gulf and
others were demanding an increased price. Tanner commented that
the renegotiation clause which Gulf was insisting upon would virtually set up that company as the rate regulating body for Trans-Canada.

These three difficulties, however, were eventually surmounted.
But the fourth, before the end of the year, was to lead to a drastic
change in the company. The steel shortage was now worse than ever.
Since the whole capacity of American steel mills for 34-inch pipe was
already sold out for the first half of 1956, and since Canadian companies could not undertake to make large-diameter pipe, it would
be necessary for the U.S. Steel Corporation to build additional mills
for the manufacture of Trans-Canada's pipe. To undertake this, and
hence ensure a start on the pipeline in 1956, U.S. Steel required a
commitment for $40 million worth of pipe by November 1, 1955.
Trans-Canada's sponsors determined to do everything they could to
meet this requirement or find an alternative. They succeeded – but
at the price of yielding temporary control to an entirely new group.
As we shall see, Trans-Canada became for the first time an American-
run company. It was not a step that augured well for passage of the
proposed pipeline legislation in the 1956 session of Parliament.

Chapter 8 "Gringo Go Home"

"I have never started anything that I could not finish," wrote C. D. Howe to Clint Murchison in the fall of 1955, "and one thing I intend is the building of the Trans-Canada pipe line. It seems to me that we have it licked for the moment." Murchison wanted to know whether Trans-Canada should get a good publicity man to cope with the mounting chorus of public criticism. "You pledged us to keep our mouths shut in answering our critics in Canada and we have diligently complied." Howe said No; action, not a battle of words, was the answer. "Adverse criticism is coming from the city of Toronto where the Consumers' Gas Company, with its advisers, Stone and Webster, is trying to stir up trouble. Consumers' Gas would like to delay your project until 1959 when they will inherit the Niagara Pipe Line. We must make sure that this does not happen."

As usual Howe did his best to look upon the bright side of Trans-Canada's affairs. He pointed out that on September 25 he had just signed a letter granting the final authority from the government for the export-import exchange of gas with Tennessee. He was impressed with Tennessee President Gardiner Symonds' confidence over obtaining early FPC approval. He assured Murchison that the final stages of the discussion between Ontario and Ottawa "have no vital bearing on the situation, for if Ontario does not join us, the federal government will finance the centre section of the line without help."

Four senior members of the American cabinet – John Foster Dulles, George Humphreys, Sinclair Weeks and Ezra Benson – had just paid Howe a visit. He hoped their talks had laid the foundation for "solving a few problems that are causing great irritation here. We had both better keep in mind the condition of President Eisenhower and Lyndon Johnson. Our friends in Washington will certainly feel the absence of the president, to say nothing of the problem of choosing another leader for the next election." It is a sad irony that on the day Howe himself died of a heart attack, New Year's Eve, 1960, Eisenhower was still President of the United States and Johnson the Vice-President-elect. Howe went on to share his conviction that Trans-Canada was the last great project of their lives. "I have never been so busy or had so many difficult problems at hand; however, I am looking forward to the day when I can return to normal life, after which I will be camping on your doorstep. We are both young men yet, but I am reaching the point where I look forward to being free to go and come as I please."

The only note of anxiety in Howe's letter had to do with the problem that was worrying Trans-Canada's Board of Directors. As long as the company could not be financed, how could it order the pipe it would need to begin construction in the spring? The U.S. Steel Corporation had set a new deadline of November 1 for a commitment from Trans-Canada for a place in its 1956 production schedule.

Since Trans-Canada was still a "paper" company, it needed powerful backing for its commitments. The American steel companies made it clear that in their view the sponsoring groups behind Trans-Canada were not sufficiently credit worthy to ensure payment for a huge steel order, even if they had been willing to take on the liability. Deane Nesbitt approached the Royal Bank of Canada on behalf of the company, but as he expected found the bank unwilling to face the prospect of owning $40 million worth of pipe should Trans-Canada fail. Neither Trans-Canada nor Howe was willing at this stage to contemplate again any form of government involvement by way of loan or guarantee. So the company was really limited to asking for help from someone who could if necessary use the pipe in some other project. Frank Schultz attempted to make an arrangement with the giant El Paso firm, but in the end Trans-Canada had to face the fact that there was only one logical partner in the affair. Tennessee Gas Transmission was the largest of all the American companies in the field. Time and again it had moved aggressively into other companies' market areas, won FPC approval, and competed successfully for business. Its president, Gardiner Symonds, was the ablest and the toughest operator in the whole business. One of the few defeats he had ever sustained in recent years was the loss of his executive vice-president, Charles Coates, to Trans-Canada. Above all, because of the export-import scheme that would help it crack the mid-western market, Tennessee had a vested interest in the success of Trans-Canada.

Gardiner Symonds was approached by representatives of the two original sponsoring groups behind Trans-Canada, Clint Murchison for Canadian Delhi and Deane Nesbitt for Western Pipe Lines. The three of them met in Murchison's suite in the Waldorf during the middle of October.

Symonds stated his terms for ordering the pipe on behalf of Trans-Canada. They were quite simple: outright control of the company during the time of the liability. Murchison and Nesbitt urged him to consider their own long and costly involvement in the company's struggle to survive. He then agreed to take a 40% instead of a 51% interest in Trans-Canada. But when the group met again a week later, they were dismayed to find that Symonds had changed his mind. During the interval he had persuaded Canada's chief potential supplier, Canadian Gulf, to become involved along with him. He now insisted that Tennessee and Gulf between them have an option on 50% of the shares of Trans-Canada's stock. He did concede after further bargaining that this half ownership of the company would bring with it a proportionate responsibility towards all future capital and operating costs. Murchison and Nesbitt phoned their partners and persuaded them that this was the only course left. They signed an agreement on November 1, 1955, and Symonds placed an order with United States Steel for Trans-Canada's 1956 pipe requirements.

He had not yet given up his original objective of gaining control, however. He continued trying to line up other Alberta gas producers, and he succeeded in involving another, Continental Oil, through its Canadian subsidiary, Hudson's Bay Oil and Gas. On December 29 he presented an ultimatum to a meeting of the executive committee of Trans-Canada in New York. He now insisted the arrangement be changed so that his liability for the steel order would be shared equally with Gulf and Continental. The three American corporations

must have 17% of the shares of Trans-Canada each, a total of 51%.
The original sponsors argued that the government of Canada could
not possibly build the northern Ontario section for Trans-Canada
if the company were controlled by three newly involved American
corporations.

After the meeting Deane Nesbitt called Ottawa and made an appointment to meet C. D. Howe the following morning. On his arrival,
after telling Howe what had happened the day before, he was dismayed to discover that Symonds had telephoned Howe the previous
evening. Howe had consented to the 51% arrangement on condition
that Tennessee and its partners would cease to control the company
after the public offering of shares, so that there would then be an
opportunity for Canadian ownership. Howe did not realize that Symonds had always accepted this condition. The original group thus
lost their only bargaining lever, and they were forced to capitulate.
They would retain 49% of the stock, 24½% each. The agreement was
not formalized until February 8. But by the end of the year Tennessee and its two allies had in effect acquired control of the company. In recognition of this, the Trans-Canada board immediately
added a representative each to its executive committee from Canadian
Gulf and Hudson's Bay to join Symonds on that body.

It was a hard blow for the original sponsors. Paul Clarke of Lehman Brothers wrote to Nesbitt on December 30, 1955, following the
meeting the previous day with Symonds: "I am 100% in accord with
the decision made but by the same token I am just about 100% unhappy with the . . . machinations which proceeded yesterday. You
have been in one of the biggest things in anybody's life for many years
now and have played in my book a very important part in keeping
the show together. In doing so you have had to face some fairly substantial decisions, and I guess they get more so rather than less as
time goes on. Certainly the one made yesterday must have been one
of the bitterest of all."

In the long run, the presence of Symonds and his allies in the
company produced two advantages which may well have been decisive to its successful financing. Symonds brought into the picture his
old associate Francis Kernan of White, Weld and Company, New
York, the man who had put together in 1947 the gas industry's first

"paper" pipeline – one sponsored by investment dealers and financed
by large investing institutions, rather than originated by a firm operating already in the petroleum industry.

In so doing Kernan set the whole pattern for the development of
this new industry in North America. Furthermore, the involvement
of Hudson's Bay Oil and Gas and Canadian Gulf in Trans-Canada,
along with Murchison's Canadian Delhi, meant that three of the four
largest gas producers in Alberta were now participating. It gave them
a direct interest in the success of Trans-Canada, and an incentive,
should the necessity arise, for lowering their gas prices in order to
make Trans-Canada financeable and its gas competitive with other
fuels in eastern Canada.

In the short run, however, the new controlling group meant even
more opposition to American involvement in the "all-Canada" pipeline and more political trouble in the offing as the federal government prepared to introduce its legislation for the Northern Ontario
Crown Corporation during the 1956 session of Parliament.

In the meantime opposition was mounting in the United States
as well, but for different reasons: the scheme would benefit Canada
to the detriment of the United States. Import of Alberta gas into
the American mid-west was denounced by a spokesman for the United
States coal producers as a "brazen attempt to force the American
people to subsidize a costly and unnecessary pipe line across Canada."
That ancient volcano of the American labour movement, John L.
Lewis, vowed with all the force of his black bushy brows and mastiff
jaw that he would stop the Trans-Canada scheme at any cost. It would
displace nearly 25 million tons of coal being shipped from the
United States into Canada. Worse still, "the importation of natural
gas from a foreign country poses a dagger at the heart of all the coal
industry in the United States and threatens to disrupt a broad seg-
ment of the American national economy.

Railroad companies and other union lobbies were equally voci-
ferous. Every few seconds' delay in hearings before the FPC meant
another ton of coal mined or a few dollars more revenue for the hard-
pressed American railroads. There was the additional incentive in
this case that the whole scheme might well collapse if resistance could
be maintained long enough.

Tennessee's competitors in the gas business were also preparing for a big battle. When Tennessee first applied for permission to import in October 1955, Gardiner Symonds was confident that he could win FPC approval for his scheme. He was known as "the real doer of the American gas industry – he has never lost a major battle before that body." During 1955 Tennessee broke into both the New England and the New York City markets against the bitter opposition of a rival gas company. But by their closing date at the end of 1955, no less than 125 interventions had been received by the FPC. It was little consolation to Trans-Canada that no one else stood a better chance than Tennessee of gaining approval for the import of gas.

By January observers in Washington were convinced that hearings could last as long as two years. Clearly a decision would not be handed down before May 1, the most recent date for proof of finance-ability granted to Trans-Canada by the Canadian regulatory boards.

On the other hand pressures in Canada to begin construction during the spring of 1956 were mounting to a new peak of intensity. On January 24 the head of the Winnipeg and Central Gas Company wrote C. D. Howe, "the 1955 delay we have swallowed. The 1956 situation is another matter. It's costing us substantial sums to keep our utility alive by continuing our coke oven operation and continuing to supply propane as an interim substitute for natural gas in new housing developments. Winnipeg builders are swamping us with orders. Our Canada Cement contract is assured only if we can start delivery of gas in the fall of 1956." The Winnipeg company publicly offered a $1 million interest-free loan to Trans-Canada as a token of its desire to get the western part of the line started immediately.

In Ontario the government was more conscious than ever of the approaching energy shortage. A bill to enable the province to participate in the Northern Ontario Pipe Line Crown Corporation was quickly pushed through the Ontario legislature, by a unanimous vote of 88 to 0, on February 22, 1956. Premier Frost urged Howe to have the equivalent federal legislation passed quickly.

Alberta producers were anxious for Trans-Canada to get going, now that their desire for an exclusively western market was ruled out. On February 25, the Alberta Conservation Board without a public hearing granted an extension of Trans-Canada's deadline.

Two days later Howe assessed the situation as he saw it in a letter to President Tanner. "I am hopeful that the Trans-Canada Pipe Lines debate may commence this week. Between Frost and myself we were able to get a unanimous vote in the Ontario house. I hope we can keep Social Credit with us in the federal house. The CCF will definitely vote against and the unknown factor is the position of the Conservatives. It is quite certain that the attack will be concentrated on the American ownership. I will take the position that I am not greatly concerned about this and that it is not pertinent to the bill under consideration." Like a watchful coach from the sidelines, Howe went on to make the further suggestion that "the Trans-Canada officers to appear [in committee] be yourself, Coates and Nesbitt." The less seen of the new American directors the better.

Until the first major clash over the bill on March 15, Howe spent much of his time in the House fending off various opposition probes for information. The more successful he was, the more exasperated they became and the greater was the pressure built up for the explosion in May.

On February 15 George Hees inquired about the chances of the application of Trans-Canada Pipe Lines being approved by the Federal Power Commission before the target date of March 1. The question was dismissed by the Speaker on the ground that the member was seeking for an opinion and not facts. When Hees pressed further, Howe rose and without bothering to tell Hees that his date was wrong simply stated, "Mr. Speaker, there is no application by Trans-Canada before the Federal Power Commission and as far as I know there never will be." Stanley Knowles then pressed in where Hees had failed. He got his facts almost right by inquiring about the present status of Tennessee's application to import gas into the U.S. from Canada. Maddeningly, but accurately enough, Howe replied, "I am not greatly interested. . . . I have not been following the matter and I have no information to give." A few minutes later the elderly Tory aristocrat J. M. Macdonnell realized that it was a Tennessee subsidiary that was making the application and framed another question. This extracted from Howe the reply, "Frankly I do not know the name of the organization, Mr. Speaker. It is a subsidiary of Tennessee. I shall endeavour to write and get the name and give it to my honourable friend." His tall, gaunt frame quivering with excitement, Macdonnell cried out, "It is coming up; it is getting hot."

The opposition for the first time sensed the possibility of a major victory in the House of Commons. They had already succeeded in the summer of 1955 in forcing Howe's first public defeat by splitting the cabinet on the issue of the indefinite extension of his powers in the Defense Production Act. Since Howe's powers as Minister of Defence Production could make him "the virtual dictator of the whole economy," as Donald Fleming put it, they dug in and fought for a compromise. Some members of the cabinet who half agreed with such criticism were a good deal more anxious than Howe to avoid a summer-long filibuster. While Howe was prepared for some concessions, he rejected the idea of any time limit on his emergency powers. During his absence over a long weekend he left the matter with his colleagues to act as they saw fit. Prime Minister St. Laurent and Opposition Leader Drew arrived at a compromise which in effect was a capitulation to Drew's terms. As one observer put it, it was "the issue on which George Drew enjoyed his greatest hour of triumph in the House." The Liberals had barely concealed division in their own ranks and then retreated despite their vastly superior numbers. Howe was furious when he heard the news, and summoned House Leader Walter Harris to his House of Commons office. St. Laurent got wind of this and within moments of Harris's arrival, slipped into Howe's office unannounced, and nodded at Harris to leave. St. Laurent told Howe that the decision to compromise was entirely his own, and there the matter ended.

But the whole issue was revived when John Diefenbaker went on the air March 9 with a blast at the government's proposed pipeline bill. He referred to the opposition victory in the Defense Production filibuster and then warned: "That battle we won. But let me tell you that the fight we put on then will appear but a mere skirmish beside the battle we will wage when the bill regarding Trans-Canada Pipe Lines comes before parliament." He spoke with supreme scorn of Ottawa's tight money policy towards western farmers and contrasted to this its "touching solicitude" for American big business. Here was a company which "would take for itself the profitable end of the project and pile the unprofitable on the backs of Canadian tax payers." Placing of Canadian natural resources in the hands of American financial interests would make this country "a virtual economic forty-ninth state." While Diefenbaker and some Conservative MP's were demanding the line be built by Canadian private enterprise, other groups, notably unions and students and such organizations as the Young Progressive Conservatives, were asking for the whole line to be built under government ownership.

Opposition Leader Drew managed to straddle both positions by stating that he doubted whether any part of the line had to be built by public authority, but that if it did, then the whole line should be so built. It could then be leased for operation by private enterprise. The main burden of Drew's attack on Trans-Canada was that it should be reorganized completely and put under Canadian ownership and control. Other opposition speakers stressed the difference between the original conception of an all-Canadian line, with no dependence on gas export, and the present position that financing the line had to wait until Washington gave permission.

The CCF leader, M. J. Coldwell, made a strong case for public ownership. He quoted arguments in favour of public utilities from former Conservative party leaders ranging back over fifty years. He pointed out that the Ontario government had originally proposed a multi-government public utility as the best means of building a pipeline, and were only accepting Howe's policy as second best. But the most passionate part of his speech had to do with Canada's alienation of her natural resources to the benefit of American private enterprise.

When C. D. Howe introduced the motion to consider his pipeline bill on March 15, he concentrated on whatever Canadian aspects of Trans-Canada Pipe Lines he could find. He pointed out that the officers were chiefly Canadian, that eleven of the eighteen members of the board were Canadian and that at least 51% of the voting shares were to be offered to the Canadian public. He stressed the benefit to Canada of what in effect would be a billion-dollar enterprise and stated that his government had never given Trans-Canada "any reason to expect any sympathy from this government unless they were prepared to meet the national policy of serving the Canadian market first, and unless they were prepared to share ownership and management with Canadians." He said he welcomed American experience and technical knowledge, and the fact that these would bring with them the loan capital which could not be raised in Canada.

"If there is some uneasiness in this country about the extent and nature of United States investment in Canada," Howe continued,

"this is the wrong place to focus it. Trans-Canada is no doubt im-
perfect, as we all are, but its willingness to share its ventures with
Canadians is not in question. It offers to other industries which have
equally strong connections beyond our borders and which for some
reason have not been subjected to the same criticism a model which
they might well study."

But Howe's strongest argument lay in the hard facts of the situation as it was in the spring of 1956, rather than in the realm of what
might have been. The company and the government and their opponents might each have exaggerated or misjudged the risks and
opportunities at various times during the five-year struggle to make a
feasible project. But by the end of March pressures building up in
favour of the Trans-Canada scheme seemed to be irresistible. First
and foremost, the provincial governments most urgently concerned
with the project were now all solidly in favour of it. While Premier
Manning may have been reluctant earlier to back an east-west pipeline, the Trans-Canada scheme was at present the only viable means
for selling Alberta gas rather than burning it off or capping the wells.
Far more than Howe, he wished to avoid government ownership of
the line. As for Ontario, it was all very well to say that Frost had
originally favoured a multi-government crown corporation. But he
had passed legislation in favour of the present scheme with the support of both opposition parties. Manitoba's Premier Campbell wired
the Board of Transport Commissioners at the end of March that his
government was "vitally interested" in the present scheme. "A start
this year is essential; low price natural gas would have a major effect
on the economy of the province."

The commissioners themselves were hearing yet another Trans-
Canada request for extension. On March 28 the chief commissioner
gave an oral judgement moving the deadline for proof of financing
from April 30 to November 1, 1956, to coincide with the extension
just granted by the Alberta Conservation Board. He remarked rather
acidly that Trans-Canada's counsel Ross Tolmie was less overwhelmed
with optimism about the situation of Trans-Canada now than he had
been during the last hearing. But in view of the fact that Trans-
Canada was the only body which had the necessary contracts, permits,
organization and material to complete the line, "to refuse an extension at this time would be to undo what Trans-Canada has already

accomplished." He said the company had done everything "it reasonably could to advance its project . . . the delays that have occurred and are occurring are largely beyond its control and not of its making."

The Financial Post of March 30 also put the case against opposition demands for a completely new approach with an editorial headlined THE MAIN THING IS TO GET THE GAS LINE BUILT. While not opposing public ownership on principle, the *Post* argued against it in this particular case, no matter how much might be said for it in the case of Canadian National Railways or the St. Lawrence Seaway. Certainly the conflicting interests of east and west and the problem of dealing with five different provinces and geographically separated producers and consumers made it quite unlike the simpler situation of, say, Ontario Hydro. "The problem of setting rates for buyers and sellers will be a contentious issue [and] difficult enough. But get this business tangled up in regional party politics and the problem assumes fantastic proportions. Add to the rate-making problem, the special pleas which would be bound to come for spur pipe lines to Pint Pot Corners and Osmosis Centre and you will have a problem in politics and administration of terrifying dimensions." The *Post* also supported the government's position on American involvement in the pipeline. "Very properly Canadians are taking an increasing concern in things Canadian and in making better use of our national resources. . . . But the pipe line is about the worst possible ground on which to take a stand against American capital in Canada." The history of other companies financed initially by foreign owners, such as the CPR and Alcan, showed that they were gradually increasing their proportion of Canadian ownership. "Anybody – Canadians, Americans, Peruvians or Cypriots – will be very welcome to buy stocks and bonds in the enterprise once it is established." But the facts of financial life remained the same whether "Trans-Canada management were overnight changed into 100% fifth generation Canadians" or not. "If the line were to be a sure-fire profit bonanza it would have been already built. The fact is that it won't be. It will be a low interest rate affair. Canadians want a pipe line. But so far it seems that we can't find Canadians willing to put up enough money to pay for the thing."

Thus by the end of March, in spite of the "longest and loudest political row of the decade" anticipated in the House of Commons, it looked as if the government would get its pipeline bill passed by the opening of the construction season on the prairies. But as the Commons moved through the April budget debate and the Easter recess it became apparent that Trans-Canada's troubles were by no means over.

Two major difficulties stood in the way. In the first place, even if the government bill passed, Trans-Canada still had no guarantee that it could raise the money to build even the western section of the line during 1956. As long as there was no assurance of sales in the American market most investors were simply not interested. This problem did not appear absolutely insurmountable until the very end of April. But the second major difficulty, the sudden leap into prominence of two purportedly all-Canadian, all-private enterprise proposals to build the pipeline, became headline news early in the month.

On March 26 the Toronto investment house of Gairdner and Company wired C. D. Howe suggesting a scheme to be financed entirely in Canada on the basis of Canadian gas sales only, Gairdner himself met Howe and Mitchell Sharp on March 28 and further exchanges of view followed over the next couple of weeks. The basic idea was to use a campaign of the kind which had been so successful in selling victory bonds during the war, but now directed to another great national project. The difficulty was that, to get its first mortgage bonds sold to major Canadian investors, the Gairdner proposal required the government to invest in unsecured junior bonds to the tune of $100 million. Trans-Canada had made a similar but better proposal fifteen months before, and the cabinet had decisively rejected it. In the light of this and the fact that Gairdner had spent almost nothing, compared to Trans-Canada's investment of $15 million and five years of time, Howe began referring to his proposal as "a scavenger operation." Gairdner replied in hurt tones that on the contrary it could prove to be "a saving grace." While the Gairdner scheme had little to recommend it, and no responsible group or newspaper made any sustained defence of it, it did lend further credence to the charge that Howe was no longer prepared to consider alternatives to the scheme he had in hand. If anything else had been put forward years or even months earlier, the opposition might have had a stronger case.

News of another and apparently more attractive scheme also

caught the public eye during the month of April. It came from the man who was already on the verge of promoting the first successful major gas pipeline in Canada, Frank McMahon of Westcoast Transmission. His projected line from the Peace River district to the Pacific coast was successfully financed during April. The idea of McMahon, a former four-dollar-a-day Alberta oil driller, taking on Clint Murchison of Texas – Canada's own native multimillionaire and oil tycoon tackling his American opposite number – appeared to catch the public fancy. As *Time* magazine put it on April 16, "If Frank McMahon is successful, as now seems likely, he will do more than spoil Murchison's dream of achievement. He may even outrank Murchison on the roster of America's biggest oil men."

Ever since 1952, McMahon had received every support and sympathy from Howe in the complicated business of getting his permits in Canada and negotiating with the American government. He discussed his new proposal to build the all-Canada line with Howe on March 28, and on April 4 confirmed it in a letter marked "private and confidential." Because of this marking, Howe managed for a time to avoid any reference to the McMahon proposal. He chose to regard it as no proposal at all until McMahon gave his permission to table it in the House a month later. By early April, however, the press was carrying reports of it, and the opposition knew its content. Howe was furious when he discovered that George Prudham, the Alberta Liberal in the cabinet, had secretly taken it to the Prime Minister at the instigation of McMahon and his Alberta friends.

Unlike Gairdner, McMahon proposed no government assistance for his pipeline, other than relief on sales tax and duties. But he did propose something similar to the old Western Pipe Lines scheme. McMahon had negotiated with four large American gas companies in the mid-west, including Trans-Canada's former ally, Northern Natural Gas of Omaha. Northern Natural and the three other American companies McMahon had lined up were already bitterly opposing the Trans-Canada-Tennessee proposal before the Federal Power Commission. Although McMahon claimed that ownership of his company would be 70% Canadian, the fact was that his scheme depended to a far greater degree on American sales than Trans-Canada's did. It would have to face the same obstacles before the Federal Power Commission, and against Tennessee's vigorous opposition.

To examine possible courses of action in the light of the Gairdner and McMahon proposals and to look at the problem of finding capital to begin the western section of the line, government and Trans-Canada officials held a series of meetings during the second week of April.

The nucleus of the group was Charles Coates for Trans-Canada and Mitchell Sharp and Douglas Fraser for the Department of Trade and Commerce. They were later joined by Gardiner Symonds of Tennessee, who controlled Trans-Canada, and at the final meeting by C. D. Howe. Also present for Trans-Canada were Ross Tolmie at the first meeting and Eldon Tanner at the last.

Coates began by asking whether in view of public criticism it was the government's desire that Trans-Canada turn over its assets and clear the way for public ownership. Mitchell Sharp replied that the government still believed that this was only a last resort, but that if delays continued and public pressure for Canadian ownership increased, the government might have to reconsider. The important thing was the construction of the western section in 1956. To do so, Coates replied, would cost about $80 million. Without a favourable FPC decision on export, raising that amount of money would be either risky or impossible. Trans-Canada was considering two means of attempting it. The first involved a $25 million guarantee by each of the three new controlling stockholders. In relation to potential returns this was a large sum. For Hudson's Bay annual gross sales only amounted to a little over $3.5 million and there was no real economic incentive for its stockholders to put up seven times that amount to gain the advantage of selling some gas a year or two earlier than otherwise. The second possible means was a purely speculative stock issue for the $80 million in advance of normal financing for the complete line. The difficulty with this was that its failure would likely prove fatal to any chance of financing Trans-Canada ever.

Sharp asked about the possibility of having Frank McMahon replace Tennessee as a major party in Trans-Canada, or alternatively, splitting the opposition and doing business with one of the American companies backing McMahon. Symonds then stated flatly that the government must be under no illusion that his departure from Trans-Canada would enable it or any other Canadian company to sell gas to his American rivals. He would fight them tooth and nail in Washington. On the other hand he and his two partners, Gulf and Hudson's Bay, would willingly withdraw from the scene entirely and transfer the assets of Trans-Canada to the Canadian government or anyone else it might designate. The three of them were "distressed and embarrassed by the 'Gringo, go home' tone of the parliamentary debates and press comments." He submitted a memorandum setting forth Trans-Canada's assets and offering to sell his group's 51% holding of company shares to the government at cost, i.e. $8 per share.

At noon on April 10 the meetings recessed and Sharp and Fraser reviewed the situation in detail. Since it was still government policy to regard public ownership as the last resort, they decided there was no point in taking up Symonds' offer to sell out just yet. They reviewed again the various forms of further government assistance to Trans-Canada which might get the western section started immediately and decided that none of them could properly be recommended to Parliament. At the same time they decided that "no other proposal presently put forward offered any real hope of earlier or sounder construction than Trans-Canada." The outcome of their discussion was that further delay appeared inevitable – though it should be "sweetened if possible." When the meeting resumed at 4 p.m. both sides agreed that the government should be given an option to acquire Trans-Canada's assets as a going concern. Furthermore Trans-Canada would provide that a majority of its directors be nominated by Canadian shareholders. In return the government would extend the northern Ontario contract with Trans-Canada to November 1, 1956, and so tie it in to the date already set by the Canadian regulatory boards. "The hope would be that no further extension would be necessary beyond that time, since by then, with FPC approval, the company would be financed."

There were several advantages in this arrangement. The company with five years of preparatory work behind it and the northern Ontario bridge in prospect could still hope to go ahead on its own without further government assistance, and eventually sign enough supply and sales contracts to establish financeability. "The fact that U.S. participants have offered to withdraw completely, up to start of construction, should silence the anti-Americans." While the government could take over Trans-Canada as a going concern at will, "it was not bound to help the company out if it got in a hopeless state. It could be allowed to collapse and a fresh start could be made."

Although it would be embarrassing for the government to have to substitute a new resolution for the one now before Parliament, the only major disadvantage to an open and flexible policy of this sort would be that a start on construction was postponed until 1957.

To consider this proposal, C. D. Howe himself was present at the last meeting on the morning of April 11. Howe had been informed of the course of the discussion, and of the group's consensus that 1956 construction should be postponed. At the risk of edging closer to outright government ownership of the line, Howe refused to accept this conclusion. He asked whether the western section could be financed and built in 1956 if the government undertook to buy it at 90% of cost if the company failed to finance the whole portion of the line within a year after the new deadline of November 1, 1956. Symonds said he could accept this proposal and that it should help him obtain a bank loan in New York to finance the western section. An agreement was quickly worked out. Trans-Canada would ask its shareholders to option their shares to the government at $8 per share until such date as the company made a firm legal undertaking to begin construction.

After the meeting had been in progress for about an hour Eldon Tanner arrived from Alberta. Premier Manning had just assured him that his government would not cancel Trans-Canada's permit and grant one to Frank McMahon or anybody else.

Coates was asked what was the latest possible date for start of construction in order to ensure completion of the line to Winnipeg this season. He replied that they would have to put six spreads in the field not later than July 1. That meant authority to go ahead on all construction contracts by June 1. Any delay beyond this involved a risk of running into winter weather. Symonds undertook to discuss the proposal with his bankers in New York on April 16 and to inform Mitchell Sharp immediately of the results. He would then plan to have a written proposal in Howe's hands by April 19. The minister would take it to cabinet the same day if possible. Sharp would prepare any necessary amendments to the resolution for establishing the Northern Ontario Pipe Line Crown Corporation already introduced in the House. As soon as the proposal was approved by cabinet, the amended legislation would be pressed through the House of Commons.

Once again there was trouble. When the executive committee of Trans-Canada met in Toronto on April 17, Gardiner Symonds had to report that his New York bankers would not loan money to Trans-Canada without the definite prospect of an American market for gas. A pipeline across the prairies to Winnipeg and the intervening markets was not a viable proposition in itself. The whole situation in Canada, both economically and politically, seemed to have too many elements of risk and too little solid prospect of adequate return of the kind necessary for a bank loan. Following the meeting, several members of the executive committee went to Ottawa to tell Howe the bad news. The company could not hope to begin construction until the following season.

Howe was shaken, but said one way or another he was determined to have construction begin in 1956. The government itself, if he had any voice in the matter, would make an immediate short-term loan to Trans-Canada, thus acting in the role that the bankers had refused, so that they could build the western section in 1956.

The prospect of facing public critism over the Northern Ontario Pipe Line bill had been unpleasant enough for Trans-Canada sponsors. The inevitable uproar over a government loan was just too much, especially now that there was a good chance of carrying out normal financing in 1957. Rather than face a national debate over the government loan, Deane Nesbitt suggested to Jack McCausland of Wood, Gundy that they take the risk of a public offering of $80 million worth of debentures and common stock to finance the western line entirely in Canada. When they had got the backing of their own firms, along with that of Trans-Canada's other two Canadian underwriters, they met Gardiner Symonds. He was already sceptical about Canadian ability to do such a thing but did agree to discuss it with his two colleagues in the 51% control and with Coates. Afterwards, none of these could recollect being consulted. Nevertheless, Symonds advised Nesbitt that he and his associates had concluded the scheme was entirely impractical. There was nothing for it now but to join Howe in the even riskier political course he had undertaken, and to ride through the storm of the coming weeks with him.

Chapter 9 The Great Debate

May Day to Black Friday, 1956: the public life of Canada has never seen anything quite like it. The House of Commons was in a continual uproar. For a whole month the days lasted three and four hours into the following morning and Members of Parliament straggled home by the first crack of light in the northeastern sky. This May had thirty-two days: for purposes of House business the Speaker declared Friday the first of June to be Thursday, and the government majority sustained his ruling. Outside in the corridors the division bells rang like fire alarms in the night, or distress signals on a ship sinking at sea.

It was a month of noises unnatural to that once sober place: cackling, whistling and catcalls, jabbering interruptions, strained laughter edging on hysteria. At the height of the tension a heavy male chorus from the Liberal backbenches, as if they were living in the Marx Brothers' Fredonia or the Land of Rudolph Friml, broke into full-throated song about the pipeline, to the tune of *There'll Always Be An England* and words even sillier than the originals.

The gestures, like the sounds, were melodramatic. The future Conservative Finance Minister Donald Fleming refused to obey the Speaker's call to order and continued to stand until there was nothing for it but to have him named and so expelled from the House. As the solemn little man turned his back on the Speaker and marched down the aisle, John Diefenbaker called out "Farewell, John Hampden"; Ellen Fairclough draped a red ensign in eloquent mourning over his empty desk. At one point the packed galleries witnessed the incredible spectacle of the venerable and scholarly M. J. Coldwell, overcome with rage, advancing towards the Speaker's chair to the very throne of the House of Commons, shaking his fist.

The language was often wild and violent. Sometimes it seemed like the product of a communal brainstorming session. Canada was renamed "the Dominion of Howe." The company was called "Anti-Canadian Pipe Lines Limited" and "a Colombo Plan for Texas tycoons." Animal imagery was particularly popular. The new Commons' bestiary included not only the cliché animals, like the leopard that would not change its spots and that obscene hybrid which was neither fish nor fowl, but also everything from jackals to magpies, from jackasses to the racehorse Citation, last winner of the Triple Crown. The leader of the opposition and the deputy chairman got into a heated debate over whether the words "trained seals" should be withdrawn. (George Drew stoutly refused to retreat from his claim that he had heard seal-like barking sounds from the Liberal backbenches.) The tread of C. D. Howe was compared to that of an elephant, and Liberals popping up and down from their desks were likened to gophers. Trans-Canada itself was called a pampered pet and a Liberal dog. Its coat of arms should be an octopus on a maple leaf shield with a background of stars and stripes.

The Social Credit MP, Rev. E. G. Hansell, said that anyone opposing the pipeline bill was following the communist line. The opposition asked whether the Liberals had not turned the House of Commons into the pre-Nazi Reichstag. The bill was "an abomination, the evil spawn of a fascist mentality." The Liberals were "rapists" of Parliament. Macbeth was quoted on the need for assassins to act quickly. References to the unnatural and the dreadful ranged from evocations of the ghost of Mackenzie King and the reincarnation of Bridey Murphy to John Diefenbaker's phrase for Clint Murchison: "the man in the shadows." You could almost see him lurking in a Gothic corner of the Commons as the debate waxed on into the night.

Before May Day, opposition pressure for information or attacks on the government over pipeline policy had been intermittent. But from then on, for the rest of the month, the pipeline was the central subject of daily concern in Parliament. On May 1 opposition members peppered the Prime Minister with questions about a *Canadian*

Press report that the government was now proposing a loan to Trans-Canada Pipe Lines. Visibly annoyed, St. Laurent replied, "I am not going to say anything one way or the other to encourage such speculation in newspapers." John Diefenbaker scoffed: "That is the usual report to Parliament." The opposition sensed that the cabinet itself was divided and had not yet made up its mind on the issue. They kept probing. George Hees asked "whether the government [was] sufficiently united on the pipeline to allow this very important question to be brought before the House the following week for debate." St. Laurent said he was sick and tired of turning away "hypothetical questions based on newspaper speculation. When there is anything firmer for them to be based upon, answers will be given in Parliament. I do not enjoy as much as you do these questions that are constantly being thrown at us."

For the time being the government was able to fend off harassment on the issue of a loan to Trans-Canada. But the opposition smelt better game on the question of Canadian ownership. The Gallup Poll of May 1 had revealed just how concerned the Canadian public was about American domination of the economy, and how effective the opposition had been in focusing that concern on the issue of Trans-Canada Pipe Lines. Nearly 75% of the adult population of the country, including nearly 90% in the four provinces most immediately involved, said they had heard or read of the project. Of those who had an opinion, 45% said they favoured a pipeline "built and run by private Canadian investment," while 29% favoured one "built by the government." Only 17% wanted a line "built partly by the government and partly by private investment in Canada and the U.S." Almost all of those who chose the first alternative were willing to stick by it even if it meant delay in building the line; 2 out of 3 favouring a government pipeline said they were willing to pay higher taxes to get it. One could read in this a clear mandate for something like either the Conservative or the CCF position, and against anything like the government's Trans-Canada proposal.

On May 2 the opposition concentrated on breaking down the government's wall of silence on this particular issue. During April press reports of alternative offers to build the all-Canadian line had prompted several questions in the House. C. D. Howe responded by tabling documents relating to the Gairdner proposal. But John

Diefenbaker repeatedly asked Howe about the existence of what he first called "documents" and later "memoranda" containing an offer from Frank McMahon. Howe said he had none.

Then George Drew asked Howe if he had "received a *letter* from Mr. Frank McMahon in regard to the proposed pipe line." This time Howe said, "I have received no letter that I am free to table in this House," and the cat was out of the bag at last. The opposition immediately pressed him about the McMahon proposal, asking whether the minister thought it was sensible or not. Howe kept repeating that he was not obliged to discuss private correspondence. Drew turned to the Prime Minister: "Do we understand that the government leaves discussions on pipe line development in Canada as private matters of ministers of the Crown?" St. Laurent replied sharply, "The government cannot prevent any Canadian citizen from addressing a confidential communication to any member of the government or to anybody else." Stanley Knowles then jumped in: "Does the Prime Minister know the nature of the letter which Frank McMahon wrote the minister?" When St. Laurent said he did not, and that he had not seen it, the government was told they had better get together and speak to each other in cabinet meetings. "They do not even trust each other," said Earl Rowe.

On May 3 Howe telephoned Frank McMahon and asked him to remove the private and confidential designation from his letter so he could table it. McMahon agreed, and he also stated that he now wished to withdraw his proposition. The opposition accused Howe of threatening McMahon with trouble over his Pacific pipeline if he did not withdraw his proposal to go east. In his public statement of withdrawal McMahon said that he would now be too preoccupied with Westcoast Transmission, which had been successfully financed towards the end of April, several weeks after he first made his informal proposition to Howe.

Once tabled, the McMahon correspondence provided the opposition with more ammunition. Howard Green asked whether the rest of the cabinet had known anything about the McMahon offer before this time. Howe replied he would be glad to discuss cabinet secrets "some time when I am no longer a Privy Councillor." Since a Privy Councillor is appointed for life, he added pleasantly, "the discussion would have to take place in the next world."

Honourable members opposite boiled over in righteous wrath. Diefenbaker accused Howe of cavalier and flagrant contempt of Parliament. Why had he denied having documents pertaining to an offer by Frank McMahon? Howe replied, "A letter addressed to me which I am not free to table is not a document of Parliament. I was asked for documents. The letter was marked private and when a letter is marked in that way, if you are going to respect a document at all, it must be private to you." "Why did you not say that," called out an opposition member. "Why did I not say that?" demanded Mr. Howe. "I get letters from my sister. I suppose I should announce in Parliament when I receive a letter from my sister."

"About the pipe line?" asked Diefenbaker, savouring his question, and as the Conservative benches dissolved in laughter, George Drew landed in heavily, "Is she advising you in regard to the pipe line?"

Drew accused Howe of double-crossing Parliament. Howe said he had never double-crossed anybody in his life. The Montreal *Gazette* commented on Monday, May 7, that Howe's position was untenable. Instead of telling the House during April that there were no McMahon documents, he should have admitted they existed – since "strangely enough the details of the McMahon proposal were widely known everywhere except in the Cabinet" – and then he could have explained that he was bound by the words *private and confidential.* "It is difficult to resist the conclusion that Mr. Howe decided to sweep the McMahon offer under the rug and let it lie there as long as possible. His tactics were not very rewarding since the McMahon correspondence will now undergo a much more minute security than would otherwise have been the case." *The Gazette's* extenuating afterthought – "that this tendency towards secretiveness represents a developing habit rather than a deliberate policy" – was perhaps the sharpest cut of all at an aging government.

As the second week of May began in Parliament, however, the opposition stood frustrated once again; McMahon's reputed offer was formally withdrawn the day before its contents were tabled. Just as the government seemed to be caught, it had slipped free.

Then, almost immediately, there was another chance for the opposition to pounce. On Monday evening, May 7, the cabinet met to make a decision on the loan proposal which was now the only means by which construction could start in 1956. According to Prime Minister St. Laurent's secretary and biographer, Dale Thomson, Howe "literally pleaded with the other ministers to let him have his way once more, to crown his career with this final splendid accomplishment for Canada. Caught between the knowledge that the delay would mean losses measured in the billions to the Canadian economy, and fear of the political repercussions of the deal, they finally took their courage in both hands and plunged." The following morning just before the announcement, the cabinet led by the Prime Minister presented a solid and confident front to the special caucus of Liberal MP's called for the purpose. The cabinet also took full responsibility for working out a plan that would enable the bill to get through Parliament by the June 7 construction deadline set by the company.

Howe then met the Commons on Tuesday afternoon May 8 with a definite statement about the government's intentions. He said Trans-Canada was asked "whether it would be prepared to construct the western section in 1956 if the government advanced a substantial proportion not to exceed 90% of the cost of construction at an interest rate of 5% for a short period. I emphasize that the approach came from the government, not from Trans-Canada. Trans-Canada was not in default. It was prepared to wait another year if necessary. The company was unable to proceed with construction simply because the FPC in Washington had not yet approved the importation of Canadian gas into the United States."

Howe urged the advantages of the scheme: the western section would get built in 1956; after that there were two alternatives at least. If Trans-Canada was successful in financing the whole line by April 1, 1957, it would repay the loan and construct the remainder as originally planned. If the company failed to repay the loan, the government could take over the whole line at 90% of its cost. In addition to the $8 million already invested, the company was pledged to put in nearly another $8 million to go with the government's loan of up to $80 million. The company thus stood to lose up to $16 million in either of two possible eventualities: first, if it could not finance the whole line quickly; or second, if it failed to complete the western section of the line, short of *force majeure* (such as a strike), during the 1956 construction season.

The prospect of risking their huge investment under such terms was not one that the sponsors were happy about. On the other hand they realized that Howe was in an extremely difficult position and that to make tough conditions was the best chance he had of getting a loan accepted by Parliament and the public. The toughness of the conditions, however, was completely lost on Members of Parliament. Now they had something definite to shoot at. Davie Fulton called the whole thing a "treaty of surrender." Drew declared that this was a general invitation to American capitalists to come to Canada "to be financed to the extent of 90¢ on every dollar and still retain control under terms that would be entirely satisfactory to them."

The rest of that week was occupied in procedural wrangles, and there was no chance for the government to introduce a motion on its revised plan. George Drew tried to get both the Gairdner and the McMahon proposals referred to a committee of the House of Commons, which would have ended any chance of 1956 construction. Other members made much of the fact that the new resolution overlapped the original March 15 proposal for the Northern Ontario Pipe Line Crown Corporation and therefore could not stand beside it on the order paper. The first one must be dealt with first. The opposition knew the government's timetable: The bill had to pass the House by June 7. The objective was therefore to take considerably longer than that to examine it. The government would then either have to back down, dissolve Parliament, or else force its bill through by an early and hence questionable application of closure. If that happened there would be plenty more to talk about besides the bill itself. In fact, the government recognized that it would be impossible to meet its deadline without applying closure at some point during the bill's three readings in the House and consideration by committee of the Whole. The House Leader Walter Harris and the other chief parliamentary strategist, Jack Pickersgill, worked out a plan, accepted by the whole cabinet, which Howe was instructed to follow when presenting the bill. Only the precise details of timing were to be left for action at the appropriate moment in the House.

When the Commons met on Monday, May 14, to hear C. D. Howe's statement in support of his revised pipeline resolution, there were at most only nineteen days left for debate in the House and Senate before the June 7 deadline. Once again after the question period there was a long wrangle over procedural matters, featuring a learned and closely contested debate between Stanley Knowles and the Speaker over the propriety of the Speaker's judgement. His rulings were challenged three times by the opposition, and three times sustained by the government majority.

The better part of the afternoon and Howe's patience were dissipated before he was finally given the floor. He referred to the last time, almost a week ago, that he had attempted to bring forward his new resolution. He had been stopped by procedural questions and a chorus of loud laughter from the opposition benches. The opposition had once referred to "the vacuous faces" of the Liberal backbenchers; Howe now picked up the phrase and threw it back at them. The derisive laughter from the opposition benches, he said, suggested the "vacancy of mind or easy irresponsibility of those who need not produce a workable course of action." In one of his most powerful speeches to the House of Commons, Howe then pounded home one simple theme: the opposition's refusal to face "certain inescapable facts," their preference for mere talk.

"Nothing that can be said in this House can change those facts. Nothing that can be said here is going to end the world shortage of steel pipe. No words spoken here can convince the owners of capped gas wells in Alberta or the would-be gas consumers in Manitoba and Ontario that there is no hurry about building an all-Canadian pipe line."

Howe reviewed "the facts" that had led the Ontario legislature to unanimous support of the bill for the northern Ontario section of the line. "In passing, I notice that members of the Opposition have fallen into the habit of calling this the unproductive section. I suppose that when such Honourable Members water their gardens they turn on the tap and walk down the garden path with the unattached nozzle in their hands. They would regard a connecting hose as unproductive.

"Another fact with which we must deal," Howe continued "was the unexpectedly long delay in the approval of the export of gas to the United States by the FPC. Perhaps the government should have foreseen this, but whether it could have or not, the point was that it was dealing with the situation as it was now." Since Trans-Canada was simply not financeable in the ordinary capital markets until FPC approval was granted, he continued, the government was in effect making a short term loan, with extremely tough conditions attached, in order to free the company and the country of dependence on decisions made by a foreign power.

Howe then turned to the McMahon proposal and stated why in his view it was "never a starter." "Although it is now history, having been withdrawn, I should like to suggest why it was never put forward by its sponsor, and why it could not have been accepted had it been presented formally." He pointed out that the "immediate and overwhelming objection to the proposal was that it was really a plan for selling Alberta gas to the midwestern United States." Of the volume of gas authorized at that time by Alberta for export from the province, McMahon was counting on four-fifths for the American market and only one-fifth for central Canada, "an amount clearly insufficient to attract capital to construct a pipe line eastward from Winnipeg and quite inadequate for central Canadian requirements. McMahon had none of the plans and permits, rights-of-way and steel pipe, required to begin construction in 1956. "As you see from the correspondence which has been tabled, his specifications were simply not consistent with the construction, even on a patchwork basis, of a line through central Canada. If any Honourable Members have studied it as closely as I have, they will, I am sure, agree with Mr. McMahon that it had now best be forgotten." In the meantime, however, talk of the scheme had "confused the issue and it has confused the Opposition in particular."

Which brought Honourable Members bang up against another hard fact. Instead of referring to Trans-Canada as the government's "chosen instrument," the opposition should face the fact that it was the "only agency which can be placed in a position to build the western part of the pipe line this year. The government has no chosen instrument. Trans-Canada is the only instrument available."

Howe pointed out how reluctant Trans-Canada had been to accept the government's terms for financing 1956 construction. "Each shareholder is required to put at risk his full investment in the company in order to build a long stretch of pipe line from Alberta to Winnipeg, which is a losing proposition unless it is completed to the United States or eastern Canada. The company knows that unless it goes on to complete the line either southward or eastward by the spring of 1957 it stands to lose its investment. If it does succeed in paying off the loan and building beyond Winnipeg, it has still a long way to go before it begins to reap any profit on it. If this were a sure thing I know plenty of people who would be only too willing to finance Trans-Canada today. But the picture of this proposal as a scheme to provide vast profits for Texas buccaneers is a fantasy, insulting to the ordinary intelligence and grossly insulting to the men who have sponsored this project with hard cash and hard work where most Canadians have been unwilling to venture."

Howe blasted those who called the proposal a sell-out of Canadian interests: "The line will be built wholly within Canadian territory . . . the entire project is subject to Canadian law . . . not a cubic foot of gas can be exported to the United States without a permit from the Canadian government. In other words, whoever may own it, it is completely under Canadian control."

As far as ownership was concerned, the offer to have 51% of the shares sold to Canadians was most unusual. "While it may yet prove necessary for us to attempt government enterprise in this field . . . , short of public ownership there is no way of guaranteeing Canadian control of the shares. We cannot force Canadians to buy them or having bought them, to keep them. If public ownership is what the Official Opposition wants, let them stand up and be counted with the party to their left, who at least advocate public ownership out of intellectual conviction, not out of intellectual confusion." He took a further dig at George Drew who had called his 51% offer of common stock to Canadians a "shallow pretence." "I am more or less accustomed to the Leader of the Opposition accusing me of misleading the House, that being his idea of statesmanship, but his inability to understand a straightforward proposition continues to amaze me." Howe concluded by describing Trans-Canada once more as an undertaking "of truly national scope, which we must either launch now or see languish for years to come. The means proposed are flexible, adaptable either to development by private enterprise, or if necessary by public ownership, which though less attractive, can still be moulded to our national needs."

As Howe finished, there was a momentary hesitation, and a sense of decision in the balance. The House was absolutely still. He leaned towards Walter Harris who had placed a piece of paper in Jack Pickersgill's handwriting on his desk. "Do I do it now?" he whispered.

Then he straightened up again, stood his ground with shoulders hunched forward and fists on the desk in this familiar debating posture and said: "Mr. Chairman, it is obvious that some Honourable Members prefer to obstruct this motion rather than debate it." He picked up the paper from his desk and read out the fateful words which changed the whole course of the debate. "I beg to give notice that at the next sitting of Committee I shall move that further consideration of this resolution shall be the first business of the Committee and shall not further be postponed."

In other words, closure – closure of a debate that had yet to begin.

Opposition members could scarcely believe their ears. The axe they expected might fall at some stage in the debate had dropped before it began – before the opposition had so much as uttered a word of criticism of the bill in the formal debate. As much in jubilation as in anger, members cried out, "The guillotine!" and "Dictatorship!" They had been handed the best issue of all, an issue which symbolized twenty-one years of continuous rule. Now it could be made clear to the whole country that for Howe and his colleagues, due parliamentary process was merely a nuisance, a tiresome matter of rubberstamping cabinet decisions by means of their huge majority.

Until that moment there was still some chance of the government's case getting thoroughly examined in Parliament and in the press. If the Trans-Canada pipeline scheme had been the central subject of debate over the next week or two, there is little doubt that its content would have been discussed, along with the difficulties of any alternative, to an extent and with a knowledge that had hitherto been impossible. Howe's "facts" would have had to be faced. As it turned out, after the middle of May, there was little thorough editorial criticism of the pipeline proposal itself.

But now, instead of coming to grips with the pipeline issue, the old criticisms could be repeated over and over again, while the focus of debate shifted away to something more general and fundamental. The government's treatment of Parliament and its right to continue in office were thrown into question as never before. The government's action had the psychological effect of telegraphing some such message as this to the Canadian public: "We are stuck with this deal now. We haven't convinced you that we are right. So we'll carry out our plan any way. We have the votes to put it through parliament, and by election time you'll have forgotten the whole thing."

It was plausible to maintain that the government had something to hide – all the more so because of its secretiveness and its difficulties over the scheme in the past. In the government's pipeline policy the opposition had not really found an adequate symbol of what was wrong. But that could now be forgotten. The Liberals had provided new evidence that they believed in their own divine right to rule. They had once again acted as if they thought that good government is better than self-government, and that national necessity overrides everything else. Blinded by the fact that most criticisms of its plans in the past had proved to be carping and shallow, the cabinet could readily convince itself that the objections to the case for closure would also prove unsubstantial. They seriously misjudged their own understanding of parliamentary government. And they faced a thoroughly roused opposition, willing to be marshalled into a brilliant delaying action by a superb parliamentarian.

Stanley Knowles had succeeded the saintly founder of his party, the Rev. J. S. Woodsworth, in his old seat of Winnipeg North Centre. A minister of the United Church, his gaunt frame, austere mien and intent singlemindedness suggested to some the puritan conscience incarnate, to others the stereotype of the socialist fanatic. By his ruthless honesty, quick mind and thorough knowledge, however, he held the respect of all members of the House, and, thanks to a quality of gentleness in his being, along with a wry and subtle humour, the affection of most as well. He did not dominate or command the House in the grand manner of John Diefenbaker in his prime. He had not been in the Commons at the time of the 1932 closure, like the lone survivor of the last Conservative cabinet, the Ontario harness racer Earl Rowe, a pugnacious participant in the new debate. He rarely spoke at length in the manner of his apt pupil and ally, Davie Fulton of the Conservatives. The twenty-one gun salute of George Drew's every utterance was totally foreign to his manner, as was the blind anger or clever inanity of many opposition interventions. Yet without in any way diminishing the position of his own leader, M. J. Coldwell, Stanley Knowles during May of 1956 became chief keeper of the liberties of the House of Commons, the effective tactical organizer of the opposition to the most powerful government we have ever had. More than anyone else Knowles was the stumbling block, the embodiment of the nemesis that effectively turned the prospect of rapid steamroller defeat into, first, a meaningful delay and finally, a kind of moral victory. Through it all he concentrated his fire on the Speaker and committee chairman, and rarely clashed head-on with the chief figures on the other side of the Commons: the silent, withdrawn Prime Minister; the long-suffering, even-tempered House Leader Walter Harris; and the member in a different orbit from the rest, C. D. Howe, who was, by turns, bellicose, bored, impatient and jovial, but always obedient as he could be to whatever plan would end all the palaver and get him his bill by June 7.

The Liberal case for the use of closure amounted essentially to this: It was not democratic practice for a minority to overrule the will of the majority. The opposition had been threatening obstruc-tion in order to block any Trans-Canada pipeline legislation ever since last March. And since the arrangements for 1956 would fall through, according to the contract signed by the government with the company, if the legislation was not passed by the agreed deadline, the only way to ensure the rule of the majority, as reflected in the present Parliament, was to apply closure. But the trouble with this was, as Eugene Forsey pointed out in his classic article on the debate, that "Parliamentary government is not [merely] a matter of counting heads . . . it is also a matter of using them. It is government by dis-cussion, not just by majority vote. Parliament is not just a voting place, it is also pre-eminently, essentially, a talking place, a *parle-ment.*" The government ignored, in its arguments about the demo-cratic practice of majority rule, the fact that it was also democratic practice for the opposition to oppose. It must not only argue against any proposed measure, but also, if necessary, use the rules of the House to obstruct the passage of major legislation which has not been previously put before Parliament or the public, until its argu-ments have been thoroughly aired. This is especially true if there is reason to believe that the public's view of the measure will run against the government. After that, if it is not prepared to amend or withdraw its legislation or put it to the test of an election, the govern-ment can reasonably move to close off debate.

The Canadian Parliament's closure rule was born in 1913 after the longest filibuster in our history. The Conservative government's naval aid bill had been under debate day and night for forty days before closure was applied. The practice had been used sparingly since, the last time being in 1932 after an eleven-day debate which stretched out over nearly a month's time. Since the government appealed to the precedent of 1932, Stanley Knowles, during the one day debate on first reading of the pipe line bill under closure, quoted the protesting words of the then opposition leader, Mackenzie King. King complained that the Conservative government had used the weapon "to end all discussion on the most important question which has engaged the attention of parliament since this ministry was formed. If ever in this world there was evidence of an autocratic power used to the nth degree we have it in what we are witnessing at the present time." And Knowles added, "If there is anything in spirits walking this earth after a man like Mackenzie King has passed on, I am sure his ghost must be haunting every cabinet minister every night during the course of this debate."

For its action, he continued, the government has used "the alleged excuse of necessity. What is that necessity? . . . the government has virtually pledged that parliament will get this measure through by June 7th. In other words, Mr. Chairman, this free and independent parliament of a sovereign nation is bound by a commitment the government has made to a private company. It is because of that commitment that we are now under not the threat but the fact of closure." Knowles quoted two of the classic statements of the rights of Parliament: William Pitt's "Necessity is the argument of tyrants" and John Pym's "Freedom of debate being once foreclosed the essence of the liberty of parliament is withal dissolved."

Under the Canadian rule once debate under closure has begun, no member may speak more than twenty minutes and the debate must adjourn by 1 a.m. of the following day, at which point the question is put. At 1 a.m. on Wednesday, May 16, the chairman of the Committee of the Whole called the question. But Fulton and Knowles between them managed to run circles around both him and the Speaker with points about proper procedure. They kept the Commons in session with division after division for nearly four hours while the chairman vainly tried to report back to the Speaker and have the motion formally put to a vote in the House. It was twenty-five minutes to five when the Speaker finally declared the first reading of the bill carried. He then put the routine question as to when there should be a second reading. Knowles cried out "Never." Some Liberal backbenchers shouted "Now." The House adjourned at 4:42 a.m.

It all made good copy for the newspapers. Parliamentary debates had not consistently hit the big black headlines for years. And, overwhelmingly, the press was critical. Even the traditionally Liberal papers like the Toronto *Star* and the *Winnipeg Free Press* denounced the government's tyranny in their editorial columns.

The government attacked the opposition for refusing to discuss the content of the bill and preferring mere obstruction instead. This approach found little support, except from one major daily, *The Montreal Star*, and from *The Financial Post*, which denounced "a violent effort by the opposition parties to mislead and befuddle the Canadian public in the hope of making political profit at the next election." In an editorial entitled THE GAS LINE, it said it would be an outrage to let "mere gas bagging in the House of Commons" result in the waste of another construction season.

While at one level the debate lay between the rights of Parliament and economic necessity, at another the old issue of anti-Americanism provided emotional fuel for the controversy. Howe himself was a prime target. He was called an American immigrant who did not understand Canada. His mail was full of letters like the one from the disgusted St. Catharines Liberal who wrote that he was fed up with "you guys giving our country's wealth to the U.S. I hope you don't sell the country away before the next election. Otherwise we'll have to fight to get it back." A motor cavalcade descended on Parliament from the Niagara peninsula to lobby Parliament against foreign capitalists.

Some opposition MP's let their imaginations run riot over American multimillionaires plotting to cheat the Canadian taxpayer. George Hees conjured up a scene in which he depicted the men behind Trans-Canada plotting to "get good old C.D." to help them out. "You can just see the boys sitting around the room cutting up the melon in advance."

Liberal John Dickey interrupted "You are one of Canada's foremost novelists." But liberal backbenchers grew increasingly dispirited and uneasy. One of the hardest things to take was the sight of their Prime Minister, suddenly aged, sitting grim and tight-lipped day after day as the debate raged on around him.

"Through all this hubbub," wrote Grant Dexter of the *Winnipeg*

Free Press, "the most arresting figure on the government side of the House was Prime Minister St. Laurent. He sat impassive, expressionless, chin in hand, an open book on his desk, silent. His aloofness is almost unbelievable."

Over and over again opposition members mocked St. Laurent for his withdrawal. Earl Rowe told him that Sir Wilfrid Laurier would be ashamed of him. Donald Fleming conjured up the real force in the government — "unrepentant over his own lust for power, the same man who said 'if we wanted to get away with it, who would stop us?' Now we see the full fruits of that attitude. The Prime Minister sits hiding behind a reckless Minister of Trade and Commerce. Behold the wantonness of power!" St. Laurent was scornfully nicknamed "Louis the Silent." One member inquired if Mr. Howe had imposed closure on the Prime Minister.

President Tanner of Trans-Canada was a man of few words and not easily moved to impulsive action. But after sitting in the galleries day and night for two weeks hearing his company denounced as "Tanner's tomboys" and "Murchison's minions," he finally decided he had had enough. He must express his feelings to someone. During the debate on second reading, before closure was applied for a second time, and after the House had adjourned at the normal hour of 10 p.m., he decided to go and see the Prime Minister. He had no more than formally met the man, and had no idea whether he would be allowed in or whether St. Laurent was even present in his office. But he went.

After he began speaking he half expected to be invited to leave — "I have never talked straighter to a man in my life." He sensed St. Laurent's Irish temper begin to flare. But then the Prime Minister subsided, not into the lassitude of his House of Commons presence but rather into the role of sympathetic and intelligent listener. In a sense both men were in a similar predicament: a situation for which they were responsible finally, as chief officers of the two contracting bodies, and yet not a situation of their own making, but one in which they had reluctantly placed themselves, out of a sense of duty to what seemed the only viable course, and out of personal regard for C. D. Howe.

As they sat alone in the silent, almost deserted building, Tanner expressed his feeling about the company's struggles of the past and its present troubles. He told the Prime Minister he was shirking his responsibility by not speaking out in the debate, and aghast at his own presumption, urged him to take a stand. He left with the sense that he had not only been listened to acutely but with great sympathy.

St. Laurent had hoped from the beginning that he would not have to speak at all in the debate, and he told his colleagues he did not plan to. But his failure to do so was now being taken as a sign of division in the cabinet and as virtual abdication of his office. He was persuaded at last to act.

When he entered the debate on the afternoon of May 22 he was his old self again. His manner was the essence of dignity and firmness, his utterance replete with lofty generality. It was almost as if he had dropped into the fray from another time and place. He spoke of implementing "what has been Canadian policy for the last half century," and of the appreciation of "future generations of Canadians." He said how much he agreed with the leader of the opposition in his desire that it be a Canadian project. He referred to the words of support from the Prime Minister of Ontario which had already been read into the House record, and of the sense of urgency felt by the Premiers of Alberta and Manitoba. He spoke of the reasonable nature of the government's agreement with Trans-Canada and the watertight protection for the Canadian public it afforded. Ultimately of course it would all be submitted to the judgment of the Canadian people in an election. But as he surveyed the great throng of Liberal MP's in the House and looked across at the small numbers of the opposition, he spoke regally of the expectation that his party would again "get the response [from the electorate] we have been getting over the past years every time we faced them." In the meantime, however, as Prime Minister his oath of office required him to do what was best in the interests of all. St. Laurent did not attempt to defend the government's use of closure nor did he even deign to mention the word. He simply spoke of never shrinking from duty, however disagreeable, and the "distasteful responsibility of having to resort to the standing rules of the House."

Just how distasteful the government's task would be was made even clearer over the next few days. The Prime Minister's stand put new life into his supporters, but its high-minded tone filled the opposition with fury and exasperation. It was 3:15 a.m. of the day following St. Laurent's speech before the House adjourned, after the passage of second reading of the pipe line bill, once again under closure. Later that day, May 23, almost all the time was spent in long debates over procedure between the Speaker and the committee chairman on the one hand and several members of the opposition on the other. C. D. Howe's chance to present the bill in Committee of the Whole was delayed yet another day.

In committee stage, normally one in which a bill is examined and discussed clause by clause in detail, Howe simply read clause one of the bill and immediately moved that "further consideration of this clause be postponed." He did the same with clause two.

This entirely unprecedented action was ruled in order by the presiding officers. As the Speaker called out for order and reminded Davie Fulton that "there are certain forms which have been traditionally followed in this House," Knowles interjected, "Tell that to the government." The Speaker pleaded with members to be "good enough to understand my position," but one of them called back, "It is our position we are concerned about." Davie Fulton committed the grave offence of refusing to resume his seat when the Speaker stood. "I have never seen this before," said the Speaker, "and I never thought I would." Fulton got away with his defiance without being disciplined, but the debate lurched and crashed on over the Speaker's rulings that Howe could in effect close off discussion of each clause in advance.

On Friday, May 25, matters grew worse. Even more deliberately than Fulton, Donald Fleming in Committee of the Whole refused to resume his seat when asked by the chairman, who in turn had to report this to the Speaker. Fleming said that he stood his ground precisely because of his respect for the chair. "There comes a time when a high duty is owed, the duty to parliament itself and to the long centuries of parliamentary freedom. Sir, the right that I assert here today, I assert not for myself alone. I assert it for all members of this House." And so on, in one mighty rhetorical swoop, culminating in "generations yet unborn" and "I abide by the consequences."

As government House Leader, Walter Harris was faced with the unpleasant task of moving Fleming's suspension for the rest of that day's sittings. He felt at the time that he was probably ending his own political career by doing so. Until then he had been considered the

Prime Minister's most likely successor. Fleming received a hero's welcome in Toronto on his return there for the weekend and the Saturday papers across the country were full of the story. Liberal gibes about "Saint Donald the Martyr" did not help their cause.

As the House met on Monday, May 28, the deadline for passage loomed closer than ever. Everything would depend on what happened in the House this week. The Prime Minister proposed a compromise whereby ample debate on the most crucial clauses of the bill could take place. It was met with scorn. John Diefenbaker called out, "The retreat from Moscow." George Drew said the only thing the opposition could accept was reversion to clause one. For two more days the government made no attempt to push through the other clauses without discussion. But this was only seen as a sign of weakness and a half-way confession of guilt. The opposition used most of the time not to talk about the bill but about the rights of Parliament. Knowles and Fulton once more referred to the debate in which closure was introduced in 1913. Fulton pointed out that its architect, Arthur Meighen, had been asked at the time whether the sort of thing actually being done by the government in 1956 was possible under his new closure rule. Knowles called out, "The Prime Minister should listen to this one," and Fulton continued, quoting Meighen, "Yes, but it would be absurdity itself . . . and could not be perpetrated except by a government that was at once insane and vicious." "That day has come," cried Fleming.

The climax of the pipeline debate centred around the person of the Speaker of the House, René Baudoin. A meticulous, handsome, proud man with a trim little moustache, he had cultivated and acquired a reputation for his knowledge of House rules and his elaborate courtesy and fairness in applying them. He was preparing a book on Commons procedure and was spoken of as a possible candidate for the office of permanent Speaker if it were created.

It became daily more apparent during the debate that Beaudoin made of himself two exceedingly difficult yet contradictory demands. One was to maintain the impartial dignity of his high office. The other was to take upon himself a part of the government's responsibility for seeing that its legislation passed through the various stages of debate in some relation to the timetable that had been set for it. To meet the second objective he almost invariably managed to rule against the many points of order raised by the opposition. To achieve the first, he entered patiently into long and learned debates with members who challenged the correctness of his decisions. In both cases he increasingly tended to regard the opposition's tactics as an assault on the integrity of his person and his office. The more he did so, the more he and his colleagues, the chairman and the deputy chairman of the Committee of the Whole, rather than the government or its legislation, became the immediate target of the opposition's attack.

Early on in the debate he turned to Stanley Knowles, who was pressing him hard, and pleaded "Would the honourable gentleman be good enough to say what the Minister could have done?" The very question is indicative of what most exasperated the opposition about his frame of mind: it was obviously neither Knowles' business nor the Speaker's to advise a minister how he could get his legislation passed in the form he wanted it.

Given the double responsibility Beaudoin had assumed, it is a wonder he did not crack sooner. By the end of May, however, he was showing signs of strain. As the impeccability of his record as Speaker and the chances of meeting the government's tight schedule eroded daily before his eyes, Beaudoin struggled all the more desperately to save the situation.

The final calamity arrived innocently enough. It began late in the afternoon of May 31. Another of the opposition's appeals against the committee chairman's rulings was being referred back to the House. Instead of putting the question immediately, as he should have done under the rules, Beaudoin mistakenly allowed the opposition to argue at length a point of order. More stratagems were devised to keep the pot boiling till the dinner break at 6 p.m. But the Prime Minister had moved closure on all clauses of the bill earlier that afternoon, and opposition members were stumped as to how to prevent the question being put when the House reconvened for the evening session.

It seemed like a shot in the dark, but why not try it? Colin Cameron of the CCF rose on a question of privilege, based on two letters he had just read in an Ottawa newspaper. He suggested that they were a reflection on the dignity of Parliament. One letter spoke of "the systematic garroting of the opposition by Mr. Speaker." The other, written by his friend, Eugene Forsey, included the statement that "the Speaker's words would seem to imply that when the rules get seriously in the way of doing something the government very much wants done, no reasonable person can expect the government to follow them or the Speaker to enforce them." Beaudoin recognized Cameron's move for the delaying tactic that it was, but the attack upon himself and his office, coming on top of all the opposition charges (Davie Fulton had just invited him to end his career as "a rapist of Parliament") was too much to take. He decided to demonstrate his impartiality in no uncertain terms, then and there. He proceeded to instruct Cameron in precise detail as to how he should make his motion, and what should be said in it. There was a flurry of excitement while the surprised member asked to borrow a pencil from colleagues nearby. The Speaker's response had exceeded Cameron's wildest hopes.

When the motion was prepared, the Speaker read it out and the leader of the opposition rose to speak to it. Horrified, Walter Harris could see a whole new debate about to begin, stretching out perhaps for days beyond the June 7 deadline. He tried to point out that under the rules of the House the opposition's appeal against the committee chairman's ruling should have been put immediately. But the Speaker cut him off before he could begin. When the debate adjourned at 10 p.m., George Drew was still on his feet talking about Cameron's privilege motion. By now Beaudoin realized not only that he had made a mistake, but how serious it was for the government's position. When Walter Harris came to visit him in his office afterwards to discuss the next day's business in his capacity as the government House Leader, neither of them could see any way out of the impasse. Harris recalled later that he left Beaudoin's office assuming that there was now no chance of meeting the June 7 deadline and that the government would have to drop the pipeline bill for the time being and turn to other business on Friday. The following morning, Jack Pickersgill, the other cabinet minister most responsible for the debate schedule, drove over to Beaudoin's house. By now however Beaudoin had worked out his own plan to redeem himself, and he refused to discuss the matter with Pickersgill at all. Nevertheless when the presence there of a cabinet minister's car was later recalled, members were free to speculate and assume the worst. George Pearkes told the Speaker, "We shall never know that sordid means were used to lure you from your path of duty." And other members asked, "What took place in the dark?" and "Why did you change overnight? Are you afraid?" There were two pipelines in the debate, "one of them running between the government front bench and the Speaker's chair."

When the House met Friday morning, before George Drew had a chance to continue his speech on Cameron's motion, the Speaker gravely interrupted him, and began to speak of his own errors of the day before. He said first he had been mistaken in ruling that Cameron's motion was in order. After a careful reading of the letters Cameron complained of, he had decided because of the unusual circumstances of the pipeline debate that they were not in fact breaches of privilege. This much produced anger and astonishment. Worse was to come. The Speaker referred to the more serious error he had committed the previous afternoon in not putting the appeal against the committee chairman to the House immediately. Lest the House suffer through his mistake, he proposed that business revert to the point where it has been on Thursday at 5:15 p.m. Amid mounting noise, tumult and song, the Speaker finally succeeded in putting what was in effect a motion from the chair, and it passed by 142 votes to 0. The opposition, for the first time in parliamentary history, refused to vote at all, on the grounds that there was no proper question before the House.

The final outburst came in a half hour of sheer chaos when the House resumed for its afternoon sitting at 2:30. The Speaker grimly proceeded with business as if it were Thursday, May 31, at 5:15 p.m. – his excursion in time travel, as one reporter called it. While Davie Fulton continued to stand and George Drew called out "You have no right to sit in that Chair," Beaudoin put the question that he should have put the day before. As the division bells rang, Conservatives and CCF'ers moved out into the centre aisle talking, shouting and gesticulating. Liberal members began banging their desks. But, as one observer recalled, they "were so stunned by what was going on a few feet in front of them that their singing this time was only half-hearted." A small group of them began *Onward Christian Soldiers* and were met with cries of "Shame! Shame!" A Liberal chorus struck up their improvised song, *We've been working on the pipeline* and others followed with whatever they could think of – *Alouette, Tip-*

perary, Home on the Range. The *Canadian Press* reported that Beaudoin "sat white-faced in the Speaker's chair looking straight ahead, at one point he tapped his left foot, at another he fiddled with his robe. He did not try to restore order." Only one Liberal member made any move towards the aisle. Rev. Dan MacIvor, at 83 the oldest member of the Commons, tried to rush forward as if to protect the Speaker, but was pulled back by the coat tails by a fellow Liberal.

When the division bells finally stopped after what seemed to many members the longest half hour they had ever spent, the vote was taken in an ominous silence more dreadful than the clamour of the preceding half hour.

For the rest of the day the opposition tried in a more orderly fashion a host of stratagems to prevent the pipe line bill passing the committee stage under closure. But the presiding officers grimly and swiftly now, with little attempt to explain or justify, continued to rule against them. Passage was completed at 1:47 a.m. on Saturday morning. The bill was given its third and final reading in the small hours of the morning of June 6. After being put through all its stages in the Senate, where its actual content was more thoroughly debated in a day than it had been during a month in the House, in less than twenty-four hours, it was given royal assent on June 7, just a few hours before the contract between the company and the government was to expire. And so the bill became the law of the land. The most tumultuous debate in the history of the House of Commons was over. At the end of the week construction crews were preparing to begin work on the western section of the Trans-Canada pipeline.

Chapter 10 To Find a Quarter Billion

"The pipeline seems to have extended from Vancouver Island to the far end of Newfoundland," said the exasperated committee chairman during the third week of the debate as he vainly tried to persuade members to return to the subject of the bill before them. The pipeline debate was in fact a kind of grand national steamletting. It was the occasion for all kinds of long-repressed anger and latent fears, frustrations and fantasies, to come shooting and bubbling to the surface in every part of Canada.

General George Pearkes, v.c., m.p., spoke of the needs of old age pensioners and veterans' military hospitals in his riding of Victoria. The former ccf hardware merchant, Ross Thatcher poured scorn on the inability of the Saskatchewan government to produce socialist shoes at $2.75 a pair and went on to attack public enterprise in general. Premier Bennett of British Columbia said that the whole debate was a death struggle of two old parties and an outmoded political system, from whose ruins Social Credit would rise triumphant. That forlorn stepchild of the depression, the Hudson's Bay Railway Association, uttered a plea for pipe to be shipped in through the port of Churchill. And of course there was coal to be considered in Cape Breton, just as sure as there were fish in the sea and outports in Newfoundland. The Toronto *Globe and Mail* and the *Winnipeg Free Press* both blasted the government from different positions on the political spectrum but saved some of their choicest invective for a feud between themselves over which paper's editorial line was the more despicable. A Montreal MP accused the Tories of deliberately planning their filibuster as part of a plot to keep federal Liberals out of Quebec during Duplessis's provincial election campaign. Two French-Canadian members became so heated in their exchange that they broke into French, a rare event in Parliament in those days. The poor chairman pleaded with them as politely as he could to speak English so he could understand what was going on.

In spite of its frequent excursions into foolishness, irrelevance and anger, it is difficult to see the pipeline debate as the national disgrace or unmitigated disaster which many participants and commentators at the time considered it to be. Certainly it had its element of personal tragedy. The career and reputation of Speaker René Beaudoin were shattered, George Drew's health was so strained that he had to resign from his party's leadership shortly after. And a few hours after the bill passed the House of Commons, the Liberal MP Jack McDougall, a lively and spontaneous person, who was highly regarded by members of every party, dropped dead in the Parliament Buildings of a heart attack.

May and June of 1956 may not stand in the best traditions of Parliamentary decorum or public debate, but the storms and eruptions of those days were, after all, a relatively mild way in which to make a break with the past and to end an era. Disorder was confined to language and noise, rather than the range of violence, from duels and fistfights to bombings and assassinations, that have been part of the pattern of politics, even in the best of democracies, at other times and places.

It is surprising, too, how quickly the bitterness of Black Friday vanished. Indeed, in some members, like Roland Michener, it had never been aroused. Although those two old warriors, Diefenbaker and Howe, could growl and thunder at each other in the House, they could still share a certain personal fondness for each other and a respect for the offices they held. To many, the great debate was in the very best sense of the word, a game, to be played fiercely and well and with a will to win. The night he trapped the Speaker in his own vanity by quoting Eugene Forsey's criticism of his conduct, Colin Cameron, like the government, was sure his shot in the dark had won the battle of the pipeline for the opposition. At 10 p.m., as the House rose, he rushed in high glee to the telephone. "Well, Eugene, I have just poured you down the drain for the sake of democracy." Delighted, Forsey had visions of becoming one of the few men in modern times to be called before the Bar of the House and there sentenced to prison for breach of parliamentary privilege.

Most of the excesses of the debate quickly found a counterbalance. A government that abused the rules to suit its own purposes quickly found that two could play at that. On the other hand, flights of opposition rhetoric could be deftly shot down by some of those on the government side who managed to keep their perspective.

Walter Harris's good-natured interjection, "Oh, act your age, John," as he was being richly insulted by the member from Prince Albert, somehow took the edge off the grandiloquent effect. A government that was supposedly fascist, tyrannical and Hitlerite, had been successfully confronted and stymied for days on end by what Lester Pearson called "the noisiest gagged men in history."

As a matter of fact, the opposition had brought the government to its knees. At the last moment they failed to deliver the *coup de grâce*. While they lost on the immediate issue of preventing the passage of the pipeline bill, they had made great political gain and won a kind of moral victory on the closure issue. More than that they had taken up so much time in the debate that the government was running out of money. It either had to have immediate passage of interim supply or else dissolve the House and face a general election. On Friday afternoon, June 8, Stanley Knowles and Davie Fulton parted on the assumption that both their parties would oppose, by delay, the government's request for interim supply. But George Drew was in Toronto that weekend and he apparently had sober second thoughts about mounting a second filibuster and facing an election after the exhaustion of the pipeline debate. Some Ontario Tories were reluctant to raise funds and fight a campaign over an issue that had brought Howe much sympathy from the business community and had divided federal and provincial leaders of their own party. Interim supply passed in time, and the government was given a breathing spell.

Nevertheless, a future abuse of parliamentary rules such as that practised by the government during May and June of 1956 was unlikely for a long time. The debates afforded a model for future presiding officers of the House on how not to act, and a warning they should take their role seriously but not too solemnly. It may have been a blessing too that the appointment of a permanent Speaker was not made in 1957 but waited for the steps that were taken in 1968 toward that end.

One of the worst and most lasting results of the pipeline debate was just the opposite to the practice of the government and the presiding officers during the pipeline debate. The opposition's stretching of the rules of the House had been so successful in humiliating an all-powerful government that the Liberals, with an even smaller guard of opposition members after the Diefenbaker sweep in 1958, regularly managed to improve upon the 1956 tactics of Knowles, Fulton and company. Once again, after 1963, through the whole five years of Pearson's minority government, members of the Conservative opposition repeatedly developed cases of pipelinitis. In the debate over the fluke Liberal defeat in the House in February 1968, one observer commented that Davie Fulton kept hunting for moose and ended up chasing hare. In December 1968 all parties agreed on the most radical set of rule changes in parliamentary history, but the opposition united in appealing to the abuses of 1956 and so prevented a majority government from putting through a rule that resembled C. D. Howe's closure in advance.

The period of the pipeline debate witnessed one of those regular ritual Canadian outbreaks of anti-Americanism. It was led by several opposition MP's. Donald Fleming spoke of "the Boston influence," and the Yankee-born Howe's inability to understand British parliamentary institutions. This sort of talk soon produced a spate of editorials attacking it. *The Vancouver Province* described Howe as a great Canadian and remarked that he was a relative of Joseph, the other famous Howe in Canadian history. The Halifax *Chronicle-Herald* recalled Howe's peril in an open boat on the high sea after his ship to Britain was torpedoed in 1941 and stated that he was "possibly the greatest Canadian of the twentieth century." The Peterborough *Examiner* delivered an eloquent lecture against that "common brand of ingrown, mean and mistrustful Canadianism which combines in a single crooked mind the idea that Canadians are superior beings and that Canadians must be frightened of the superior cleverness of everybody else."

Howe was particularly sensitive to the anti-American talk directed at him. One of his frequent replies to the flood of criticism was that "the American type of filibuster has been imported into the House of Commons." He defended the government's use of closure as "the British answer" to this abuse.

Howe's own assessment of the political consequences of the pipeline debate is interesting. An old friend wrote to tell Howe to keep "that worthwhile smile" but also observed that "the government would have been wiser to wait a couple of days before calling closure." In his reply Howe said "I doubt if the sudden application of closure made much difference in the long run. Both the Tories and the CCF had announced that they intended to block passage of the Bill, and we were working against the deadline. The main thing is the pipeline is now under construction. I must say I enjoyed the battle, and the newspaper criticism does not bother me. I feel that the end will justify the means."

To Alan Williamson, who was in hospital, Howe wrote, "I find that all our business friends are supporting the idea of the government, though we have lost some ground with labour and the man on the street. I think that this ground can be regained in time but I would not like to face an election at the moment. Fortunately, we do not have to do so. I have a feeling that the long term reaction will be definitely against the Conservatives. Drew has split with Frost on this issue and will get no help from provincial sources. Green has kept silent throughout. The Tories have done everything possible to discredit Nickle of Calgary and done themselves a lot of harm in Alberta. It looks to me as if we will be net gainers by next June. Obviously we have no intention of having an election in the meantime."

What pleased Howe most was that the amount of gas being signed for by customers in the east after passage of the bill was far beyond the volume anticipated. "Officers of the company are confident that we no longer need to depend on exports to the U.S.," he wrote, "which is an ideal situation as far as I am concerned. I would like nothing better than to tell our U.S. friends that we have nothing to offer them. This is not to say that if we get a proposal in time to be of any use, we would turn that down." But he went on to voice concern about getting the financing under way immediately and said "You will appreciate the government, and incidentally myself, will be in serious trouble if the $80 million loaned cannot be repaid."

As far as the company itself was concerned, neither the political side of the debate nor the struggle to survive and prepare for financing were over on June 7, 1956. It was at best the end of the beginning. In the long run Trans-Canada could look forward to another round of anguish and embarrassment when the next election rolled around and the pipeline debate was fought all over again. For the company officers in Calgary, some of them Americans who had decided to make their lives in Canada, the prospect of another round of "dirty Yank" written in weed killer on their lawns, or their children sent home beaten up and crying from school, or of being politely ostracized by their super-patriotic Canadian neighbours, was not a pleasant one.

The immediate business began well enough, however. The seven directors selected for the Crown Corporation were now formally appointed. They were chiefly members of Howe's two departments. Its president was David Golden, a young Rhodes Scholar from Winnipeg who was deputy minister of defence production. Large-diameter pipe from the United States Steel mill in McKeesport, Pennsylvania, began moving towards Saskatchewan within hours of the final agreement being signed by Trans-Canada and the new Crown Corporation. Before the end of June, contracts for over half of the western section of the line had been awarded. Negotiations on sales contracts also proceeded well during the month. Another contract was signed with Union Gas and one with Ralph Farris's Northern Ontario Natural Gas, whose shares were later the focus of a political scandal involving several local politicians and whose identity sometimes became confused in the public mind with the Northern Ontario Pipe Line Crown Corporation. The biggest potential customer, Consumers' Gas of Toronto, was still a holdout. Even so, the new contracts were large enough that Trans-Canada might now perhaps hope to finance on the prospect of Canadian sales alone.

Financing was in any case the company's most urgent business. Failure this time would finish Trans-Canada for good. During late May the Board of Transport Commissioners held hearings in order to allow a decision on the company's request to build only the western section of the line in 1956. The difficulty ahead in financing was well summed up by Chief Commissioner Kearney's comment to Trans-Canada's counsel, Ross Tolmie, during the hearings when he said "Heaven help you if you don't deliver the goods. This is a tough agreement." He went on to estimate that shareholders would only get about four dollars a share, if the company failed to finance itself or to construct the western section in 1956, and so defaulted to the government.

C. D. Howe recognized that he had staked not only his own reputation but the government's fate in the next election on Trans-Canada's success. On June 22 he wrote to Deane Nesbitt, "You no doubt realize the importance to me and to the Liberal party of arranging the financing. Every effort must be made to that end, even though it must depend on Canada for all the funds required."

"I understood that Gardiner Symonds had promised to attempt a compromise with the Chicago people [his competitors for the midwestern American market] after the pipeline bill was passed. I have heard of no effort to that end. Please convey to Gardiner Symonds my insistence that something must be accomplished before November 1st."

Only if the rivals worked out some sort of agreement over the Chicago market, could an FPC decision on the import of Canadian gas follow in time to be of any use. Howe had been in touch with his old friend, the former American Ambassador, Hon. Douglas Stuart. On June 22 Stuart asked him, "Have you any objection to my talking to Gardiner Symonds about working out some sort of compromise? If I were in his position, I would [agree to one]." Howe replied, "As you say, the pipeline battle was an epic. I'm afraid the future of our government depends to a considerable extent on the ability of Trans-Canada to finance the pipeline and pay off the government loan. It would be a great help if Gardiner Symonds would compromise with his opposition and get FPC approval. His right to an export permit for gas from Canada ends on November 1st. I know a compromise will relieve the FPC. I doubt if the latter will make a decision if the present battle continues."

Pressure on Symonds had already met some success, however, and Howe followed up with another letter to Stuart telling him that Symonds was now ready to come to an agreement along with two of his rivals, but that the third "refuses to talk with Gardiner Symonds or with an intermediary. Anything that can be done to induce a compromise would be most helpful all around. It occurs to me that since the First National Bank does business with both parties, it might be possible to get the Bank to intervene in a manner that would be helpful to both their customers."

By July there was more trouble ahead for Howe and Trans-Canada when a steel strike closed all the big American mills. The manufacture of Trans-Canada's pipe ground to a halt. Unless the strike could be settled quickly, there was little chance of the pipeline being completed to Winnipeg before the ground was frozen solid in November. Since a strike had been already described in the contract as one of those conditions under which Trans-Canada was not obliged to complete the western section in 1956, the company's survival was not directly at stake, but politically, it put the government and the company in an embarrassing position.

"The battle of the pipeline in Ottawa is not over yet," Howe commented. The better part of several summer days in Parliament was spent debating the position of the company or discussing the government's and the Speaker's behaviour in the pipeline debate. When U.S. Steel could not deliver the rest of the pipe, the opposition suggested, incorrectly, that the company had never really optioned it. Nevertheless, in the spring Howe had left many people, including the Prime Minister, with the impression that Trans-Canada's pipe had actually all been manufactured and was stock-piled waiting to be put into the ground.

The critical concern now, however, was to place the company's bonds on the American market. A significant new factor here was the presence of Francis Kernan, a New York Irishman from Harvard and long time partner of the investment firm of White, Weld and Company, who had acquired a reputation as the ultimate wizard in the financing of pipelines. Kernan was engaged as consultant to Trans-Canada by Gardiner Symonds with whom he had worked in the initial arrangements for Tennessee during the war. And in return, Kernan received an option on 40,000 Trans-Canada shares at $8, the same price as the shares for the original sponsors.

Kernan was the man who had set the pattern of the industry's financing in the United States during its tremendous expansion in the early fifties. He had arranged the first purchase of natural gas securities by an insurance company in 1936. In 1948 he put together the first "paper" line, a company called Trans-Continental. It was the first natural gas pipeline ever built without the backing of either a government or a powerful company already in the field. Tennessee's big line built during the war had been backed by a government agency, the RFC, under an emergency certificate. The large oil companies, as in Canada, were able to build their own pipelines. But there were no private organizations between 1945 and 1960 in a sufficiently credit worthy position to put up the hundreds of millions of dollars required for gas pipeline bonds, none, that is, except the largest insurance companies. It was to them that the investment bankers turned in order to finance their pipelines. As a result of wartime savings, money in the early fifties was cheap. The relatively high 4% rates going for pipeline bonds were attractive to insurance companies in times when "better paper" brought only $2\frac{1}{2}\%$ or 3%. Kernan had the trust of the insurance companies as well as the experience in pipeline financing to enter into the tough negotiations with them. He approached Metropolitan Life which along with Prudential was one of the two companies accustomed to leadership in the financing of pipelines. After his appointment in March of 1956, one of Kernan's first acts was to ask Trans-Canada to engage Commonwealth Services of New York for an overall feasibility study of Trans-Canada. There had been studies of various kinds at several stages in the company's history, but if Metropolitan Life were to back the company they would require first a complete and up-to-date report such as he could expect from Commonwealth.

By the time Trans-Canada's board was ready to appoint a finance committee, relations between Gardiner Symonds, the American gas chief who held effective control of the company, and Deane Nesbitt, the most active of the Canadian financiers on the board, were such that Symonds would not have Nesbitt as a committee member. An independent chairman, T. H. Atkinson, former general manager of the Royal Bank of Canada was offered an option on 5,000 shares of Trans-Canada stock and invited to join the board so that he might act as chairman of the finance committee. As it turned out, however, Nesbitt and Kernan got along extremely well, and in practice, Kernan worked more closely with the Canadian underwriters than with the finance committee. Both of them were in close touch with Paul Clarke of Lehman Brothers in New York. Throughout the summer of 1956, Kernan, assisted by Clarke, Nesbitt and others, was negotiating with Metropolitan Life.

Trans-Canada's executive committee met in New York in September to examine the detailed requirements and conditions necessary to satisfy the insurance company. Commonwealth Services' feasibility study had now been presented and it predicted, after deducting the company's operating costs, an annual short-fall in meeting interest obligations on bonds and debentures of about $8 million during the first couple of years of the pipeline's operation. Metropolitan Life therefore insisted that the sponsoring group of shareholders put up an additional $21 million in case cash was needed to cover interest on the debt. Among Metropolitan's many other requirements were the sale of the Montreal gas system by Quebec Hydro to Quebec Natural Gas Corporation prior to the take down of any bonds, and evidence that the Alberta Gas Trunk Line Company was adequately financed for the volume of gas delivery required by the Commonwealth study. At a later point Metropolitan required an arrangement to ensure that no one of the three chief sponsors – Gardiner Symond's new controlling group, the Canadian sponsors of Western Pipe Lines, and Clint Murchison, for whom Metropolitan chairman Harry Hagerty had an abiding dislike – gain control of Trans-Canada at some future date after public financing. Most important of all, Metropolitan Life insisted on a renegotiation of gas supply contracts which had so far been settled on the basis of a price comparable to what suppliers were receiving in Texas and Louisiana.

Alberta suppliers, including such backers of Trans-Canada as Canadian Delhi and Canadian Gulf, were not pleased. But since the Canadian government had the power to license exports there was no other market for their gas, and the eventual result was that approximately 5% was shaved off the well-head price of gas on most of the renegotiated contracts. When it was all over, Francis Kernan commented that it was the toughest set of bargaining sessions he had ever been through.

When arrangements to meet Metropolitan's many requirements had been agreed to in October, Trans-Canada drew up a schedule for financing. It was already established that the total amount needed was approximately $370 million. Of this, the Crown Corporation took care of $120 million, and $16 million had already been paid in over the previous half decade by the original sponsors. That left an estimated $234 million to be obtained by public financing. It was determined that $144 million of the total should come from first mortgage bonds, $60 million from subordinated debentures and $30 million from common stock. Kernan's experience was also helpful in the sale of debentures and stock. Several years before, he had conceived the idea of selling these two types of security in a single package so that there would be no danger that the one might be fully subscribed without the other. He noted that Trans-Canada debentures were particularly unattractive to investors, so he decided to include a fairly high proportion of common stock in the package. The 2 to 1 ratio he chose (each $150 unit containing one $100 debenture and five shares of stock at $10 each) represented the highest proportion of common stock he had ever used. But he was greatly relieved, after a meeting in Montreal attended by investing firms from both Canada and the United States, to see that he had hit the proportion just right.

By late summer there was great interest on the part of insiders to buy large blocks of common stocks. One director asked Nesbitt whether the group he represented might receive some $20 or $30 million worth of equity in the company before any offering was made to the public. Nesbitt reported to Howe, "I advised him that I did not think this would look well at all. If as shareholders they felt entitled to this amount, perhaps Tennessee, Gulf and Continental and other shareholders might also come in for large amounts, leaving nothing for public offering. I told him that it was essential for us to live up to representations made earlier that we were going to offer to the Canadian public. If there was tremendous over-demand later for stock, we would be subject to a great deal of criticism if we had reserved such a large block." Howe replied that he agreed that any such proposal would be "shocking to the Canadian people" and he added that Trans-Canada "will not be permitted to overlook the fact that the agreement with the government provided that 50% of all equity stock will be offered to the Canadian public.

Other insiders, expecting a common practice to be followed, put forward their claims to stock at a reduced price before it was offered to the public. One original sponsor, Ray Milner, wrote asking for a special price on some shares for his International Utilities, and Nesbitt had to point out the political impossibility of such a proposal. He also had to win a point with Francis Kernan who asked that the number of institutions buying first mortgage bonds be kept to a minimum in order to limit the problem of making modifications to the trust deed in future years. Nesbitt again urged the political aspect of Trans-Canada's financing and the very close scrutiny it would be under. "No matter what we do there will be criticism," he said, "but the good will created in involving as many Canadian institutions as possible will be extremely valuable." The Canadian underwriters had to fend off a host of requests from investment dealers in both the United States and Canada with a promise to do their best to include each of them when the time came for public sale. The Canadian underwriters also insisted that the Canadian market could take a much larger share than the Americans thought possible. In all of these assertions they could count on C. D. Howe's firm support.

By the time of the October Trans-Canada board meeting in Toronto, the directors had good grounds for optimism. Though there was still no sign from Washington of an FPC decision to allow import of Canadian gas, and though the U.S. steel strike meant there was now absolutely no possibility of completing the western section of the pipeline in 1956, the prospects for successful financing seemed brighter than ever before in Trans-Canada's history. Most of the stiff conditions laid down by Metropolitan Life were in the process of being met or lay within the realm of possibility. The elaborate documentation needed to satisfy the Securities and Exchange Commission in Washington was well on its way to being prepared, as were the simpler requirements for the prospectus in Canada. Early in October Trans-Canada's largest potential customer, Consumers' Gas of Toronto, finally signed a contract to take $82\frac{1}{2}$ million cubic feet of gas a day during the first year of the pipeline's operation and double that amount by the fifth year.

Once again nemesis appeared. Just five days after the board meeting, an international crisis radically changed the company's prospects. On October 29, Israeli troops moved across the Egyptian border into the Suez Canal Zone. The next day, the British and French governments presented both combatants with an ultimatum to withdraw on twelve hours' notice, and following Colonel Nasser's reluctance to remove his army from the invaded portion of his own country, landed their paratroops. Moscow promptly threatened to rain rockets on London and Paris and the prospect of a thermonuclear World

War III was closer than it had been since the atomic age began in 1945. Thanks to the restraint of the two atomic powers and the solution devised at the United Nations on the initiative of Lester Pearson the worst of the crisis swiftly passed.

The recovery in world financial markets was not so rapid. The American owners and financial advisers of Trans-Canada wanted to postpone financing indefinitely until international markets had resumed some sort of order. But the Canadian underwriters hurriedly called a meeting in New York, and after a long and difficult session, during which they offered to sell all the junior securities in Canada if necessary, they managed to persuade their American colleagues that Trans-Canada's only hope of success lay in going ahead with plans to finance even under the adverse conditions that prevailed.

The underwriters found that American interest in Trans-Canada stock had greatly diminished, although this was not the case in Canada. But much more serious was the problem of floating Trans-Canada's bonds. For several weeks after Suez, many new issues were unsaleable at any reasonable price. Francis Kernan had been hoping that the American bonds would go at about $4\frac{3}{4}\%$. This figure was now raised to $5\frac{1}{4}\%$, with customary $\frac{1}{4}\%$ higher for the parallel Canadian issue. Metropolitan Life held firm to the $40 million initial commitment it had promised, but other companies which had been counted on for amounts of between $1 and $10 million, now showed considerable reluctance to invest at all, or else a desire to scale down their purchases drastically.

Under these circumstances the psychological effect of a rapid FPC decision to allow Canadian gas import once more appeared to be critical, since it was the United States market which was counted on for over four-fifths of the total sale of Trans-Canada bonds.

C. D. Howe again entered the fray to put further pressure on Gardiner Symonds and his mid-western rivals to arrive at some sort of agreement. On November 28, he told Symonds that when he was in Chicago, he had urged compromise on the group there. He now did the same to Symonds. "To date we have tried to assist you in your efforts to enter the midwestern market. However, we have been forced to note that your forecasts which induced Trans-Canada to enter into your contract, and induced the government to agree to an export licence for Tennessee, have so far not been justified." Howe urged upon Symonds his moral obligation to make some sort of settlement. He continued with a veiled threat. "The Government cannot proceed with the Northern Ontario section until the money on loan to Trans-Canada is returned. The helpful attitude the government has taken on behalf of Trans-Canada could easily turn into determination to build the line as a government project, which we will both regret. Trans-Canada publicity here continues to be very bad indeed. Parliament will meet on January 8th, and I hesitate to think what could happen in a session that will end in a general election."

On December 13 Howe received word from the Canadian embassy in Washington that Dean Acheson, Tennessee's lawyer, had proposed a compromise which would give Tennessee's three rivals a minority interest in the stock of a merged operation but equal representation on the board, with a neutral director agreeable to both sides holding the balance. Acheson added that he hoped Howe would further settlement on that basis should the opportunity offer, and that he would be glad to go to Ottawa if Howe wished to discuss it. On December 15 Howe replied to the Canadian Ambassador that he and Acheson had had a talk by telephone and that now "Acheson must be told Canada has reached the end of its patience and that unless the Chicago talks lead to a settlement, action must be taken to end the export permit to Tennessee. Export is helpful only at the time of financing the pipeline, and if it is not forthcoming in time we are better off without it. Financing of the pipeline is to be completed during the latter half of January. The situation will not go unnoticed by Parliament which has always been hostile to export. Nineteen fifty-seven being an election year, the pressure will be that much more intense. Tennessee would be very unwise to pass up any chance of settlement, even though some loss of prestige is involved. We cannot concern ourselves about empire-building by Tennessee in the middle west."

Two days later, on December 17, Howe wrote to his fellow Liberal Senator Peter Campbell, who had resigned from Trans-Canada's board when the pipeline bill came before Parliament, to tell him of his warning to Tennessee. "Now you warn the Chicago group," he told Campbell, "there may be no Canadian gas unless there is a quick settlement. Our job must be to make sure both sides realize it is now or never. Salvation must lie in the fact that the two parties will continue to meet without lawyers until an agreement is reached.

Lawyers can then put the agreement into proper form but I think that in the meantime they can only muddy the waters."

Howe had also been busy during December doing his best to help Trans-Canada with the difficult task of selling as much as possible of its $144 million in bonds in Canada. He suggested among other things that the Alberta and Ontario governments might take a sizeable quantity. But both of them avoided the issue by pointing out that they had no power to take such action without the approval of their legislatures, which were not scheduled to meet until February.

By fervent appeals to patriotism, the Canadian underwriters managed to get commitments for $33 million worth of the bonds in Canada, which was $8 million more than the originally projected Canadian sales total. But large American institutions were still reluctant to take Trans-Canada bonds, and the country was scoured for bond sales in smaller quantities. By early January it was obvious that the potential market had been saturated and that little more could be done to move past the $94 million mark then reached. In other words, $50 million would somehow have to be found within a couple of weeks, or the public financing would be a failure.

The underwriters cast about for some means of coping. Since the international situation had improved, the demand for Trans-Canada stock was showing signs of renewal. So they decided to risk increasing the total amount of junior securities offered from $90 million to $110 million. To go higher than that might so dilute the stock that sales of the units of junior securities would also fall short.

That left $30 million to be accounted for. Francis Kernan, after being refused a loan by Chase Manhattan, managed to persuade three U.S. banks, National City Bank of New York, Morgan Guaranty Trust and Mellon Bank of Philadelphia, to loan Trans-Canada $20 million against the security of that amount of Trans-Canada bonds.

To obtain the last $10 million, the Canadian underwriters suggested that R. A. Brown Jr. of Calgary be offered one third of the $15 million in common shares he had earlier requested, provided he would also agree to take $10 million of first mortgage bonds. Francis Kernan put the idea to Tennessee, Gulf and Hudson's Bay, who turned it down. The Canadians then asked Kernan to present the American companies with an ultimatum. Either the three companies should accept Brown's participation or else put up the $10 million in first mortgage bonds themselves. Kernan was sympathetic, but told the Canadians that it would be easier for him if the Canadian sponsors would agree to subscribe $1 million immediately first. Within twenty-four hours, Nesbitt replied favourably and with this commitment in hand, Kernan was able to raise the final $9 million worth of bonds from among the three American sponsors.

At the January 16 board meeting, the directors also agreed to a proposal that an extra $2.5 million should be raised in the units of junior securities in order to cover possible extra construction costs. In the previous few days, there had been a sudden spurt of public interest in these, and there was no doubt that an additional cushion to cover possible increases in construction cost would be useful. The board also formally confirmed an interest rate of 5.85% on the Canadian debentures and 5.6% for the American series, and it was agreed that $81.25 million worth of the units would be available in Canada and $31.25 million in the United States. A target date of February 11, 1957 was set for public offering of the junior securities.

As rumours of the company's successful bond financing spread, there was a storm of demand for Trans-Canada stock, which of course could only be obtained by purchasing the units. Brokers everywhere were besieged with orders. Investors recalled the way in which West-coast Transmission stock had shot up from the original offering price of $5 per share to several times that amount on the market soon after public financing in 1956. By late January, there were hundreds of letters and wires requesting small amounts of the Trans-Canada units. Million dollar orders from Canada, London, New York, and centres in Europe were not unusual.

On January 18, C. D. Howe wrote Eldon Tanner to congratulate him on the company's apparent success in having worked out its financing. But he added, "I am receiving a great number of letters from small people across Canada who would like to invest in the junior securities. Some of them are quite bitter when they find that brokers give them little hope that they will receive no more than a small part of the securities for which they subscribed. I am conscious of the fact that during the pipeline debate I promised a wide distribution of the securities in Canada. Therefore, I trust that you will be able to arrange with your brokers that subscriptions up to and including $5,000 will be filled in full. If there is to be a cut back I suggest that it be confined to the larger subscribers." Asked by Tanner to reply, Deane Nesbitt wrote Howe that the underwriters had arranged for the widest possible selling group, including not only all members of the Investment Dealers Association of Canada, but also a great many other dealers from coast to coast as well as numerous members of the country's stock exchange. While it would be impossible to police such a large group, numbering over four hundred dealers in all, each one was being asked to do his utmost to confirm all small orders in full. "It seems desirable to omit the figure five thousand dollars. It might suggest to people the idea of putting in a number of five thousand dollar orders with different dealers and getting a fill on each. As there is a demand for the units, none of these dealers will be satisfied with their participations, but with the exception of very few of them, none of them have done anything so far to help Trans-Canada. There has also been a lot of complaining from individuals whose amounts are cut down, but if everyone were satisfied with what they received, there would be no after-market for the securities. The fact that people will be allotted less than they subscribed for merely indicates a successful offering."

A successful offering it certainly was. Investors, small and large, descended upon the underwriters. "Schoolmates showed up in droves; casual acquaintances recalled meetings in airports and railway stations where they had expressed their support of the company's policy. Politicians who had voted in favour of legislation supporting Trans-Canada; producers who had sold the company gas; distributors who had negotiated successfully with the company; investment dealers who had shown their complete sympathy; all of these now came forward demanding their right to participate in the equity financing." It was no small task to placate some of them with amounts far less than they wanted and still keep their good will for the future. Over-the-counter traders, at the mere prospect of getting hold of shares in the unit, nominally priced at $10 a share, managed to raise the price on an if-as-and-when basis to $20 a share, thus giving a theoretical value of $200 to each $150 unit of the junior securities. Those selling the securities had to do their best to separate requests to purchase which were of investment quality from those which were merely attempts to get a quick profit. By closing date on February 26, allotments had been made to over 35,000 individuals and corporations.

In the history of financing in Canada, this represented the largest number of individual shareholders to whom a new issue had been allotted. Its only peer in the total amount of junior securities sold to Canadians has been Canadian Pacific Investments, in their October 1967 financing.

By the end of the month the proceeds were pouring into the company treasury, and Trans-Canada was able to repay, with interest, the loan it had received from the Crown Corporation. The shares of the original sponsors which had been placed in escrow as security for the loan were returned to their owners. Underwriters could now turn to their final task of clearing up the last major conditions precedent to the delivery of Trans-Canada's first mortgage bonds. The most difficult of these proved to be the successful placing of $25 million worth of Quebec Natural bonds on the market. With all financial hurdles cleared at last, the Trans-Canada board meeting of June 12 turned to a whole new set of problems posed by the building and operation of the pipeline.

On that same day, Prime Minister St. Laurent telephoned John Diefenbaker in Prince Albert to congratulate him on the results of the June tenth Canadian general election and invite him to his office in Ottawa. It now seemed certain that Trans-Canada's severest critic would be the man in charge of Canadian energy policy and of the conditions under which the company must operate in the years ahead.

Chapter 11 Son of the Great Debate

Successful financing did not end Trans-Canada's stormy career in politics. The publication of the company's prospectus in February 1957 opened up a whole new dimension of it. Critics seized on an issue which provided fuel for the coming election campaign, work for a major Royal Commission, and problems for a new government. During the 1956 debate and after, the opposition had found the pipeline scheme difficult to attack except by general invective; they concentrated their arguments on the government's attitude to Parliament and its use of closure. Now however they spotted something that might justify the invective. What Trans-Canada's prospectus revealed was that the company's chief officers, President Eldon Tanner and executive Vice-President Charles Coates, when they were engaged in 1954, were given future options to purchase stock at the same price ($8 a share) the sponsors had paid during the years when it was potentially worth very little. These options were exercised during February 1957 at the time of public financing. By the end of the month speculative fever over Trans-Canada stock had driven its trading value up to some $20 a share. The opposition saw a golden opportunity at last to show the electorate that their resistance to the pipeline scheme the previous spring had not been "mere gas bagging"; the whole proposition had turned out to be, as one of them put it, "even more iniquitous than we realized at the time."

It was Stanley Knowles who first spotted the political value of the prospectus. In order to make the most of the issue he began by digging a trap for the Minister of Trade and Commerce in question period on February 19. His victim jumped in feet first. Annoyed by the way Knowles put his question, Howe impulsively told the House that there were no stock options available to officials of Trans-Canada the previous May. On February 25 however he had to confess, "I now find that my memory was at fault, and that in fact when the government entered into the agreement on May 8, 1956, a copy of which was tabled in the House on May 9, I was aware of the fact that there were options outstanding." Howe apologized to the House, but immediately took a swipe back at Knowles. He pointed out that the existence of options was known at the time to any member who took the trouble to read the agreement; in any case the success of such a business operation as Trans-Canada depended upon its chief officers having stock options.

After Howe had extricated himself from the preliminary trap, the main debate began, and it raged all through the rest of that day's sitting. Knowles moved adjournment of the House to discuss a matter of "urgent public importance." He quoted a statement of Howe's made on Black Friday, 1956: "this idea that the insiders are making a 'killing' is absolutely wrong." He pointed out that the information tabled in May did not show *how many* share options were held by Tanner and Coates, but that the minister knew – "on his own admission today." They held these options right through the pipeline debate "when they were pieces of paper" of little or no value. Then, after the bill was passed, and the financing was a success, they were able to exercise these options, or, in other words, "to do exactly what on June 1 last year the Minister told us could not be done; they made a killing as a result of support from the public treasury made available to Trans-Canada. . . . I understand prior to his entry into provincial politics [Tanner] was a school teacher. The fact that a school teacher is now able to buy $440,000 worth of stock is something I'm sure that will amaze the school teachers who are in this House." Knowles also pointed out that the prospectus revealed Tanner was "enjoying a salary of $35,000 a year guaranteed for five years" and, if this was not renewed, would get a separation allowance of $15,000 a year over the subsequent five years. "This is the poor hard up company that last year we were called upon to aid by a loan of $80 million."

Knowles' colleague Colin Cameron concentrated his fire on Howe's failure to retain any knowledge of such an important matter. While he accepted the apologies of the minister, he was also "obliged to accept the tragic fact that Right Honorable Minister of Trade and Commerce is now past his ability to be of service to the Canadian people. . . . In other parliaments such a situation as this would result automatically in the resignation of the Minister, yet when this was suggested to him, he merely smiled quite merrily at this House."

The socialist attack was mild compared to that mounted by the official opposition. The new leader, John Diefenbaker, struck out with his broad sword at the perpetrators of "the gigantic trick played on parliament." He described Clint Murchison "as a man who possesses the popular Texas ambition of buying the rest of the United States," whose companies are "as varied as a pirate's treasure and who is able to put $1 by $1 and make $11 million. Messrs. Tanner and Coates did not do that, but they made a fairly good attempt. . . . They risked nothing but their signatures and they reap fabulous profits. . . . I ask the minister to say what risk did these buccaneers take?"

Howe's reply was a lecture on stock options as a necessary incentive in the free enterprise system. He praised the restraint with which it has been used in the case of Trans-Canada Pipe Lines.

"What is the crime now being discussed? Certain gentlemen undertook to promote a work of great national importance. Certain of them contributed money. . . . But you cannot build with money alone. You must also have brains and experience." The two accused had held secure and attractive positions in a growing oil company and the world's largest gas transmission firm. To join this marginal and risky enterprise in 1954 they were offered salary and stock options in some degree equivalent to the ones they held previously. They bought their stock at $8 a share at the same time as the public bought theirs at $10. In fact "the Treasury of the Company received nine dollars a share from the ten dollar price, the extra dollar representing the cost of distribution to the public. So the cost to the company of these options was one dollar a share. That might be a killing. I do not know. It seems to me it is a reasonable reward for four years of hard work. If that is a crime then the company to my knowledge has committed a crime."

Howe contrasted Trans-Canada with the financing of Frank Mc-

Mahon's Westcoast Transmission. He pointed out that McMahon got his shares for 5¢ a piece, that they were sold to the public for $5 and were now listed on the market at $35. "That is several thousand percent difference." Finally, "it is somewhat important that Trans-Canada has been successfully financed. I think the fact that the project is being built will impress the public more than the quibbling and bickering about ways and means. At two o'clock tomorrow afternoon a cheque is going to be put in my hands for the full amount of the [government] loan plus interest at five percent plus the expenses incurred by the government. . . . In the meantime, the transaction is what it is, I have explained it as it appears to me. . . . On the hustings I will talk about this great Canadian project and the opposition it has encountered at all stages. The Opposition can tell the electors how much trouble they were able to create in the House of Commons. And we will let the voters decide."

The debate swirled on for several hours, focusing more and more on the character and reputation of Eldon Tanner. Conservative William Hamilton pointed out that Tanner went "straight from the Social Credit cabinet as Minister of Mines to a company doing business with the Social Credit government. Then about two years later he leap-frogged from there into a company doing business with both the federal and provincial governments. . . . I forbear to suggest why Mr. Tanner got that stock option. It does not seem to me he got it for the ability he had demonstrated to that date, yet I would not want to think he got it because he had been Minister of Mines in the Social Credit government of Alberta and thus facilitated certain negotiations with Trans-Canada. . . ."

The Social Credit leader Solon Low replied with a long emotional speech about the integrity of a man he had known intimately since schooldays. Conservative Carl Nickle of Calgary praised Tanner as the minister who had coped with the sudden and enormous consequences of Leduc in the first six years of the oil boom — "and without a breath of scandal in his department." As for Trans-Canada's stock trading at $20 because of speculators' eagerness for a quick turnover, he doubted whether it was worth more than $12. Given the uncertainties ahead for Trans-Canada, he would be reluctuant himself to pay much more than the $10 price at which they had been initially sold to the public. For anyone who bought shares as an investment in the long term future of the company, it meant waiting at least five years before dividends could be expected, and five years loss of interest on the money invested. As it turned out, it actually was five years before dividends were paid, and the stock dropped as low as $16 in 1960 and $18 in 1962 though it briefly shot up to a high of $38 in the fall of 1958.

Most Conservatives who attacked Trans-Canada were in the somewhat awkward position, as Liberal John Dickey put it, of favouring free enterprise and stock options in general, without agreeing that "the system should be admitted to work in this instance." By contrast, the CCF attacked the system itself: It was no justification of free enterprise or Trans-Canada for Mr. Howe to get up and "claim that what other companies had done was a thousand times worse."

The Prime Minister concluded the debate by stating once again why his government refused to take over the pipeline as long as private enterprise could possibly be enabled to do the job. As with the issue of railway freight rates, a government carrier caught between the pressures of eastern consumer and western producer would almost certainly cost the Canadian taxpayer a great deal of money.

Less than seven weeks later the House of Commons was dissolved and the election campaign, of which the February 25 debate had been a preliminary, began. By the time Prime Minister St. Laurent opened his campaign on April 29 in Winnipeg, preparations for completing the western section were well under way. It seemed certain now that gas would be flowing into Winnipeg well before the end of the year. St. Laurent attacked those who had tried to obstruct a great national project during the pipeline debates. Hecklers yelled back at him, "Closure!" and "Guillotine!" and "Supermen!"

The Conservatives concentrated, above all other issues, on the government's abuse of Parliament. Their headquarters produced a pamphlet and an ad for insertion in local newspapers. Both were entitled *Black Friday*. But the Liberals could easily console themselves that the public's interest in the pipeline debate was limited and its memory short. Results were what counted. The project was now past its worst crisis, and soon its consequences would be manifest in another increase in the Gross National Product. Trans-Canada's apparent success could not help but increase the Liberals' conviction of their own indispensability to the well-being of the nation. They had little appreciation of John Diefenbaker's capacity to dramatize his own giant-killer's role and the sacredness of Parliament as antidotes to a tired and aging tyranny. There were signs of protest in the air, but sensible political observers did not take them seriously. *Spring Thaw's chef d'oeuvre* for 1957 was a satire on the pipeline debate, and the Governor General in *My Fur Lady* brought the house down with his phone call to the Prime Minister: "Hello Louis! How(e)'s everything?"

At the polls, just a year and ten days after Black Friday, the electorate provided both the experts and the government with a rude surprise. For the first time in twenty-two years, the Liberals were rejected by the Canadian public. C. D. Howe himself went down to personal defeat.

Whether or not it was the pipeline controversy itself or those aspects of the Liberal government it symbolized that chiefly contributed to the result, there was no question that the new régime had a mandate, even a commitment, to investigate Trans-Canada and the arrangements that Howe had made with it. At this stage, however, since there was no clear alternative to the company continuing to build the line, and since Liberal policy on the pipeline might well prove to have been sound after all, the safest thing to do was to turn the problem over to a Royal Commission. At the very least its existence could postpone any vindication of Liberal policy and Trans-Canada until after the next election. At best its findings might provide ammunition for that occasion. Diefenbaker, the prairie radical, made an astute political move by appointing the Toronto Tory and nephew of a former Conservative Prime Minister, Henry Borden, as Chairman of a Royal Commission on Energy. The selection of Borden could not easily be criticized by the Liberals or Conservatives, since he was the head of the giant Canadian-owned utility, Brazilian Traction, and a highly respected businessman committed to the principles of private enterprise. He was little likely to sympathize with threats to punish Trans-Canada that had been made in the heat of the election campaign.

The creation of a Royal Commission was roundly criticized, however, in two quarters. The CCF saw it as evidence that the government was prepared to betray the Canadian people by continuing Liberal policy. They finally succeeded in forcing a vote in the Commons. To the embarrassment of the Conservatives, they were joined by the Liberal and Social Credit parties in order to defeat a CCF motion calling for public ownership of Trans-Canada Pipe Lines.

At the other end of the political spectrum, in Alberta, there was a strong attack on Diefenbaker's government for using the Royal Commission to postpone decisions on the development of Alberta petroleum resources. The *Calgary Albertan* called it "a far worse setback to Alberta than anything else that could have happened."

On October 31, 1957, the *Albertan's* worst fears were realized when Diefenbaker stated that his government was not bound by C. D. Howe's 1955 letter to Trans-Canada promising an export licence for Canadian gas. The Prime Minister said he would await the findings of the Royal Commission before deciding. His statement brought consternation to those interested in the Trans-Canada-Tennessee scheme to supply the American mid-west. Francis Kernan, who was testifying on behalf of Tennessee's request for an import licence before the FPC, stated that without a prior commitment from the Canadian government, it would be hopeless to try to raise money for the line into the United States. He pointed out that the Trans-Canada line itself could not have been financed but for American bond investors' belief that a commitment by the Canadian government to export already existed. There was now no chance of selling Alberta gas to the United States through Trans-Canada until after the Royal Commission reported.

Its appointment, however, did effectively take Trans-Canada out of the headlines for the balance of 1957 and during the March 1958 general election. Because of this, and with successful financing behind it, the company could turn to its own internal development and the normal problems of a going concern rather than those of a "paper" company whose survival was in doubt from one month to the next.

As a reflection of the crucial position of gas sales in the eastern market, the company moved its head office from Calgary to Toronto. And because construction would be the central concern of the company during the next two seasons, the experienced pipeline engineer Charles Coates was elected President and Chief Executive Officer in June 1957. Eldon Tanner retained only his position of board chairman.

There were also important changes in the company's ownership and Board of Directors during 1957 and 1958. Both Hudson's Bay and Tennessee began to reduce their common share holdings in Trans-Canada. The president of Hudson's Bay, R. C. Brown, said in his letter of resignation as director and member of the executive committee that since financing has been successfully completed, his company's objective in coming into Trans-Canada had been realized. It would now be best to turn the use of his own time and his company's money to their basic function, petroleum exploration and production. Gardiner Symonds also resigned from the board and Tennessee began to sell its Trans-Canada's shares. Tennessee's annual report for 1957 showed a profit of almost $2.5 million made on this sale which amounted to over $7 each on shares for which Tennessee had originally paid $8.

The shares sold by these two companies were mainly acquired by the largest independent Canadian petroleum company, Home Oil, whose president, R. A. Brown Jr., had been turned down in his bid to obtain a large block of Trans-Canada's shares in the original allocation. Home Oil's holdings eventually reached a million and a quarter shares. By the end of 1957 Home Oil had become Trans-Canada's largest shareholder, and Brown was appointed to the board and its executive committee.

The third member of the American trio controlling Trans-Canada in 1956-57 did not leave, however, although its money might well have been more profitably invested in petroleum properties. In 1969 two representatives of the Gulf Oil Company were still members of the Trans-Canada board. One other resignation took place in early 1958, that of H. R. Milner, president of the two major Alberta utilities. He was now interested in developing another pipeline to use Alberta gas. Since his controlling company, International Utilities, was also partly American-owned, American holdings in Trans-Canada stock were further reduced, and by early 1958 over 75% of the shares were owned by Canadians.

Trans-Canada's construction programme for 1957 was one of staggering proportions. It involved building only a part of the main line, but even this was longer than most major pipelines then in existence, and some of it was to travel through territory such as the veteran construction crews had never experienced before. Pipelines had been built over desert, in the southern swamps of the United

States and through the passes of the Rocky Mountains, but never before over such a vast wilderness of muskeg and solid rock, over so many lakes and rivers, and in such northerly climates and terrains.

The target for 1957 was the completion of a 34-inch line from the Alberta border through Regina to Winnipeg; a 30-inch line from Winnipeg to the Lakehead, including the westernmost portion of the Northern Ontario Pipe Line Crown Corporation's line from the Manitoba border eastwards; and a 20-inch line from Toronto to Montreal, with a spur up to Ottawa. This last section was to be hooked up to Trans-Canada's first pipeline built in 1954 from the middle of the Niagara River to the outskirts of Toronto and would continue to use American gas until the rest of Ontario was bridged in 1958. In all, some 1400 miles of line – 60% of the total – were to be built. If it could be done, well over 90% of the population to be served by Trans-Canada would receive natural gas by the end of 1957.

The chief incentive to complete the first stage of the programme was the need to pay bond interest immediately, and common share dividends as soon as possible, on the quarter billion dollar investment. But there was also the spur of the Conservatives' criticism of the company's past performance, and concern over what they might do if the company's construction schedule were not met.

Only 225 miles of the western section of the line had been completed before freeze-up in 1956. All through the winter and early spring of 1957 the pace of preparation was intense. Most of the route had already been surveyed in detail and the formidable task of negotiating for right-of-way with landowners across Canada was well under way. Clearing right-of-way went on through the winter, stock piling of pipe began again once the U.S. mills were free of the strike, roads were cleared into the bush and through prairie fields, and necessary field camps and offices were moved in. Early in May trenching operations began in the prairies. An enormous trench, eight feet deep and three feet wide, had to be dug all the way from Alberta to Montreal. Forty-foot lengths of pipe were strung along the entire route and the sections welded together. Pipe was to be cleaned and installed and, after the trench was refilled, tested under conditions more rigorous than ever expected in actual operation. Over some of the wider rivers a double line had to be constructed in order to insure safe and uninterrupted delivery. As the crews reached the Laurentian

Shield they found they had to blast out the rock in thousand foot stretches. For a fifth of a mile, at twenty-two inch intervals, eight-foot holes were drilled three abreast down into the solid rock. Each of the holes was then filled with dynamite. The whole section was blown by electrical wiring in one glorious bang. Up to thirty thousand sticks of high explosive were used for one mile of trench.

In some regions there were no inhabitants but moose and bear to hear the sound of the blast. In populated parts of the Lake of the Woods region it was a noisy summer for cottagers and the residents of towns like Kenora.

On the prairies the construction of the line gave a great boost to temporary employment. Wages ran at an unheard of minimum of $1.65 for the most unskilled jobs up to $4 for the most experienced American welders and operators of pipelaying machinery. Skill was in such short supply that some of the greenhorn Canadians would stay up all night to teach themselves to operate one of the pipelaying machines. For them a normal day began along the Saskatchewan portion of the line at the first crack of prairie dawn before 5 a.m. After wolfing down breakfast and packing a lunch, there was perhaps a twenty- or thirty-mile trip to the site of the day's activities from the town where the crew happened to be boarding that week. The first man back around 9 or 10 p.m. would begin making dinner. Many of the American veterans, however, had their family trailers along and lived closer to their daily work.

On September 27, permission was given by the Board of Transport Commissioners for the first gas to come into Winnipeg under low pressure. By December 1 the Toronto-Montreal line had been completed and tested. By Christmas eve it looked as if the last portion to be completed, from Winnipeg to Port Arthur, would be bringing in gas to the Lakehead before the end of the year. That night high-pressure testing was taking place near Dryden, Ontario. The line installed in its coffin-like rock ditch was being tested to a pressure of 1030 pounds per square inch. At a pressure of $1028\frac{1}{2}$, there was a tremendous roar, the ditch heaved, the cover of soil and rock flew upwards, and the pilot of a TCA aircraft saw a long flash of light leap from the earth below him. The longest pipeline break in history, some three and a half miles, took place instantly.

Fortunately there was no fire and no one was hurt. But over Christmas there was a desperate rush to get the pipe replaced and the line retested so that the last target for 1957 could be met. Men were working at night in weather down to 56° below zero. The sideboom tractor lowering the pipe had to have three tractors trailing it to hold it from skidding into the ditch. A gravel pit was purchased to provide soft material for padding and lining the trench but even this had to be constantly heated and unfrozen before it could be poured in. The job was completed by New Year's, and Port Arthur was supplied with natural gas for the rest of the winter. As an engineer in private life over a generation earlier, C. D. Howe had built the giant Lakehead grain elevators that stood as one monument to his career. Now they were joined by another. And natural gas was used to keep the grain dry.

During the winter, clearings of right-of-way continued through the waste land of northern Ontario from the Lakehead to North Bay. Crossings of highways and farms were prepared north of Toronto. Some of the final negotiations with the last hold-outs on right-of-way were difficult and delicate. In the end these real estate transactions involved some five thousand individuals. Many of them were bitter about the idea of their orchards or gardens being ripped apart by an eight-foot ditch. In the end there was only one person for whom the pipeline had to make a major rerouting, Mrs. Ann Sugarman in Vaughan Township west of Richmond Hill. Her four acres as she said, "bloomed with trilliums in the spring which make your heart leap." She was determined not to have the moisture removed from the top of her hill and risk destroying her flowers. She spoke of "tantalizing Trans-Canada officials with trilliums and apples." She ultimately won her point and the red construction flags were moved off her property. Given the nature of such negotiations, it is remarkable how little ill will was generated. Congratulations on their fairness and efficiency were received by the company from Saskatchewan's socialist government, among others. The land around the buried pipe soon reverted to its normal functions of growing wheat or fruit or flowers. Still, the maintenance roads and the metering stations *en route* formed a permanent addition to the scene, as were the aircraft daily patrolling the length of the line for signs on the earth of a pinhole leak — like a patch of dying vegetation — that could be easily spotted from the air.

One of the tasks during the 1958 construction season was to build a half-dozen compressor stations along the route. During the 1957 season gas came originally all the way from Alberta to Port Arthur under its own well-head pressure. To compress it and drive it further east in large quantities, however, powerful reciprocating engines later replaced by gas-fired turbines had to be used.

During the summer of 1958, the wettest in living memory, several crises developed as the muskeg swallowed up pipe, or the rivers and rock formations of Northern Ontario posed their own new problems. In some places the pipe had to be welded in mile-long segments and then moved into place in one piece. But at long last, on October 10, 1958, in the midst of a wild sleet and rain storm, the last weld of the Trans-Canada line was finished near Kapuskasing. The line was complete from Alberta to Montreal. The final testing was carried out, approval was given by the BTC, the flow of American gas from across the Niagara River was stopped, and on October 27, the first Alberta gas came east. The ten-year-old dream of power from the west moving right across Canada to the markets of Toronto and Montreal had come true.

The pipeline has some claim to be ranked with the St. Lawrence Seaway and the building of the CPR as one of the great physical accomplishments of Canadian history. At its peak the army of construction workers numbered five thousand men. Nine million cubic yards of earth and rock were excavated, and over 650,000 tons of pipe was laid into the 2200-mile ditch. The line crossed 8 lakes, 99 rivers and countless streams, roads and rail lines.

In meeting the deadline, within cost estimates, Charles Coates had done a remarkable job. Amid predictions of delay or disaster from many experienced pipeliners in the United States, and attacks on natural gas as a public danger by heating competitors, Coates still managed to cope with the heavy schedule of testifying before the Borden Commission, supervising relations with customers and suppliers and running headquarters operation for construction.

Throughout it all he would find a few days every month to tear off to northern Ontario and do what he liked best: checking on the crews in the field. He would drive from one sixty-mile spread to the next, examining the operations of each contractor on the spot without comment; then, as he turned to leave, he would list to the field superintendent the exact amount of additional help and equipment which was needed – "by tomorrow night" – to meet the deadlines.

Credit for the completion of the line belongs to many people besides Coates, from the sponsors to the construction crews. But most of all perhaps, the ultimate victory was C. D. Howe's. Just as he had predicted three years before, the line was completed by October 1958. He did not guess that he himself would no longer be in power. But he could now look back at the building of the longest natural gas pipeline in the world as his last and possibly greatest single feat. All the skills and experience of his life, as engineer and business man, as organizer of a nation at war, as politician and cabinet minister and general manager of a whole economy, all of his capacity for absorbing criticism and his stubborn refusal to accept defeat, had gone into this last achievement.

A magazine which chose C. D. Howe as its Man of the Year for 1958 stated that "when the final weld was made near Kapuskasing in October, it rivalled in historic significance the driving of the last spike in the trans-Canada railway line." If the praise and congratulation that were now showered upon him seem fulsome, they must be set against the attacks he had continued to receive, even in defeat. The year before, after the 1957 election and the end of Howe's political career, *The Globe and Mail* published a triumphant editorial called THE GREAT MAN. It attacked all and sundry who were willing to accord that title to C. D. Howe, and stated that only "in the constant enlargement of his own power . . . did Mr. Howe show authentic genius. . . . Never before has a minister of the Crown ruled with so much authority. Never before have so many Canadians feared, so many Canadians bowed the knee before, one man. Perhaps that was his greatness. But it is not the type we wish to see enshrined in this country's history."

On October 27, 1958, the very day that Alberta gas arrived in Toronto and Montreal, the first report of the Royal Commission on Energy appeared. Publication of the Borden Report marked a turning point in the history of Trans-Canada and Canadian energy policy. Its most important general recommendation, later adopted by the government, was the creation of a National Energy Board to examine all proposals for the use of Canadian energy resources. It also recommended that the Board of Transport Commissioners, subject to the jurisdiction of Parliament, regulate the rates charged by gas pipeline companies. The main purpose of the interim report, however, was to deal specifically with uncertainties over the past and future of Trans-Canada Pipe Lines.

The commission had begun hearings on Trans-Canada in February 1958, and all through the spring and summer it conducted an exhaustive inquiry into every aspect of the company's activities. Company officers welcomed the inquiry because they felt that past accusations would be put into proper perspective by bringing all the facts under scrutiny. The original promoters were particularly conscious, for example, of the fact that they had paid $8 for their shares at a time when they risked losing everything. If the cost of interest were added to the money invested earlier in the decade, they had in effect by 1957 paid more than the public offering price of $10. Compared to the insiders' price for shares on other promotions this was an unusual record. On every point but one in its review of the company's history, the Royal Commission gave Trans-Canada, and hence indirectly the Liberal scheme, what amounted to a complete exoneration. The commission commented favourably on the Northern Ontario Pipe Line Crown Corporation and its relationship to Trans-Canada as well as the terms of the loan that had been made and repaid. It also justified the option to purchase the northern Ontario section given to Trans-Canada. Furthermore it stated that if the government had not acted as it did in the spring of 1956 "the Commission is of the view that construction on the western section of the line by Trans-Canada would have been indefinitely delayed."

There was no reference at all in the report to the alternative proposals which had been presented by Gairdner and McMahon in 1956, nor to schemes for a north-south exchange arrangement considered in 1955. The commission looked at the existence of gas purchase contracts entered into by Trans-Canada with certain of its major shareholders, but concluded no special action need be taken to safeguard the interests of Canadian producers or consumers, provided the BTC were asked to regulate rates.

The commission also examined closely the public financing of the company and the share ownership of Trans-Canada as of January 31 and February 28, 1957, immediately before and after public financing. It noted the wide distribution and that the company was more than 75% Canadian-owned.

When it came to the question of share options the commission declared that the price set of $8 per share was reasonable and that options were one of the normal tools used by corporations to attract key executives. With respect to Tanner and Coates, however, while it noted that they were offered salaries and options roughly equivalent to those which they had been granted by their previous employers, it concluded that the management contracts assuring their salaries for five years placed them in an entirely different position from all other shareholders. The commission concluded that "the government of Canada should have insisted, as a condition of financial assistance that steps be taken, or that the two men should have voluntarily taken such steps, as would preclude them from reaping large capital profits from the purchase of shares in a company by which they were employed and which was being financed, in an essential part and at a critical time, with public funds."

It is curious that the commission did not attack Trans-Canada's board, who were after all ultimately responsible for the options, nor the other persons such as Francis Kernan, T. H. Atkinson and other employees who received them. It looked unpleasantly like an attempt to find and identify the "buccaneers" so eloquently evoked during the pipeline debates. Charles Coates as a Texan and Eldon Tanner as a former Social Credit cabinet minister, appear all too much like convenient political scapegoats. There was another round of criticism in the press.

As it happened, both Tanner and Coates had decided to leave their posts once the line was completed. By early autumn a committee of the board was looking for a new chief executive. Had there been any doubt, the Borden Report would have settled the matter. Tanner and Coates could henceforth only deal with the Diefenbaker government from a vulnerable position, and were clearly a political liability to the company. They were in any case heartily sick of seeing their names in the headlines. Their resignations as chairman and president respectively were received and accepted in December 1958, as the company began a new phase of its history as an operating utility.

Chapter 12 The Great Lakes Affair

Early in October 1958, James Kerr of Canadian Westinghouse received a call from his friend and fellow engineer, Geoffrey Gaherty of Montreal, chairman of Calgary Power Limited who asked if he could come to see him in Hamilton. Kerr assumed that he was interested in buying equipment for his company and offered to drive over to Toronto instead. When he arrived at the Royal York Hotel, Kerr found that his friend had something quite different in mind. He was introduced to a colleague of Gaherty's, R. A. Brown Jr. of Calgary, and asked if he would accept the presidency of Trans-Canada Pipe Lines. Gaherty and Brown were the newest members of Trans-Canada's board. They had replaced the heads of two of the three large American firms who controlled the company during 1956 and part of 1957 – Gaherty because of his experience in engineering and Canadian utilities, Brown as an Alberta petroleum man and president of Home Oil, Trans-Canada's largest shareholder. Kerr agreed to think the matter over and to meet the other board members responsible for choosing a new chief executive.

Born in Hamilton, Kerr joined Westinghouse in 1937, the year after his graduation in electrical engineering from the University of Toronto. He rose to the rank of squadron leader in the RCAF during the war, returned to Westinghouse afterwards, and in 1956 at the age of 41 became a divisional vice-president. He had his doubts about joining a firm with as uncertain a past and future as Trans-Canada and also about entering an industry entirely new to him. Gaherty told Kerr that this was the type of thing he himself would like to take on if he were younger. Kerr would probably not have as good a chance again to take charge of a giant firm, owned and controlled in Canada, nor such an opportunity to apply his convictions about the ability of Canadian engineers and manufacturers to pioneer industrial research in the country and apply it in new ways and on an unprecedented scale. Kerr also consulted his old friend Richard L. Hearn, the chairman of Ontario Hydro, who strongly urged him to accept. He was appointed to the presidency at the Trans-Canada board meeting of December 3, 1958. Charles Coates was moving back to Texas to take over a consulting business but he agreed to continue for a time as Trans-Canada's board chairman, a post which Kerr assumed some sixteen months later in addition to the presidency.

An intense, reserved, cautious man, Kerr presented a contrast to the large ebullient Texan whom he succeeded. Coates' manner of running the company, with little formal structure, often with no agenda for important meetings, reminded one colleague of a college quarterback calling plays for his football team. Kerr was more like a chess player methodically planning his moves, calculating all the possibilities before taking action. Another analogy also has some truth in it: that of a bush pilot flying by the seat of his pants and inspiring others to follow him, in contrast to the commander of a giant passenger jet guided by ground control, radar and a complex instrument panel. What both presidents had in common was an engineering background, a fascination with new technology and a concern for applied research. Each man had a strong if different kind of commitment to team management, but tended in practice to act more like a powerful prime minister than as the executor of a managerial consensus.

The company was faced with a huge operating deficit over the next two or three years. It had to build investors' confidence before further large-scale borrowing to expand facilities and to buy out the Cown Corporation. Kerr's first priority was to take a careful look at operating costs. He realized he would have to make some decisions that would likely be unpopular inside the company. During the construction period, time was more valuable than money and spending tended to be free. One of the first things he did was to sell the company's DC3 aircraft which had been used for freighting and inspection during the construction phase, as well as rushing company executives back and forth across the 2,200 mile pipeline.

As for longer term objectives, Kerr hoped to make the company more Canadian — both in its purchasing policy and its personnel. He was concerned to experiment continually with new engineering methods for driving a larger volume of gas through the system more efficiently and for controlling its flow more precisely. There were advantages to natural gas for which many customers would be willing to pay a premium, but the survival and growth of the company essentially depended on whether the price of gas could be kept competitive with that of other fuels.

In the meantime, however, three of the company's perennial problems were lying in wait for the new president as he prepared to take over. These were, first, that of export permits from the authorities in Washington and Ottawa; second, signing up for an adequate gas supply with the petroleum companies and gaining provincial permission to remove it from Alberta; and third, coping with Trans-Canada's nine major Canadian customers, most of whom like Trans-Canada still had their growing pains ahead of them.

The Borden Report recommended that C. D. Howe's 1955 conditional export permit be withdrawn and the whole matter re-examined by a new National Energy Board. This immediately had the effect of killing the current application of Midwestern, Trans-Canada's American customer, before the FPC. Another application would have to be prepared, and a whole new round of hearings begun.

Before the new FPC hearings convened in July 1959 there were two favourable developments. As it became clearer that American demand for natural gas was increasing and long term American reserves were relatively smaller than the potential of Canadian gas fields, one of Midwestern's chief opponents in Washington switched sides and came to an agreement on sharing imports. Midwestern and the Michigan Wisconsin Pipe Line Company now went before the FPC as allies rather than enemies.

The prospect of Trans-Canada getting a bigger volume of gas out of Alberta also improved. There were many months of fierce competition with Alberta rivals who planned to export gas directly south to the western United States, e.g. Alberta & Southern, a new firm with which former Trans-Canada director Ray Milner was associated. But by mid-1959 the Trans-Canada purchasing team in Calgary had signed nearly another hundred gas supply contracts, twice as many as were in force at the time of the company's original financing in 1957.

The difficulty was that, as the November 1 expiry date for Trans-Canada's American sales contract approached, neither the provincial nor the federal government was ready to decide on export permits. The new National Energy Board, legislated into existence by Parliament in May, was not fully set up and ready for business until November. The FPC came through at the last possible moment — Hallowe'en 1959, and granted permission for Canadian gas to enter the United States. The Alberta Conservation Board brought down a favourable report on December 31, 1959, and Premier Manning granted Alberta's export permit on January 13, just as the first hearings before the National Energy Board in Ottawa began.

Here another major delay loomed up as the municipalities of northern Ontario prepared a massive intervention under the leadership of Trans-Canada's customer in the area, Northern Ontario Natural Gas (NONG).

The eventual effect of Canadian export to the United States would be to stimulate the exploration for Alberta gas and make possible increased volume and lower prices. But there was concern in northern Ontario lest export increase competition for the presently available supply in Canada and so raise its price. The provincial government also asked for reassurance that the National Energy Board was considering the overall future needs of Ontario – which accounted for over 80% of Trans-Canada's total sales in 1959 – before allowing export. Once the lines were built, and American customers had come to depend on Canadian gas, the commitment would be irreversible. After a vigorous two-month battle, Trans-Canada and NONG resolved their dispute by negotiation. The National Energy Board reported favourably, and in April of 1960 the Canadian government finally granted a licence for export at Emerson. Eleven years after the original export proposal had been conceived, Trans-Canada could look forward to selling as much as one-quarter of its volume to the United States during 1961, and so help reduce its large operating deficit.

During 1960 Trans-Canada's sales were running as well as projected, except to NONG, Consumers' and Quebec Natural Gas. None of its nine original Canadian customers was in a safe position, however. The risks, like the potential, were high. Six of them were distributing natural gas in new territory for the first time. No less than seven were new companies. They faced the same problems as Trans-Canada in borrowing the huge sums of money required to initiate or expand their operations. They were all competing against established energy sources whose performance, costs and administrative and legal requirements were better known. In spite of the great care taken in drawing them up, the original gas contracts were bound to contain flaws and omissions. By 1960 many of the key staff who had worked out the original arrangements during the mid-fifties were no longer with their companies. There was continual dispute over the precise meaning of words: exactly what volumes of gas, at what pressure, with what thermal content, at what times and prices, had been contracted for? And in what ways were the penalty clauses to be interpreted under entirely new and unforeseen circumstances?

The managements of all customers but one were able to navigate through the early difficult years without a major disaster. But the predicament of that one was enough to shake Trans-Canada to the foundations; it became the chief preoccupation of company officers for over two years.

On June 20, 1960, James Kerr was at the Manoir Richelieu in La Malbaie, Quebec, dressing for the annual dinner of the Canadian Gas Association, when he received a long distance call from Leonard Milano, Quebec Natural's chief executive officer. Mr. Milano had news. His company could not pay its gas bill for the month of May.

Within a matter of minutes, Kerr and his two senior vice-presidents were on their way by rented car to Montreal. At the same time Milano also informed his board (which included three Trans-Canada directors) that the company could not meet its next payroll or debt interest obligations, both due at the end of June.

Quebec Natural's trouble had many roots. The initial price paid to Quebec Hydro for the old manufactured gas system was exorbitant. For years Quebec Hydro had been allowing gas customers a minimum billing of 50¢ a month, and this practice was continued by Quebec Natural even though other Canadian companies used a minimum of

$1.50 to $2.50. After the Suez Crisis was over, the world price of fuel oil fell. Montreal had the closest Canadian refineries to supplies of Venezuelan and Middle Eastern crude, and hence was a particularly difficult area for natural gas to compete in. On top of all this, Quebec Natural's top management (found for the firm by Commonwealth Services of New York) proved inadequate, as did its accounting system, which for a time obscured its financial difficulties. An extra $15 million acquired through the sale of preferred stock in 1959 for the purpose of capital expansion was entirely used up in operating costs within a few months' time. Trans-Canada had some warning of its customer's plight as early as the fall of 1959 when Quebec Natural failed to take the full volume of gas for which it had contracted. Trans-Canada undertook to act as Quebec Natural's agent in selling the gas to other customers.

When the final crisis came in June 1960, Quebec Natural's bankers acted swiftly to enable it to meet its immediate obligations and so avoid bankruptcy for the moment. Its board received Milano's resignation and put the company in the charge of two experts from a firm of Chicago engineering consultants assigned to undertake a complete assessment of the company's position. The two men, Glen Maddock and Carl Horne, were later appointed its president and executive vice-president. To avoid conflict of interest in the critical period ahead, two Quebec Natural board members, Asselin and McCausland, resigned from the Trans-Canada board, and the third director common to both, Frank Schultz, from Quebec Natural's board.

On June 22, two days after Milano's call to Kerr, the Union Nationale, in power since 1944, was defeated at the polls. The most radical government in provincial history took power and with it began the exciting experiment of the Quiet Revolution. Quebec Natural Gas became one of the symbols of the discredited Duplessis régime. During the election campaign, Le Devoir, for long the Union Nationale's only press opposition, published the news that government members in the Quebec legislature and certain party officials and civil servants had purchased Quebec Natural stock at the time of its public sale. Though the stock fell later as low as $3 a share, reflecting a truer value of the company, its market price zoomed upwards to $18 in the first fever of speculation. That newspaper story alone may have provided the extra spurt of energy to the Liberals' campaign that made possible their narrow victory over the entrenched and apparently unbeatable Union Nationale machine.

One of the Liberal government's first important acts was to appoint a Royal Commission, chaired by Mr. Justice Elie Salvas, to investigate Quebec Natural's entire history. It would obviously be impossible for the company to set its affairs in order and refinance on a long term basis until the Salvas Report was brought down. In the meantime Quebec Natural could not even gain an increase in the minimum billing that had contributed to its difficulties. After two long hearings before the Quebec Electricity and Gas Board, fought every inch of the way by Mayor Jean Drapeau of Montreal, the company was awarded an increase from 50¢ to $1, and finally to $1.40, still the lowest figure in North America, on June 26, 1962, two years after the initial disaster.

Throughout that period, Trans-Canada was faced with the dilemma of whether and how to continue carrying Quebec Natural's unpaid bills. At one point Quebec Natural owed nearly $8 million to Trans-Canada, a larger sum to the Royal Bank (some of it in unsecured loans), and a total of $25 million in all. Trans-Canada's own deficit for 1960 ran to nearly $3 million. In the political climate of Quebec with another election in the offing, there was obviously no guarantee that the government would allow the rate increase that was essential for Quebec Natural's survival.

Yet for Trans-Canada to shut off gas at the border would ensure the permanent destruction of an essential customer. It would be a breach of faith with Montreal manufacturers and home owners dependent on gas supply. If that happened, there would be no opportunity for any enterprise, private or public, to bring natural gas into the province again for a long time to come. Trans-Canada and the Royal Bank decided to risk everything to keep the company afloat.

Early in 1962 a representative of the bank along with President Maddock of Quebec Natural, and Deane Nesbitt and James Kerr of Trans-Canada, called on Premier Lesage. They wanted to know if he still agreed with the principle of a reasonable rate of return on investment which had been set up as the yardstick for its judgement in the legislation creating the Quebec Electricity and Gas Board. Lesage said that he did, and later stated his position publicly. Trans-Canada kept its other customers across the country fully informed at every stage. Their refusal to criticize or complain made matters easier. The pipeline had locked Canadians from Alberta to Quebec, whether they liked it or not, into yet another network of interdependence. The utilities knew that none of them could risk a break anywhere without danger to them all.

The Salvas Commission reported on July 27, 1962. It went back to early beginnings and criticized Quebec Hydro for failure to sell its manufactured gas in the 1950s at a level that would show a satisfactory rate of return on assets. Its manner of selling those assets to Quebec Natural was also criticized. So was Edouard Asselin's action in remaining Quebec Natural's counsel while piloting its legislation through the Upper House as government leader there. The report castigated the share purchases by public servants and party officials. It did not criticize Quebec Natural itself, and praised the promoters of Trans-Canada ("who, in spite of numerous difficulties, have accomplished a colossal task which reflects credit on them") for their part in bringing natural gas to Quebec.

Thanks to the Salvas Report, the Quebec Board's ruling on rate increases, and the effects of two years of good management, Quebec Natural's affairs already showed signs of improving by the end of 1962. There was one further difficulty experienced over refinancing. Investors panicked at the prospect of Quebec's remaining private electric utilities being nationalized, which was the chief Liberal platform for the November 1962 provincial election. Premier Lesage uttered some reassuring words about natural gas, however, and appointed another commission to consider the future of gas utilities in Quebec. It eventually reported that they would be better left in the hands of private enterprise.

Nineteen sixty-one marked the first year of Trans-Canada operation in the black. From a net loss of nearly $3 million in 1960 the company's income, after paying out debt interest, amounted to over $2 million. This was a reflection of a dramatic increase in Canadian gas sales and of the first full year of American export. For the next six years the rate of sales moved up on an average of about 15% a year, with exports accounting for between one-sixth and one-fifth of the total volume. Net income rose to $13 million in 1964, and the company paid its first dividend on common shares.

The year 1961 also saw changes on the Board of Directors. With their own interests now entirely outside Canada and James Kerr no longer new to his command, Coates and Tanner resigned from the board. Clint Murchison had been weakened by a stroke and he left the board early in the year to be replaced by the operating chief of Canadian Delhi in Calgary, his long-time associate Smiley Raborn who had settled in Calgary permanently and was in the process of becoming a Canadian citizen. The only major change of the sixties in Trans-Canada's ownership began in 1965 when Murchison's American Delhi firm was acquired by another oil company. Beginning in that year, most of the former Canadian Delhi shares were eventually acquired by Canadian Pacific Investments. Thus the only two large Canadian-owned petroleum companies, the CPR and Home Oil, became the two largest shareholders of Trans-Canada, owning about 30% of the company between them. While the total number of shareholders remained relatively constant – in the 31,000 to 36,000 range – throughout the decade, dropping only slightly as early speculators sold out, the percentage of Canadian ownership climbed steadily towards 90%. The president of Canadian Pacific, Ian Sinclair, was invited to join Trans-Canada's board, and eventually did so in 1966.

In the meantime, however, the size of the board had been increased to nineteen members, and strengthened by the addition of presidents Neil McKinnon of the Canadian Bank of Commerce, William Scully of the Steel Company of Canada and Marcel Vincent of Bell Telephone. The Commerce, as Canadian Delhi's banker, had since 1954 shared 50% of Trans-Canada's banking business with the Royal Bank, who had been Western Pipe Lines' banker. Stelco was responsible for the first Canadian production of large-diameter pipe and for metallurgical research into new types of steel specifically to meet Trans-Canada's needs. As for Marcel Vincent, his presence meant that there was another experienced utilities man on the board, and indicated the role that communication systems were to play in the future development of Trans-Canada.

With its first operating profit behind it and the danger past of losing its whole Quebec market, Trans-Canada could make plans for its next major financing. Original estimates called for the purchase of the Crown section of the pipeline some time late in 1961. The sooner it was bought the better for the company, since the agreement provided for a progressive increase in rent. The recession in the Canadian economy and the difficulties with Quebec Natural Gas however required the date to be moved ahead. In May of 1962 the devaluation of the Canadian dollar increased the cost of carrying long term debt to American bondholders by nearly $1.5 million per year. By the spring of 1963, however, arrangements had been made with Metropolitan Life and other leading American and Canadian institutions for the sale of $145 million worth of first mortgage bonds, to be preceded by the sale of $25 million in convertible debentures. One of the first acts of the new Liberal government's Minister of Trade and Commerce Mitchell Sharp was to supervise the sale at full contract price plus interest of the assets of Northern Ontario Pipe Line Crown Corporation to Trans-Canada. From that time on, not a year passed without Trans-Canada resorting to the Canadian and American money markets for more working capital.

The company could not remain profitable, let alone survive, without continual pressure to make more efficient use of the original line and to discover and install equipment adapted to the needs of the Canadian situation. Such is the geography of Canada, the length of the line and the relative sparseness of population and industry, that the company is far more dependent on such pioneering of new technology than any of its American counterparts, who usually could rely on the simpler solution of looping the original line as soon as demand appeared likely to outpace capacity.

Beginning in 1962 the line was internally coated with a hard epoxy resin; four years later a process of sandblast cleaning was developed which could gradually reduce the inner surface roughness and so increase the flow capacity by over 10%. It was estimated that it would have cost five times the money to achieve the same result by adding to existing power facilities, and even more than that in terms of the cost of laying more pipe. Much of the company's engineering research was aimed at devising more efficient power units for its compressors, culminating in the use of a jet aircraft type of turbine which drastically reduced capital and labour cost over the original reciprocating engines. In order to avoid the installation of permanent standby equipment at every compressor station to meet emergencies, Trans-Canada developed mobile compressor units small enough to be moved in by road as they were needed.

Prolonged spells of twenty and thirty below weather at compressor stations from the Alberta border to North Bay presented operating problems not encountered in the U.S. In co-operation with the Canadian steel industry and various government bodies, special research was done on the metallurgy of pipe to withstand the severe climate and the unusually high pressures used on the system. In 1957 no large-diameter pipe was available in Canada for construction of the original line. But as replacement or looping became necessary, Trans-Canada was able to arrange for all its purchases in Canada. As early as 1963, President Kerr was able to announce that of the total cost of equipment purchased by the company its Canadian component had risen to 83%, as compared to 28% in 1956.

Trans-Canada entered the computer age in the sixties. A highly sophisticated system for controlling and measuring the flow of gas in the whole line from one despatch centre in Toronto was devised, the first applied to a pipeline anywhere. The Toronto despatcher could thus start and stop the engines at compressor stations across the continent. The computer could control output and produce varying flows anywhere in the system from the Alberta border to the province of Quebec. An hourly log over a 6,000 mile telemetry loop records conditions across the whole pipeline. Any major changes are automatically brought to the despatcher's attention by means of a scan of the complete system every five minutes.

At an early stage Trans-Canada was concerned with the development of a chemical industry in the west to use natural gas by-products. By 1962 the company had signed an agreement with Pacific Petroleums for the construction of an extraction plant at Empress, Alberta, and the building of a six-inch pipeline from there to Winnipeg paralleling the Trans-Canada system. The Empress plant could initially extract propane, butane and other liquids from over a billion cubic feet of natural gas daily.

Another element in Trans-Canada's growth was an aggressive gas purchase policy. The problem of gas supply was a recurring one in the company's history. First there were the difficulties in 1950-52 in gaining permission from the Alberta government to take any gas out of the province at all. Later, the refusal of major petroleum companies to bind themselves to contracts for shipping gas east in 1954 and 1955 was perhaps the greatest single barrier in the way of arranging to finance the pipeline. Then, after the company was successfully launched, there were several difficult periods, not for the lack of gas in the ground or capped wells waiting to be put into production, but because it was obviously more tempting for producers to hold out for freedom to sell in the western American market as long as there was any prospect of doing so. As a result, it became company policy to buy up first any and all amounts of gas that could be had at potentially competitive prices, and only then worry about selling whatever was available in eastern markets. The close relationship between purchasing and sales policy was more formally recognized when Vernon Horte was made group vice-president in charge of both. Horte was the young man who had patrolled the streets of Calgary with Nathan Tanner during the mid-fifties, calling over and over again on the many petroleum companies in their attempt to nail down the first supply contracts.

As late as 1959 an aggressive examiner for the FPC was able to put Trans-Canada on the spot over its export application, because the Alberta Conservation Board was dragging its heels on dedicating additional supplies for American export. "Let's deal with realities," he said. "Have you got any gas?" Until permits were granted in 1960 the answer, embarrassingly enough, was No. After that, however, once additional supply contracts were signed and export had begun, the pace of exploration and discovery also increased. It became clear that the first Trans-Canada line would only tap a small supply compared to the potential production of Alberta gas that might be developed. The eastern Canadian market was shaping up better than all expectations. Even so, after 1961, it could hardly absorb more than a 20% annual increase. The obvious place for a fast growth rate in sales was the much larger American market.

In December of 1960, just over a month after the first gas flowed across the border at Emerson, feasibility studies were authorized to consider ways of tapping the vast reserves of the Peace River district in northern Alberta and northeastern British Columbia and linking them up to the great markets around Chicago and Detroit, still out of reach of Trans-Canada's first American customer. The studies also looked forward to the day when Trans-Canada's own main line to southern Ontario would have to be looped. Would it be better to duplicate the existing line across northern Ontario or build south of the upper lakes and back into Canada at Sarnia? Co-operating in these studies was Trans-Canada's original customer, Midwestern, along with some Chicago companies who later dropped out, and American Natural Gas of Detroit through its subsidiary, the Michigan Wisconsin Pipe Line Company.

Building south of the border would mean a shorter route. It would avoid the problem of blasting through the solid rock of the Shield. Above all the extra American sales of gas along the way would be a boon to the economy of the whole company and help keep down the price of its product throughout eastern Canada.

Eventually, when no initial agreement could be reached with American Natural on volumes and timing of gas purchase or on the question of joint ownership of the project, Trans-Canada decided to go ahead on its own. In 1964 Great Lakes Gas Transmission, a wholly owned American subsidiary, was incorporated. It requested authority from the FPC to construct a 36-inch pipeline through Minnesota, Wisconsin and Michigan, across the Straits of Mackinac at the meeting of the upper Great Lakes and down to the St. Clair River and the Canadian border just south of Sarnia, Ontario. There would also be a spur line up to the important industrial centre of Sault Ste. Marie, Ontario, which was not yet supplied with natural gas.

American Natural and Midwestern filed a counter-proposal with the FPC in May 1965. Further discussion took place, however, before the FPC hearings scheduled to begin in the summer of 1965. The Americans pointed out to Trans-Canada why their Great Lakes scheme had little chance before the FPC. Trans-Canada in turn argued that the American plan for a long term exchange of gas would be wholly unacceptable in Canada. In a different form it had already been rejected by the Canadian government in the 1950s. Any proposal for building the major Canadian supply line through the United States would have to include at least two basic requirements: first, that the eastern Canadian market be supplied with gas from western Canada; and second, that Trans-Canada participate in the ownership and management of any line built through the United States for this purpose.

The result was stalemate. The two parties then worked out a plan involving 50% control for each and construction of the line in two stages.

First the existing American line would be extended across the St. Clair River to bring larger supplies into the eastern Canadian market prior to the completion of the entire system. Midwestern would take the equivalent amount of Canadian gas at Emerson. The following year the two systems would be joined together by a line south of Lake Superior and across the Straits of Mackinac. At this point, Trans-Canada's old American rival, Northern Natural Gas of Omaha, which had a monopoly in northern Minnesota, Wisconsin and upper Michigan, became alarmed. Northern Natural intervened and gave notice to the FPC that it would file a counter-proposal. The rivals now settled down for a long winter's siege in Washington. But Trans-Canada and their American allies had good grounds for counting on a favourable decision in time to put the first stage of the Great Lakes proposal into effect by the end of 1966 and complete the second in 1967. Their opponent could not come up with any better alternative than the old chestnut of a continental exchange — but of course without any assurance of co-operation from Trans-Canada or the Canadian authorities.

Trouble arose from an unexpected source. In March 1966 hearings began before the National Energy Board to gain Canadian permission for the Great Lakes project. While the NEB was receiving briefs and examining witnesses, the government was pressed in the House of Commons to take a stand on the issue. The senior Conservative critic, Alvin Hamilton, urged official Canadian support for the Great Lakes project in Washington, though his basic view was that such an important matter should be the subject of a treaty between the Canadian and U.S. governments. The NDP attacked Great Lakes as strongly as Hamilton supported it. Two years earlier the Ontario NDP leader, Donald MacDonald, urged the building of a system much like Great Lakes in order to make better use of the storage fields of southwestern Ontario and to supply the area with cheaper energy. But by 1966 he and the federal NDP were supporting northern Ontario's demand for looping the original line through Canada rather than building through the U.S. Liberal M.P.s from the area took the same stand.

Northern Ontario had benefited most from the immediate impact of pipeline construction in 1958. Local merchants and motel owners prospered as the Trans-Canada crews spent their wages there. Local cement dealers had a banner year, when the company desperately tried to get enough ballast to weigh down their pipe in the muskeg during the rainiest summer in living memory. In over half the municipalities it crossed, Trans-Canada became the largest taxpayer. Much more important, the lasting benefits of cheaper energy became more important every year. For the first time, thanks to the price differential between gas delivered in the north and in the south, northern Ontario towns reversed their former energy disadvantage in competing for new industry. Any move that appeared to threaten this favourable situation was bound to bring fierce opposition.

The government replied to its critics that there would be no statement on policy while the board was reviewing the case. But when hearings ended and the summer came and the commissioners retired to write their report, the matter tended to drop out of sight. There was no extended public debate on the matter at all.

In mid-August the NEB submitted its report to the government, stating that there were no economic objections to the Great Lakes scheme. The government of course had to take final responsibility for issuing an order-in-council to approve construction, and had to face the political consequences for doing so. Since the Great Lakes line was to be six inches in diameter larger than the original line across northern Ontario and to be half-owned by an American company, approval of the new scheme meant not only facing the wrath of northern Ontario M.P.s but also a national debate on whether Trans-Canada's main line should be allowed to pass through the U.S. at all. The Liberals felt they could not risk anything that might be turned into a repeat performance of the 1956 drama. It seemed doubtful whether the minority government could survive an accusation, whether justifiable or not, of contemplating the sellout to American domination which their party had begun a decade earlier.

When the Cabinet met on Wednesday, August 24 to make its decision, they were preoccupied with the more immediate crisis of an impending national railway strike. They were also concerned about their reputation for indecision and the risk of leaks in cabinet secrecy. They decided to act immediately and decisively on the NEB report. A statement flatly rejecting the Great Lakes scheme was prepared that evening and released to the press Thursday morning.

The effect on Trans-Canada was, to put it mildly, electrifying. All that day and night there was great activity on the top floor of the Trans-Canada building in Toronto. Phones rang; emergency consultations were held; the government's statement was examined under a microscope for possible loopholes, lines of retreat, or any way in which the decision might be reconsidered or compromised. An emergency board meeting was called for Friday morning in

Toronto and an appointment in Ottawa made with the Minister of Energy and Resources, Jean Luc Pepin, for James Kerr and Ross Tolmie late the same afternoon.

As a result, by Friday evening, there was some faint possibility of a new approach in sight. Pepin showed interest in Kerr's suggestion that the Great Lakes line should never carry more than half of Canada's gas supply east. It was obvious that the northern Ontario line would be looped eventually, so that a Trans-Canada commitment to keep its main route in Canada was quite feasible.

With opposition parties calling for debate on the Great Lakes decision, the company's most immediate concern was to keep open the possibility explored by Pepin and Kerr before the government became completely entrenched in its position. A high level meeting was arranged for September 9 between senior cabinet ministers and one of the most formidable groups of Canadian businessmen ever assembled for such a purpose. In addition to the Trans-Canada board members most involved and knowledgeable in the matter, there were the heads of the Steel Company of Canada, Bell Telephone, the Canadian Imperial Bank of Commerce, two Montreal and Toronto investment houses, and Trans-Canada's four largest customers. President W. O. Twaits of Imperial Oil, representing the Canadian Petroleum Association made a strong statement in favour of the Great Lakes scheme. A few days later during the federal-provincial conference in Ottawa, the prime ministers of Ontario and Quebec, who were concerned over the threat of higher energy costs for central Canada, were persuaded to lend their verbal support to the pressure being mounted by the premiers of Alberta and Saskatchewan for reconsideration of the final decision. A group of Western Conservative M.P.s secured John Diefenbaker's support for a statement in favour of the Great Lakes proposal and asking the government to change its mind. On September 19, Alvin Hamilton released their statement to the press.

Prime Minister Pearson replied that his government was examining a proposal being submitted by Trans-Canada. Finally on October 7 the government announced that the revised Great Lakes application had been accepted. In this, Trans-Canada agreed that at all times over 50% of its gas delivered to Ontario and Quebec would be transported through northern Ontario, to be increased to 60% by 1976, with an ultimate objective of 65%. Looping the northern

Ontario section would begin no later than 1970, and the major part of gas for Ontario and Quebec would always be transported through Canada. Trans-Canada would not dispose of its 50% ownership in Great Lakes without consent of the Canadian government.

The new decision was attacked by the *Toronto Daily Star* and a number of Liberals and NDPers as a sellout of northern Ontario to big business and American influence. In reply, it was Alvin Hamilton who made the best case against economic nationalism in this particular instance. Without Great Lakes, he argued in the House of Commons, Pennsylvania coal and overseas oil would remain seriously competitive with western Canadian gas in the Ontario and Quebec market. There would be pressure to bring cheaper Texas gas across the border from Detroit. He also pointed out the dubious and reactionary American company, including the U.S. coal lobby, in which Canadian opponents of the Great Lakes scheme found themselves. It was significant that Northern and Central gas argued publicly against the politicians and contractors in their own area who were attacking the scheme. Without Great Lakes, northern Ontario, like the rest of the country, would pay more for its gas.

The real difficulties over the next two years lay in Washington. The debate in Canada provided material for Great Lakes' opponents to prolong objections before the FPC and eventually to make a case in American courts which might not be settled until some time in the 1970s.

In January 1967 Pepin advised Trans-Canada that an alternative plan (in case the FPC refused Great Lakes) for looping the northern Ontario line would have to be submitted if the government were to keep alive its permits on the Great Lakes project. It was agreed that, if Washington failed to act, northern construction would have to begin by July 1 at the latest to be finished in time to meet a critical energy shortage in Ontario projected for the winter of 1967-68.

In the nick of time, on June 20, 1967, the FPC came through with a strongly worded 5 to 0 decision in favour of Great Lakes. A great many factors, from private warnings that Canada was about to proceed on its own to the indirect effect of the Arab-Israeli June War, may have affected the last minute speed and forcefulness of the decision. But the chief influences were essentially the obstructive character of alternative American plans to Great Lakes, the obvious need of the area it traversed for more gas in the near future, and

Ontario's clearly established and immediate demand for additional natural gas. Trans-Canada had to buy expensive American gas at Niagara during 1967 and sell it at a loss in Canada in order to keep up with its customers' demands.

The first phase of the Great Lakes project was begun immediately and completed by the fall of 1967, so that Ontario avoided a severe energy shortage that winter. Its opponents still had an important last resort, however. They went before the U.S. Court of Appeal in the District of Columbia in an effort to block the second phase of Great Lakes. In the meantime the FPC refused to order a halt in construction, and finally, with the judicial prospect improving but the case not finally settled, construction of the Great Lakes system was completed in October 1968. The first gas came through from Alberta to Ontario exactly ten years from the opening of the original Trans-Canada line in 1958. Another milestone was reached in December 1968. Exactly ten years after his appointment to the presidency of Trans-Canada, James Kerr was succeeded by Vernon Horte, though he remained the company's chairman and chief executive officer.

December 31, 1968, marked the end of Trans-Canada's first full decade of operation. In that time it had seen the volume of gas sales increase from 75,000 to nearly 520,000 million cubic feet per day, its operating revenues from $30 million to almost $200 million per year, and its net income from a deficit of $8.5 million to a surplus of $17.5 million. At the same time its prices had remained relatively stable and its average number of employees increased only from 700 to 1,100. The capital intense nature of the company was further indicated by the fact that its compressor horsepower along the pipeline had increased from a total of 75,000 to 710,000, while its average capital cost per horsepower had decreased from $450 to well under $200. The gross value of plant, property and equipment had increased from one-quarter to nearly three-quarters of a billion dollars.

The total number of shareholders had remained remarkably stable and was back to the original number of 35,000 to 36,000, though the proportion of Canadian ownership had increased to 94%. All of the company's new pipe was being manufactured in Canada in 1968 in addition to 50% of the pipe used in the U.S. construction of Great Lakes.

The more general effects of Trans-Canada Pipe Lines on the Canadian economy are difficult to calculate but the amount of foreign exchange saved on the American coal and gas and overseas crude oil that would have otherwise been imported can be guessed at by looking at projected sales for 1970. The company expected to sell $164 million worth of gas in Ontario and $27 million in Quebec. The estimate of 1970 gas export sales to the U.S. was over $45 million.

The total assets of gas distributing utilities and transmission companies in Canada amounted in 1967 to nearly $2.75 billion. The amount of new investment in the gas industry as a whole – from exploration and drilling to consumers' appliances – that resulted from the building of the pipeline to the east is almost impossible to calculate, but it had clearly made the natural gas industry one of Canada's largest in terms of total capital investment. The effects on other industries, from the creation of chemical plants in the western provinces to refining and pulp and paper in northern Ontario and steelmaking and other secondary manufacturing in the urban east, have also been enormous.

On the threshold of the 1970s the central problems facing Trans-Canada were chiefly those which had been critical in the past. The pace of exploration and production in the west had to be sufficient to maintain high volumes and low prices in competition with other fuels in eastern Canada and with American natural gas in the north central United States. In an industry with huge capital demands, the company had to calculate its every entry into the securities markets with great precision and a fine sense of timing. But of course increased demand did not often coincide nicely with the best opportunities to find cheap money. Immediately ahead there was the obligation to finish looping the northern Ontario line so as to ensure continued delivery of the greater proportion of eastern Canada's gas supply via the all-Canadian route. More capital would also soon be needed for the Great Lakes project. Beside the need to win final clearance for Great Lakes in the U.S. courts there would be future dealings with the FPC and regulatory bodies in Canada as export opportunities increased.

As the NEB increased its staff and gained more experience it would inevitably examine and regulate Trans-Canada's gas contracts and rates of return. One response to this, as well as to other corporate needs, would be for the company to step up the pace of the diversification programme it had already begun. Large transmission companies in the United States, like the railroads in an earlier period, were findings by the late fifties that they could not remain profitable easily now that their routes and rates were closely regulated by the FPC. Most of them did their best to follow Tennessee Gas Transmission, now Tenneco, towards enterprises in unregulated fields. Partly for this reason, but more immediately because of the need for greater gas supplies, Trans-Canada had already invested in gas extraction plants — begun with the Empress plant in 1964; and in gas exploration — begun with the creation of Banner Petroleums in 1966. Provision of consulting and pipeline engineering services was another obvious way to diversify into related fields. By the end of the sixties Trans-Canada was recognized around the world as a pioneer in pipeline technology, and its incorporated engineering subsidiary was acting as consultant to major operations in the U.S.A., the U.S.S.R., Australia and many other countries.

The essential challenge for the Company in the future, however, lay not in diversification, but in developing and expanding the role for which it was originally chartered — the moving of Canada's most important new energy supply from west to east across the centre of the continent. By 1970, Trans-Canada had only just begun to tap the immense reserves of the western provinces and the arctic territories.

Furthermore, the full potential of American markets for Canadian natural gas had scarcely been tapped at all. Up to December 31, 1968, licences granted to export natural gas for sales in the United States totalled fifteen and a half trillion cubic feet. Of this amount, three trillion cubic feet had been already delivered over the whole past history of the Canadian gas industry. The remaining twelve and a half trillion cubic feet still to be delivered would sell for some three and a half billion U.S. dollars. And yet, in 1969 alone, Canadian pipeline companies made application to the National Energy Board for permission to export about nine and a half trillion cubic feet, worth another three billion U.S. dollars, during the next twenty-five years. Even allowing for the greater diversity in the modern Canadian economy, it was still true that natural gas could well take a place in Canadian economic history not unlike that held by the great staple exports of the past, upon which the fabric of the nation was built.

At the end of the 1960s, it was clear that Trans-Canada Pipe Lines had entered its second decade of operations with the struggle to survive safely passed, and that it could remain one of the nation's major corporations which was both Canadian in management and control, and a world leader in its field.

Reflections on the Narrative

The instrument that finally emerged in 1957 as the means of marketing Alberta natural gas in central Canada and the American mid-west
was different in many ways from the two original concepts of 1949-
50. Trans-Canada Pipe Lines, as it existed in May 1957 at the point
of successful completion of public financing and commencement of
the first full year's construction, bore the marks of the many converg-
ing and conflicting forces that had gone into the crucible of its making. There were elements still of the two original schemes conceived
by the Western Pipe Lines and Murchison groups. Plans for export
to the American mid-west still loomed large in the company's future
and the expectation of their fulfillment was in fact the only thing
that had made Trans-Canada's bonds saleable. Still present was the
powerful influence of east-west nationalism, as first expressed in
Murchison's plan and in the demands of several western opposition
MP's in Ottawa, then in the pressure from groups of every sort in
northern Ontario, and finally in the decisions of the federal and
Ontario governments to rule out proposals for a north-south continental exchange every time these were advanced. The idea of provincial control of natural resources assumed a further dimension in
Premier Manning's decision to keep gathering facilities under the
control of a provincial corporation created for the purpose. The idea
of public ownership of utilities was reflected in the plan for the
northern Ontario bridge, an idea that had its roots both in the half
century's experience of Ontario Hydro and in the federal tradition

of using the crown corporation as a means of achieving public goals in projects that did not attract private capital. The idea of federal aid to transportation systems linking the provinces – as old as the Intercolonial and Pacific railways for binding together the new Dominion – though it did not take the form of a grant or a bond guarantee, was also present in the 1956 government loan to Trans-Canada and in the company's temporary freedom from income tax. Finally the fact that Trans-Canada during its most critical period in 1956-57 was controlled, neither by the two original sponsors, nor by the government, but by an alliance of three giant American corporations, is also, unfortunately, very much in the mainstream of modern Canadian history. The provision for Canadian ownership at the time of public financing, however, was an untypical assertion of economic nationalism against the dominant trend towards American control of industry.

The complicated structure of 1957 was the product of the many intentions and accidents, pressures and principles, that were part of Trans-Canada's stormy history. Things need not have happened the way they did. It seemed entirely likely at certain points, even to C. D. Howe and the most committed of the original sponsors, that the east-west pipeline would never be built at all. It is worth asking what were the real alternatives to the structure that actually emerged in 1957. What might have been the advantages and disadvantages of each of them, both in terms of the national interest and of the shareholders who have owned the company since 1957. How feasible were they? Would it have been better if different decisions had been made and history had taken a different course?

I begin by making certain assumptions. These can be challenged and argued at length, but I do not propose to do so here. I assume first that any just action towards maintaining the existence of Canada as a viable political and economic entity is a good thing. Secondly, I assume that by 1953 Canadians wanted, and were prepared to pay a price if necessary, to keep control of a new means of transportation for a new source of energy in their own hands. Thirdly, I assume that the economic and political advantages of having an east-west pipeline on Canadian soil outweighed the disadvantages. To protect national sovereignty and maintain a better bargaining position it was preferable to have at least one of Canada's two greatest potential sources of energy under Canadian control. The industry of central Canada would be less completely dependent on American supplies of coal and natural gas or upon seaborne petroleum and liquid natural gas brought in by tanker to the port of Montreal.

Without questioning further then the decision in favour of an east-west pipeline, I shall look briefly at four means by which it might have been built, but was not: first, by a large established private corporation in a related field; second, by a crown corporation; third, by a private enterprise with the aid of a government agency's investment in its securities; fourth, by a private company created for the purpose but without any significant form of financial aid from government.

As for the first alternative, there is little question that a large petroleum company such as Imperial Oil or a transportation company such as the CPR would have been sufficiently credit worthy to establish financeability far sooner than the sponsors of a "paper" company such as Trans-Canada could have done.

A large petroleum company, furthermore, might have been able to establish more proven reserves and lower prices for gas earlier and so been able to sign up sales contracts sooner than was actually the case with Trans-Canada. On the other hand, the largest petroleum companies have not been Canadian-controlled, whereas Trans-Canada since 1957 has been. There is an advantage, at least in theory, in having suppliers, transmission company and distributors separate from each other and therefore more open to government regulation in the public interest. If an oil company were transporting natural gas, problems could also arise from the fact that its distribution and retail operations in petroleum products were in conflict with the interests of the utilities marketing its natural gas.

As far as the railways are concerned, both the national systems owned rights-of-way that could conceivably have been used in laying the pipeline. But in fact, because of certain physical difficulties, natural gas lines have not normally been built beside railway roadbeds in North America. Nevertheless the Canadian National or Canadian Pacific (the latter increasingly one of Canada's most important oil companies) might have built the pipeline over an adjacent route. The idea was seriously entertained by C. D. Howe and was also discussed publicly by many people and privately by at least some of the railway directors. The railways decided that they had enough problems without taking on something so radically different and risky. On the other hand if the senior management of either had taken the initiative in entering this new field of transportation, it is entirely possible that the pipeline would have been operating effectively two or three years sooner than it actually was.

The second alternative, a federal crown corporation, is on the face of things, perhaps the simplest and most attractive solution. If the two chief parties responsible for energy and transportation permits – the federal and Alberta governments – had been as keen on the idea as Premier Douglas of Saskatchewan, or as Howe himself had been in the case of Trans-Canada Airlines and the other crown corporations he founded, this solution might have been considered as something other than the last possible resort. But in fact Premier Manning of Alberta was opposed in principle to any form of government control and there is no reason to believe that he or his electorate would have been prepared to agree to this solution without a fight. Both St. Laurent and Howe were concerned over the inherent conflict between eastern consumer and western producer, as well as the potential expense to the federal taxpayer that a crown corporation such as the CNR could involve. There was the further difficulty that a new federal corporation operating in the province of Quebec or in any other province where the idea of provincial rights was politically attractive, would operate under a severe handicap. As for the idea of a multi-government crown corporation, it had never been tried before, and no serious proposals for one were made by the provinces of Ontario and Saskatchewan where it was vaguely considered.

My own view is that, in the circumstances of the 1950s, the only form of public ownership that could have worked well was an Ontario crown corporation, and preferably one which built the line and then leased it for operation to a private company. It was Ontario which would be the market for about 80% of the Alberta gas sold in Canada and which was suffering the most acute energy shortage. An Ontario corporation bargaining with Alberta oil companies and the Alberta Gas Trunk Lines would have avoided the most awkward problem faced by a federal corporation. The initial objections of Alberta petroleum companies to dealing with a crown corporation could only have been surmounted of course if the federal government used its control of exports across provincial boundaries to help overcome those objections in the interests of the nation as a whole. The problem of finding first-rate management — a Donald Gordon or Fred Gardiner — to run the crown corporation might have proved difficult, but surely not insuperable. It is more questionable whether an experienced American pipeliner of the calibre of Charles Coates would have joined a public enterprise in Canada. As it was, three others refused the job before he was approached. The most serious objection to an Ontario crown corporation would have been in the problem of its relations with Quebec. But with a private company actually operating the line under lease even this difficulty might well have been resolved.

As for the third alternative – a degree of public investment in a private company, it was nearly adopted in March 1955. Trans-Canada had accepted in principle the scheme negotiated between its representatives and the Industrial Development Bank when difficulties at the eleventh hour persuaded the directors to withdraw. That scheme would have had the advantage of enabling a start on construction in 1955, and if enough pipe had been produced before the July 1956 strike, possible completion of the line in 1956. On the other hand the nature of the proposed financial structure might have frightened off the large institutional investors necessary for a successful offering of securities or have posed serious problems to Trans-Canada later on. If, however, there had existed in 1955, not a small subsidiary of the Bank of Canada, but something like the Canada Development Corporation with an experienced research staff equipped to examine the problem dispassionately and work out flexible structures and conditions for investing in such giant new enterprises as Trans-Canada Pipe Lines, the whole history of the company and the country might have been radically different — from the episode of Tennessee's taking control right through the 1956 debate and 1957 election. One might speculate further however that the very attempt to create a Canada Development Corporation, as long as C. D. Howe was a member of the government, might itself have been the issue on which cracks appeared within the cabinet and the Liberal party. This in itself might have been the issue on which the opposition succeeded in staging a great debate to put the old régime on trial.

The fourth alternative means of building the pipeline to be considered is that of private enterprise without financial aid from government. Conceivably, if the federal government had moved to support the original Trans-Canada scheme immediately after Canadian Delhi began exploring for gas and Murchison proposed the pipeline to Howe in 1950-51, and if the Alberta Conservation Board had not been so cautious in its approach to licensing natural gas exports from the province, the all-Canada line might have been built at the quarter billion dollar cost estimate of its consulting engineers Ford, Bacon and Davis (which was over one hundred million less than the actual cost in 1957-58) , and interest rates might just possibly have been low enough to enable the company to compete profitably in the Ontario energy market. But the possibility, if it ever existed, of a purely private enterprise building the line, had disappeared by 1953. During 1954-55, Trans-Canada made sustained and costly efforts to establish financeability without government aid; and there was no one else competing for the right to do the same thing until the prospect of government aid became definite in 1956. At that point Gairdner and Co. hastily assembled a plan which was an inferior variant on the deficiency proposal of January 1955 — quite justifiably called a scavenger operation by Howe. At the same moment Frank McMahon, with the support of several large American gas companies, informally offered a plan that looked like the old 1953 Western Pipe Lines scheme; it counted on delivering gas to the American mid-west first and only building across northern Ontario much later. The only way that a private corporation could have been successfully begun by 1956 was for it to have been allowed by the federal government to postpone the northern Ontario line indefinitely or else to build south of the Great Lakes through Michigan in the manner of the interprovincial oil pipe line. But as we have seen, long distance supply lines for natural gas are more like lines for transmitting hydro-electric power in that their financing makes them dependent on sales to customers along their route. In any case there was little prospect of getting early FPC permission to build and sell in the U.S. Thus the alternative of leaving it to private enterprise would have meant in effect a decision not to build an all-Canadian pipeline at all.

Finally it may be worth speculating on the outcome of the Trans-Canada scheme as it had actually developed by April of 1956 if the alternative proposed by both the company and Trade and Commerce officials led by Mitchell Sharp, then overruled by Howe, had been accepted. Because the prospect of raising enough money to build across western Canada seemed poor without FPC approval of U.S.

imports, it was proposed that public financing be postponed until the original pipeline bill had passed Parliament and more Canadian contracts were signed. Gardiner Symonds' offer to sell out the controlling American interest to anyone named by the government made this alternative reasonably attractive. Howe's rejection of this and his option for immediate construction by means of a short term government loan made mandatory the strict Parliamentary timetable of May 1956 though not necessarily the closure tactics. But it both forced and enabled the successful financing of February 1957 and made irreversible the commitment to build the line in 1957-58. Whether the line would ever have been built under the next government, Liberal or Conservative, after the 1957 elections and with an economic recession beginning and still no permit forthcoming from the FPC, is a question with which we may cease this speculation in historical might-have-beens.

One point which emerges from any study of what has actually happened in the recent history of gas transmission is that the distinction between a public and private enterprise is apt to be very blurred. Whatever the ownership of the pipeline corporation, it is still required to make its case to regulatory bodies and governments before getting clearance to sign gas contracts, build, alter or remove pipelines or earn a different rate of return on its investment. In that sense there is no such a thing as purely private enterprise in transportation or in resources utilities.

A Note on Sources

Most of the documentary material I have used is available to anyone interested in using it: the hearings and decisions of the Alberta Conservation Board, the Board of Transport Commissioners, the National Energy Board, and the Federal Power Commission; the reports of the Royal Commissions mentioned in the narrative; Hansard and the material on Trans-Canada Pipe Lines tabled in the House of Commons; the proceedings of the Standing Committee on Railways, Canals and Telegraph Lines; and the prospectuses, annual reports and other material published by Trans-Canada Pipe Lines. A substantial body of material used which was not previously open to scholars is in the Howe papers in the Public Archives of Canada. I also had access to correspondence, minutes and other files in the head office of Trans-Canada, and to notes, memoirs or transcribed interviews given to me by A. D. Nesbitt, Dale Thomson, Ronald Hambleton and Michael Barkway. In addition to these primary sources I used material on Trans-Canada in the *Toronto Daily Star, The Globe and Mail, The Montreal Star, The Financial Post,* and during a few key periods, a number of other Canadian newspapers.

The chief problem lay in making some sense and order of the vast quantity of written evidence. For this purpose, interviews with persons (see Acknowledgements) who played a part in Trans-Canada's history or observed closely the events as they happened have been extremely helpful. Differing or conflicting accounts and interpretations presented not so much a problem as an opportunity. It was useful to be able to move from the interviews back to the written sources, and if necessary, back again to the persons interviewed. Occasionally the result was a reconstruction or an interpretation of events different from anything either the participants or I had originally expected.

As for secondary sources, articles by Hugh Thorburn ("Parliament and Policy Making: The Case of the Trans-Canada Gas Pipe Line," *Canadian Journal of Economics and Political Science,* Vol. XXIII, No. 4), Eugene Forsey ("Constitutional Aspects of the Canadian Pipeline Debate," *Public Law,* Spring, 1957), J. R. Mallory ("Parliament and Pipeline," *Canadian Bar Review,* Vol. XXXIV, No. 6), Eric Hanson ("Natural Gas in Canadian-American Relations," *International Journal,* Vol. XII, No. 3), and portions of books by Dale Thomson (*Louis St. Laurent: Canadian,* Toronto, 1967), Christina and Peter Newman (*Historic Headlines,* edited by Pierre Berton, Toronto 1967), and Leslie Roberts (*C. D.: The Life and Times of Clarence Decatur Howe,* Toronto, 1957) all deal directly with the political side of the pipeline issue. John Meisel's *The Canadian General Election of 1957,* Toronto 1962; James Eayrs' *Canada in World Affairs 1955-1957,* Toronto, 1959; C. D. Howe's "Industry and Government in Canada," *Messel Lecture,* Society of Chemical Industry, London, 1958; Michael Barkway's "The Fifties: An Ottawa Retrospect" in *The Waterloo Review,* No. 5, Summer, 1960; and my own chapter on the history of the 1950s in *The Canadians: 1867-1967,* edited by Careless and Brown, Toronto, 1967; all deal more generally with aspects of the period covered by this book.

On the natural gas industry in North America see Stotz and Jamison's *History of the Gas Industry,* New York, 1938; Leeston, Crichton and Jacobs' *The Dynamic Natural Gas Industry,* Norman, Oklahoma, 1963; Eric Hanson's *Dynamic Decade,* Toronto, 1958; John Davis's *Canadian Energy Prospects,* Ottawa, 1959; and Richard Haley's *Financing the Natural Gas Industry,* New York, 1961. There is an article by Alan Phillips on the competition for Alberta gas supplies in *Maclean's Magazine,* October 1, 1953, and an unpublished M.B.A. thesis by Ralph Thrall Jr. on the history of Trans-Canada Pipe Lines in the library of the Wharton School of Finance and Commerce, University of Pennsylvania. There is a chapter on Lehman Brothers of New York in Joseph Wechsberg's *The Merchant*

Bankers, Boston, 1966, and a two-part article by Freeman Lincoln on Clint Murchison in *Fortune,* January and February, 1953.

Some of the issues involved in this book are treated more thoroughly or in a more general analytical way in such works as *Nationalism in Canada,* Toronto, 1967, edited by Peter Russell (see especially the articles by A. Rotstein and M. Watkins); Harry Johnson's *The Canadian Quandary,* Toronto, 1964; *Approaches to Canadian Economic History,* Toronto, 1967, edited by Easterbrook and Watkins (see especially the article by H. G. J. Aitken); the report of the Canadian Institute on Public Affairs Summer Conference, 1968, *The U.S. and Us;* and J. H. Dales: *Hydro Electricity and Industrial Development: Quebec, 1898-1940,* Cambridge, Mass., 1957.

Three relevant scholarly articles are J. H. Dales: "Fuel, Power and Industrial Development in Central Canada," *American Economic Review,* Vol. XLIII, No. 2; H. G. J. Aitken: "Government and Business in Canada: An Interpretation," *Business History Review,* Spring 1964, pp. 4-21; and H. G. J. Aitken: "The Midwestern Case: Canadian Gas, and the Federal Power Commission," *Canadian Journal of Economics and Political Science,* Vol. XXV, No. 2.

There are sections on the IDB and the NOPLCC in C. A. Ashley and R. G. H. Smails: *Canadian Crown Corporations,* Toronto, 1965.

On the writing of business history see *Proceedings of the 14th Annual Meeting of the Business History Conference,* London, Ontario, 1967, especially John Dales' "Business History and Economic Theory," Richard Overton's "Company-Scholar Relations," and F. H. Armstrong's "The Historian's Approach," which includes a valuable bibliography, as does the Easterbrook and Watkins work cited above.

Acknowledgements

I should like to thank the officers and directors of Trans-Canada Pipe Lines for making this history possible by agreeing to finance my research, to open the company's records to me and to let me quote or paraphrase any material I chose, other than matter of immediate present concern such as negotiations pending.

My work owes a special debt to a carefully documented memoir concentrating on the formative period, 1954-58, prepared by A. D. Nesbitt and to his generosity in allowing me to impose freely on his time whenever it was asked for. If my narrative shows a bias towards his own views or actions in certain of the events recorded, that is of course my responsibility. It is only his kind of complete understanding of the need for business history to be written with whatever objectivity the professional historian can bring to it that can give such works as this potential permanent value.

The company and author agreed, in case of a dispute between them, to seek the mediation of a third party. One of North America's most experienced business historians, Professor Richard Overton of the history department, the University of Western Ontario, kindly consented to act in this capacity. While neither party had occasion to ask for his mediation, I am grateful for his willingness to be involved, as well as for the example he has set for all historians practising in his field.

I should like to thank the Chairman of Trans-Canada, James W. Kerr, for his warm support and Douglas Simpson, my official liaison with the company, for his invaluable assistance and advice at every stage. Donald Johnston was kind enough to advise me on many matters and in particular to assist with some of the material I used in preparing the history of Great Lakes Gas Transmission Company in the last chapter.

I should like to thank the many persons who helped by submitting to my questioning or in other ways. While I shall not attempt to record every debt here, I should particularly like to mention Michael Barkway, W. J. Bennett, John Blaikie, R. A. Brown Jr., R. W. Campbell, Hon. M. J. Coldwell, A. R. Crozier, Hon. John Davis, Rt. Hon. John Diefenbaker, George Ferguson, Eugene Forsey, Douglas Fraser, the late Blair Fraser, Hon. Leslie M. Frost, Hon. Davie Fulton, the late Grant Glassco, Carl Goldenberg, Hon. Walter Gordon, Monroe Gutman, Eric Hanson, Hon. Walter Harris, V. L. Horte, Francis Kernan, E. L. Kennedy, Stanley Knowles, Hon. Maurice Lamontagne, Hon. Hugues Lapointe, Bruce MacDonald, Robert Macintosh, James Mahaffy, Hon. Ernest C. Manning, N. J. McNeill, H. R. Milner, Morris Natelson, Hon. J. W. Pickersgill, Mr. Justice M. M. Porter, Smiley Raborn Jr., Rt. Hon. Louis St. Laurent, James Saks, Hon. Maurice Sauvé, Frank Schultz, Hon. Mitchell Sharp, William Stuart, N. E. Tanner, Dale Thomson, J. R. Tolmie, the late Hon. Robert Winters and G. W. Woods.

I should like to thank Ronald Hambleton, Ralph Thrall Jr., Norman Depoe and Michael Barkway for making available to me unpublished material of theirs relating to C. D. Howe and the history of Trans-Canada; Eugene Forsey and Eric Hanson for permission to quote from their published work; the executors of the estate of C. D. Howe for access to the Howe papers and permission to quote from his writing; Macmillan Co. of Canada for permission to quote from E. J. Pratt's *Towards the Last Spike*; the staff of the Public Archives of Canada and the Canadian Petroleum Association, and the librarians of Trans-Canada Pipe Lines, the American Gas Association, for their courteous assistance; Ronald House and Tillo Kuhn of York University, for providing me with stimulating advice at the beginning of my work; Abraham Rotstein of the University of Toronto, for his most helpful reading of and comment upon Chapters I-IX and Dr. Eugene Forsey for the same with Chapters IX-XI; Marina Franco for typing the manuscript into fair copy; and my wife, Elizabeth, for typing, criticism and support at every stage.

Statistics

TRANS-CANADA PIPE LINES LIMITED / ANNUAL GAS SALES 1959-1968 ($14.73\ psia$)

By Distributor
Volumes in Millions of Cubic Feet

	1959	1960	1961	1962	1963	1964	1965	1966	1967	1968
Saskatchewan Power Corporation	772	2,512	2,977	2,955	2,958	3,279	3,399	6,224	13,020	17,417
Plains-Western Gas (Manitoba) Ltd.	1,076	1,035	1,577	1,406	1,530	1,980	2,456	2,588	4,553	6,565
Inter-City Gas Limited	863	1,401	1,596	1,784	1,892	2,145	2,474	2,885	3,117	3,296
Greater Winnipeg Gas Company	6,421	9,087	13,262	15,604	19,108	23,467	27,406	33,255	34,480	35,628
Northern and Central Gas Corporation Limited	20,699	28,981	32,549	38,427	42,240	48,226	51,882	56,257	64,791	70,521
The Consumers' Gas Company	33,214	41,192	51,584	61,535	73,294	82,860	96,707	105,301	112,604	120,610
Union Gas Company of Canada, Limited	2,561	16,113	20,582	25,525	33,264	43,533	54,041	65,768	70,142	86,736
Kingston Public Utilities Commission	212	345	443	616	1,006	1,224	1,489	1,555	1,550	1,586
Augusta Natural Gas Limited	1,950	2,162	2,939	4,076	4,290	4,823	4,992	5,266	5,298	5,284
Quebec Natural Gas Corporation	6,690	12,205	23,780	23,120	27,036	31,737	36,308	41,149	41,114	41,153
Total Canadian	74,458	115,033	151,289	175,048	206,618	243,274	281,154	320,248	350,669	388,796
Total for Export	–	12,485	59,139	62,211	64,472	73,444	77,132	80,789	88,325	127,163
Total Sales	74,458	127,518	210,428	237,259	271,090	316,718	358,286	401,037	438,994	515,959

By Geographical Area
Volumes in Millions of Cubic Feet

	1959	1960	1961	1962	1963	1964	1965	1966	1967	1968
Saskatchewan	772	2,512	2,977	2,955	2,958	3,279	3,399	6,224	13,020	17,417
Manitoba	8,360	11,523	16,435	18,794	22,530	27,592	32,336	38,728	42,149	45,489
Ontario	58,636	88,793	108,097	130,179	154,094	180,666	209,111	234,147	254,386	284,737
Quebec	6,690	12,205	23,780	23,120	27,036	31,737	36,308	41,149	41,114	41,153
Total Canadian	74,458	115,033	151,289	175,048	206,618	243,274	281,154	320,248	350,669	388,796
Export – Midwestern United States	–	12,485	59,139	61,954	62,785	71,366	73,988	77,148	83,718	117,197
Export – State of Michigan	–	–	–	–	–	–	–	–	–	3,665
Export – State of New York	–	–	–	257	1,687	2,078	3,144	3,371	3,994	4,849
Export – State of Vermont	–	–	–	–	–	–	–	270	613	1,452
Total Sales	74,458	127,518	210,428	237,259	271,090	316,718	358,286	401,037	438,994	515,959

Source: Trans-Canada Pipe Lines Limited

TRANS-CANADA PIPE LINES LIMITED / *10 Year Statistical Review*

Income (in Thousands of Dollars)	1968	1967	1966
Operating Revenues	$ 195,659	168,122	154,131
Operating Profit	38,348	37,176	38,666
Net Income	17,274	14,859	16,501
Balance Sheet (in Thousands of Dollars)			
Plant, Property and Equipment			
— Gross	$ 731,455	648,851	617,578
— Net	620,025	553,051	536,250
— Annual Additions	83,300	31,800	30,700
Long Term Debt	350,026	365,424	359,237
Shareholders' Equity	230,762	175,539	171,504
Statistics			
Gas Sales Volumes — MMcf Annual	515,959	438,994	401,000
Maximum Day Delivered for Sale and Transportation	2,045	1,694	1,356
Initial Marketable Reserves Under Contract Year-End Volumes in Tcf @ 14.40 psia	19.7	17.6	17.1
Miles of Pipeline (including loopline)	3,425	3,107	3,073
Compressor Horsepower	710,560	643,360	574,160
Gross Plant Investment per Employee (in Thousands of Dollars)	$ 653	639	647
Gas Sales Revenue per Employee (in Thousands of Dollars)	174	165	161
Operating Expenses per Employee (in Thousands of Dollars)	140	129	121
Number of Employees — Average	1,121	1,014	954
Common Shares Outstanding Dec. 31st	8,258,776	8,232,749	8,225,499
Shareholders Dec. 31st	32,586	35,472	35,241
Common Stock Prices — High	39-3/4	33-1/4	39-1/2
Common Stock Prices — Month of the High	October	June	January
Common Stock Prices — Low	23-3/4	24-1/4	23-3/8
Common Stock Prices — Month of the Low	March	January	December

Source: Trans-Canada Pipe Lines Limited and Toronto Stock Exchange

1965	1964	1963	1962	1961	1960	1959
136,973	119,612	102,523	87,834	77,108	49,157	29,589
38,157	36,117	28,278	19,970	14,581	8,406	3,347
14,170	13,243	8,928	6,066	2,076	(2,911)	(8,411)
587,644	562,329	512,682	329,420	298,028	286,954	262,087
520,074	507,840	470,177	306,503	281,558	277,590	257,598
26,000	51,000	184,000	31,800	11,500	30,800	5,500
391,819	365,779	376,812	214,319	222,185	229,622	208,873
103,263	95,453	60,832	50,344	45,833	43,757	46,668
358,300	316,700	271,100	237,300	210,400	127,500	74,500
1,249	1,196	941	813	744	639	359
16.0	12.5	10.1	8.6	8.5	8.4	8.0
2,882	2,753	2,604	2,399	2,340	2,340	2,290
545,060	523,510	363,810	270,910	196,510	148,585	75,500
640	645	637	456	411	409	372
149	137	127	121	106	70	42
108	96	92	94	86	58	37
918	872	805	723	726	702	704
7,594,735	7,534,529	5,861,383	5,861,183	5,861,183	5,861,183	5,861,183
33,829	30,107	32,009	31,864	32,931	35,686	35,203
42	45	36	27¾	27¾	26	31
January	October	October	January	December	January	January
33-¼	34-⅛	21-¼	17	19-⅜	16	22-½
June	March	January	October	January	June	September

NATURAL GAS RESERVES AND PRODUCTION

	Canadian Yearend Reserves Billions of Cubic Feet 14.65 psia	Canadian Production Billions of Cubic Feet 14.65 psia	Trans-Canada Gas Purchases Western Canada 14.73 psia
1968	47,666	1,395	527
1967	45,682	1,216	452
1966	43,450	1,125	431
1965	40,354*	1,251	405
1964	43,391	1,114	354
1963	36,960	1,066	294
1962	35,436	973	260
1961	33,538	732	231
1960	30,674	582	132
1959	26,605	477	82
1958	23,295	401	26
1957	20,742	286	4
1956	18,894	220	–

Source: Canadian Petroleum Association and Trans-Canada Pipe Lines Limited
* Reserve estimates changed to proved remaining marketable basis

CANADIAN NATURAL GAS UTILITY SALES
BY CLASS OF SERVICE / *(in Billions of Cubic Feet at 14.73 psia)*

	Total	Residential	Commercial	Industrial
1968	765.8	214.6	144.0	407.2
1967	697.9	204.7	133.9	359.3
1965	573.0	187.3	101.0	284.7
1960	320.7	108.3	49.9	162.5
1955	117.8	45.3	23.3	49.2
1950	58.1	26.5	13.5	18.1
1945	33.9	16.9	8.2	8.8

Source: Canadian Gas Association

NATURAL GAS AVERAGE PURCHASE
AND SALES PRICES / (in Cents per Mcf at 14.73 psia)

	1968	1964	1959
Wellhead Price	15.09	14.23	10.76
Price Entering Pipeline at			
Alberta/Saskatchewan Border	18.61	17.80	15.09
Average Selling Price to			
Distributor — Toronto area	41.94	41.48	41.63
Average Selling Price to			
Distributor — Winnipeg area	33.33	34.56	28.48

Source: Trans-Canada Pipe Lines Limited

CANADIAN NATURAL GAS EXPORTS TO U.S.
(in Billions of Cubic Feet at 14.73 psia)

	Total	Trans-Canada	Alberta and Southern	Westcoast Transmission	Other
1968	604.4	122.9	291.7	148.8	41.0
1967	513.3	84.3	253.7	140.5	34.8
1965	404.7	74.0	195.2	103.1	32.4
1960	112.5	12.5	16.9	80.5	2.6

Source: Canadian Gas Association

CANADIAN ENERGY CONSUMPTION / TRILLION B. T. U.*

	1958	1960	1965	1968	1975	1980	1985	1990
Petroleum Fuels	1490.8	1667.6	2216.2	2626.2	3136.5	3763.8	4454.3	5299.2
Natural Gas	240.9	381.3	746.3	1031.7	1497.2	1904.0	2411.3	2942.5
Coal and Coke	646.6	564.8	645.4	655.7	885.9	1245.8	1405.9	1606.2
Hydro-Electricity	298.1	347.5	403.4	461.1	654.4	737.2	882.6	951.3
Nuclear	–	–	–	–	62.3	138.6	323.6	722.2
Total	**2676.4**	**2961.2**	**4011.3**	**4774.7**	**6236.3**	**7789.4**	**9477.7**	**11521.4**

SHARES OF TOTAL PERCENTAGE

	1958	1960	1965	1968	1975	1980	1985	1990
Petroleum Fuels	55.7	56.3	55.2	55.0	50.2	48.3	47.0	46.0
Natural Gas	9.0	12.9	18.6	21.6	24.0	24.4	25.4	25.5
Coal and Coke	24.2	19.1	16.1	13.7	14.2	16.0	14.8	13.9
Hydro-Electricity	11.1	11.7	10.1	9.7	10.5	9.5	9.3	8.3
Nuclear	–	–	–	–	1.1	1.8	3.5	6.3
Total	**100.0**	**100.0**	**100.0**	**100.0**	**100.0**	**100.0**	**100.0**	**100.0**

Source: National Energy Board, 1969

* N.B. The use of b.t.u.'s as the common denominator has the disadvantage of underestimating the relative importance of hydroelectric power to the Canadian economy, since most electricity is used to produce lighting and power. For a discussion see J.H. Dales: "Energy Sources in Canada," *Canadian Journal of Economics and Political Science*, Vol. XXIII, No. 2, and the subsequent replies.

Glossary of Natural Gas Terms

BCF	Billions of cubic feet.
BTU	British Thermal Unit: the amount of heat required to raise the temperature of one pound of water one Fahrenheit degree. One cubic foot of natural gas contains approximately 1,000 BTU's.
Commercial Service	Natural gas service to restaurants, retail stores, institutions, etc.
Compressor	A mechanical device for raising the pressure of gas with a decrease in volume: used to move natural gas through a pipeline.
Compressor Station	Building or group of buildings housing engine-driven or turbine-driven compressors and auxiliary equipment.
Distribution Company	A natural gas utility company which purchases gas from a pipeline and obtains its major operating revenue from retail gas sales to ultimate consumers.
Domestic (or Residential) Service	Natural gas service to households for space heating, water heating, clothes drying, refrigeration, incineration, and air conditioning.
Extraction Plant	A plant or group of structures for the separation of liquid hydrocarbons from a natural gas stream.
Gas Turbine	Power equipment of the turbine type which utilizes the available energy in hot combustion gases as a motive force.
Gathering System	A network of small lines which connects producing wells with a transmission system.
Industrial Service	Natural gas service to factories, mines, pulp mills, smelters, etc.

Looping	Paralleling an existing pipeline by another line to increase capacity.
MCF	Thousands of cubic feet.
Maximum Day Sales	The largest amount of natural gas sold in a single 24-hour period.
MMCF	Millions of cubic feet.
Natural Gas	Combustible gaseous hydrocarbons occurring naturally in the earth's formations, released through drilling and made available through pipeline and distribution facilities.
Natural Gas Liquids	Liquid hydrocarbon mixtures recovered by condensation and absorption from natural gas, including natural gasoline, butane, iso-butane and propane.
Peak Shaving	Supplying gas to a system from an auxiliary source, during periods of maximum demand, to reduce the load or demand on the primary source of supply.
Pipeline	Continuous pipe conduit, complete with necessary facilities, for transporting natural gas or fluids, usually from the source of supply to the points of utilization.
PSIA	Pounds per square inch absolute.
TCF	Trillions of cubic feet.
Transmission Company	A company which transports gas in a pipeline, usually from the source of supply to the distribution companies.

List of Directors and Principal Officers

Name	Office	Dates	City	Principal Occupation
TOLMIE, J.R.	Director	1951-	Ottawa	lawyer
MURCHISON, C.W.	Director	1951-61	Dallas	oil and gas executive
	President	1951-54		
SCHULTZ, F.A.	Director	1951-	Dallas	oil and gas executive, geologist
MILNER, H.R.*	Director and Vice-Pres.	1954-58	Calgary	utilities executive, lawyer
TANNER, N.E.	Director	1954-61	Calgary	executive,
	President	1954-57		former Alberta
	Chairman	1957-58		cabinet minister
WILLIAMSON, A.H.*	Director and Secretary-Treasurer	1954-55	Vancouver	investment dealer
ASSELIN, E.	Director	1954-60	Montreal and Quebec	lawyer, government leader of the Legislative Council, Quebec
BICKLE, E.W.	Director	1954-61	Toronto	investment dealer
CAMPBELL, G. Peter	Director	1954-56	Toronto and Ottawa	lawyer senator

* Also a Director of Western Pipe Lines 1949-54 before its merger with the original Trans-Canada Pipe Lines

Name	Office	Dates		Principal Occupation
FELL, John R.	Director	1954-61	New York	investment dealer
MacPHERSON, M.A.	Director	1954-66	Regina	lawyer
NESBITT, A.D.*	Director Secretary-Treasurer	1954- 1955-56	Montreal	investment dealer
OSLER, G.P.*	Director	1954-	Winnipeg Toronto	executive (finance)
TIMMINS, JULES	Director	1954-	Montreal	mining executive
COATES, Chas. S.	Director Executive Vice-President President Chairman	1954-61 1954-57 1957-58 1958-61	Calgary Toronto Houston	transmission company executive
McCAUSLAND, J.K.	Director	1955-60	Toronto	investment dealer
SYMONDS, Gardner	Director	1955-57	Houston	transmission company executive
BROWN, R.C.	Director	1956-57	Calgary	oil and gas executiv
LOUGHNEY, E.D.	Director	1956-	Calgary Pittsburgh	oil and gas executiv
ATKINSON, T.H.	Director	1956-	Montreal	banker
BROWN, R.A. Jr.	Director	1957-	Calgary	oil and gas executiv
GAHERTY, G.A.	Director	1958-64	Montreal	executive, engineer
KERR, J.W.	President Chairman and Chief Exec. Officer	1958-68 1961-	Toronto	
GAGNON, Hon. W.	Director	1960-63	Montreal	bank chairman, companies director
SCOTT, W.P.	Director	1960-	Toronto	investment dealer
RABORN, S. Jr.	Director	1961-	Calgary	oil and gas executiv
CAMPBELL, R.W.	Director	1961-	Calgary	oil and gas executi
KENNEDY, E.L.	Director	1961-	New York	investment dealer
MATTHEWS, Beverley	Director	1961-	Toronto	lawyer
McKINNON, N.J.	Director	1961-	Toronto	banker

Name	Office	Dates	City	Principal Occupations
SCULLY, V.W.T.	Director	1961-68	Hamilton	steel executive
VINCENT, Marcel	Director	1964-	Montreal	telephone executive
THOMPSON, G.H.	Director	1964-	Calgary	utility executive
SINCLAIR, Ian D.	Director	1966-	Montreal	railway executive
McNEILL, N.J.	Secretary Vice-President and General Counsel	1956-65 1956-67	Toronto	
	Director	1967-	Detroit	
	President- Great Lakes Transmission Company	1967-		
HORTE, V.L.	Vice-President Group Vice- President	1961-66 1966-68	Calgary and Toronto	
	President	1968-		
	Director	1968-		
WOODS, G.W.	Treasurer Vice-President and Group Vice-President	1959-66 1966-	Toronto	
	Director	1968-		

Footnotes

Page *Line* CHAPTER I ONCE UPON A TIME

8   29   Lafayette quoted in Stotz and Jamison: *History of the Gas Industry*, p. 70.

11   All quotations on this page are from Eric Hanson: *Dynamic Decade*, pp. 41-58.

CHAPTER II RIVALS IN THE WEST

13   The original of S. Bilderijst's letter (paraphrased here) is in the C. D. Howe Papers, 8-2-1, Folder #23, Public Archives of Canada. The Howe Papers in the Public Archives will be hereafter referred to as CDH.

20   3   Howe to Tanner, Sept. 16, 1950, CDH, 8-2-1, Folder #23.

     16   Tanner to McKinnon, Sept. 20, 1950, CDH, 8-2-1, Folder #23.

CHAPTER III THE SLEEPING DRAGON

23   2 ff E. J. Pratt: *Collected Poems*, revised edition, with Introduction by Northrop Frye.

27   37 ff L. D. M. Baxter mimeographed letter to Western M.P.s; CDH, 8-2-1, Folder #22.

CHAPTER IV "OUR SORT OF FOLKS"

33   1 ff House of Commons Debates, May 9, 1952, p. 2077.

33   29   H of C Debates, May 6, 1952, p. 1923.

34   8   H of C Debates, April 20, 1950, p. 1716.

35   1 ff Howe to Manning, Jan. 2, 1953, CDH, 8-2-1, Folder #20.

     32 ff H of C Debates, March 6, 1953, pp. 2704-10.

36   1 ff H of C Debates, March 6, 1953, pp. 2704-10.

     17   H of C Debates, March 17, 1953, p. 3026.

     20 ff H of C Debates, Dec. 11, 1953, p. 620.

36   32   Hugh Thorburn: "Parliament and Policy-making," *Canadian Journal of Economics and Political Science*, Vol. XXIII, p. 520.

Page Line
37   1   ff   Williamson to Howe, March 19, 1953, CDH, 8-2-1, Folder #20.
      8   ff   Howe to Williamson, March 19, 1953, CDH, 8-2-1, Folder #20.
     30   Murchison to Eakins, April 16, 1953, CDH, 8-2-1.
38   23   Howe to Wrong, March 28, 1953, CDH, 8-2-1, Folder #19.
     27   Wrong to Howe, March 30, 1953, CDH, 8-2-1, Folder #19.
39   2   ff   Wrong to Howe, April 17, 1953, CDH, 8-2-1, Folder #19.
      6   ff   Howe to Wrong, May 5, 1953, CDH, 8-2-1, Folder #19.
     13   ff   Murchison to Howe, April 9, 1953, CDH, 8-2-1, Folder #20.
     20   ff   Howe to Murchison, April 14, 1953, CDH, 8-2-1, Folder #20.
     38   ff   Murchison to Howe, April 15, 1953, CDH, 8-2-1, Folder #20.
40   1   ff   Murchison to Howe, April 15, 1953, CDH, 8-2-1, Folder #20.
     23   ff   Murchison to Howe, April 16, 1953, CDH, 8-2-1, Folder #20.
41   5   Murchison to Howe, Aug. 27, 1953, CDH, 8-2-1, Folder #19.
     13   ff   Milner to Howe, Aug. 1, 1953, CDH, 8-2-1.
     25   ff   Williamson to Howe, Sept. 2, 1953, CDH, 8-2-1.
     33   Howe to Williamson, Sept. 4, 1953, CDH, 8-2-1.
43   12   ff   Howe to Frost, Dec. 14, 1953, CDH, 8-2-1, Folder #1.

CHAPTER V A STRANGE STORY
51   15   ff   H of C Debates, March 9, 1954, p. 2817.
52   12   ff   H of C Debates, March 9, 1954, p. 2822.
     22   ff   H of C Debates, March 30, 1954, p. 3491.
56   36   Williamson to Howe, Oct. 1, 1954, CDH, 8-2-1, Folder #14.
57   1   ff   *Ibid.*
     16   ff   Howe to Williamson, Oct. 12, 1954, CDH, 8-2-1, Folder #14.
58   17   ff   Interview with F. Schultz and R. Tolmie.
59   6   Interview with F. Schultz and R. Tolmie.
      9   Interview with F. Schultz and R. Tolmie.
61   Harris to Howe, Jan. 12 and 13, 1955, CDH, 8-2-1, Folder #14.
62   8   ff   Howe to Harris, Jan. 15, 1955, CDH, 8-2-1, Folder #14.
63   1   ff   Howe to Harris, Jan. 15, 1955, CDH, 8-2-1, Folder #14.
64   27   Interview with D. Nesbitt.

CHAPTER VI COYNE'S BANK
65   25   Nesbitt memoir, p. 33, Trans Canada Pipe Line files, quoting Coyne to Tanner, Jan. 1955.
68   23   ff   *Financial Times*, Calgary correspondent, Feb. 11, 1955.
     36   ff   H of C Debates, Jan. 28, 1955, p. 621.
69   1   H of C Debates, Jan. 28, 1955, p. 621.
      6   H of C Debates, Feb. 4, 1955, p. 846.
     15   ff   *Winnipeg Free Press*, March 11, 1955.
70   2   ff   Lee Smith of the Federal Power Commission quoted in *The Montreal Gazette*, March 12, 1955.
71   1   ff   Williamson to Howe, Feb. 15, 1955, CDH, 8-2-1.
73   22   ff   Bryce to St. Laurent, Jan. 26, 1955, CDH, 8-2-1, Folder #13.

Page	Line		
74	11		Nesbitt memoir, p. 45.
75	15	ff	Coyne to Tanner, March 16, 1955, quoted in Nesbitt memoir, p. 46.
	29	ff	Tanner to Coyne, March 16, 1955, *Ibid.*, p. 48.
76	13		TCP press release, March 17, 1955.
77	5		H of C Debates, March 18, 1955, p. 2153.
	10	ff	*Financial Post*, March 26, 1955.
	39	ff	*Myers Oil Quarterly*, April 22, 1955.
78	3		Carl Nickle quoted in *Winnipeg Free Press*, March 30, 1955.
	15	ff	*Financial Post*, April 2, 1955.

CHAPTER VII "DAMN RHODES SCHOLARS"

Page	Line		
80	14		M. Barkway memoir.
	21		Interviews with R. Tolmie and J. Davis.
81	1	ff	Interviews with R. Tolmie and J. Davis.
	16		Interview with M. Sharp.
82	16		Tanner to St. Laurent, March 22, 1955, CDH, 8-2-1, Folder #13.
	22	ff	Murchison to Howe, March 23, 1955, CDH, 8-2-1, Folder #1.
83	24		Howe to Murchison, March 24, 1955, CDH, 8-2-1, Folder #13.
	34	ff	Tolmie to Schultz, March 24, 1955, TCP files.
84	32	ff	Howe to Nesbitt, March 30, 1955, Nesbitt memoir, p. 59.
	39	ff	Howe to Tanner, March 31, 1955, CDH, 8-2-1, Folder #12.
85			E. C. Manning quoted in Nesbitt memoir, p. 57.
86	4		Merriam to St. Laurent, May 17, 1955, CDH, 8-2-1.
	12		Merriam wire to Trans-Canada, TCP files.
87	34		*The Globe and Mail*, May 31, 1955.
88	11	ff	Dr. Kerr Dewar, President of the Northwestern Ontario Liberal Association, to Howe, June 17, 1955, CDH, 8-2-1, Folder #24.
89	31		Interviews with M. Sharp and L. St. Laurent.
90	13		Tanner to TCP directors, Aug. 15, 1955, TCP files.
92	2		Minutes of Sept. 27, 1955 meeting of Sharp, Crozier, *et al*, CDH, 8-2-1, Folder #11.
93	8		Howe to Jones, Oct. 7, 1955, CDH, 8-2-1, Folder #11.

CHAPTER VIII "GRINGO GO HOME"

Page	Line		
94	1	ff	Howe to Murchison and Murchison to Howe, Sept. 30, 1955, CDH, 8-2-1.
95	2	ff	Howe to Murchison, Sept. 30, 1955, CDH, 8-2-1.
97	24		Clarke to Nesbitt, Dec. 30, 1955, quoted in Nesbitt memoir, p. 83.
98	22		T. J. McGrath quoted in "How U.S. Opposition Plan to Wreck Our Pipeline," *Financial Post*, Dec. 24, 1955.
	28		John L. Lewis quoted *Ibid.*
99	18	ff	President, Winnipeg and Central Gas Co., to Howe, Jan. 24, 1956, CDH, 8-2-1, Folder #10.
100	1	ff	Howe to Tanner, Feb. 27, 1956, CDH, 8-2-1, Folder #10.
	24	ff	H of C Debates, Feb. 15, 1956, p. 2165-6.

Page Line
101   5   H of C Debates, March 10, 1955, p. 1907.
       14   D. Thomson, *St. Laurent*, p. 397.
       27 ff Diefenbaker, CBC Radio, March 9, 1956.
102   30 ff H of C Debates, March 15, 1956, p. 2165.
103   1   ff H of C Debates, March 15, 1956, p. 2166.
       25   Campbell to Board of Transport Commissioners, March 1956, CDH, 8-2-1.
104   1   ff BTC Proceedings, March 28, 1956.
       6   ff *Financial Post*, March 30, 1956.
105   Gairdner to Howe, March 26, 1956, CDH, 8-2-1, Folder #8.
108   4   ff Minutes of April 6-11, 1956, Meetings, CDH, 8-2-1.

                CHAPTER IX THE GREAT DEBATE
112   15 ff H of C Debates, May 15, 1956, p. 3895.
       26   H of C Debates, May 15, 1956, p. 3933.
113   2   ff H of C Debates, May 1, 1956, p. 3436.
       7   ff H of C Debates, May 4, 1956, p. 3570.
       21 ff Gallup Poll, May 1, 1956, as reported in *The Montreal Star*, May 2, 1956.
114   4   ff H of C Debates, May 2, 1956, p. 3462.
       36 ff H of C Debates, May 4, 1956, p. 3570.
115   21 ff Montreal *Gazette*, May 7, 1956.
116   3   ff D. Thomson, unpublished draft of *St. Laurent*.
       16 ff H of C Debates, May 8, 1956.
117   13 ff H of C Debates, May 14, 1956, pp. 3850-65.
118   *Ibid.*
119   *Ibid.*
120   *Ibid.*
121   *Ibid.*
123   22 ff Eugene Forsey, "Constitutional Aspects of the Canadian Pipe Line Debate," *Public Law*, 1957, p. 12.
124   9   ff H of C Debates, May 15, 1958, pp. 3927-8.
125   32   H of C Debates, May 18, p. 4089.
       34   H of C Debates, May 18, p. 4089.
126   1   Grant Dexter, in the *Winnipeg Free Press*, May 23, 1956.
       27 ff Interviews with N. E. Tanner and L. St. Laurent.
127   14 ff H of C Debates, May 22, 1956, pp. 4173-4.
128   10 ff H of C Debates, May 24, 1956, p. 4293.
128   29 ff H of C Debates, May 25, 1956, p. 4342.
129   20   H of C Debates, May 31, 1956, p. 4514.
130   10   H of C Debates, May 14, 1956, p. 3849.
132   28   H of C Debates, June 1, 1956, as reported by *Canadian Press*, June 1, 1956.
133   2   ff Montreal *Gazette*, June 2, 1956.

Page	Line		

CHAPTER X TO FIND A QUARTER BILLION

134	1		H of C Debates, May 30, 1956, p. 4480.
135	38		Interviews with Eugene Forsey and Stanley Knowles.
136	15		H of C Debates, June 5, 1956, p. 4742.
137	24		H of C Debates, June 5, 1956, p. 4692.
	32		Halifax *Chronicle-Herald*, May 19, 1956.
	33		Peterborough *Examiner*, June 8, 1956.
138	2		Howe to E. L. Blair, June 6, 1956, CDH, 8-2-1, Folder #6.
	7		D. R. Harrison to Howe, July 12, 1956, CDH, 8-2-1, Folder #7.
	9	ff	Howe to D. R. Harrison, July 18, 1956, CDH, 8-2-1, Folder #7.
	16	ff	Howe to Williamson, June 9, 1956, TCP files.
139	38		Kearney, as reported in *The Montreal Star*, May 24, 1956.
140	7	ff	Howe to Nesbitt, June 22, 1956, TCP files.
	21	ff	Howe-Stuart correspondence, June 1956, CDH, 8-2-1.
144	20	ff	Nesbitt memoir and TCP files.
145	5		Nesbitt memoir and TCP files.
146	34	ff	Howe to Symonds, Nov. 29, 1956, CDH, 8-2-1, Folder #1.
147	19	ff	Howe to Heeney, Dec. 15, 1956, CDH, 8-2-1, Folder #1.
	34	ff	Howe to Senator Peter Campbell, Dec. 17, 1956, CDH, 8-2-1, Folder #1.
149	30	ff	Howe to Tanner, Jan. 18, 1957, TCP files.
150	9	ff	Nesbitt to Howe, Jan. 23, 1957, TCP files.
	21	ff	Nesbitt memoir, pp. 144-5.

CHAPTER XI SON OF THE GREAT DEBATE

153	5	ff	H of C Debates, Feb. 29, 1957, p. 1599.
	18	ff	H of C Debates, Feb. 25, 1957, pp. 1602, 1603, 1605.
154	3	ff	H of C Debates, Feb. 25, 1957, p. 1609.
	11		H of C Debates, Feb. 25, 1957, p. 1608.
	22	ff	H of C Debates, Feb. 25, 1957, pp. 1610, 1611.
155	1	ff	H of C Debates, Feb. 25, 1957, p. 1611.
	18		H of C Debates, Feb. 25, 1957, p. 1627.
	32		H of C Debates, Feb. 25, 1957, p. 1633.
156	22	ff	Cf. J. Meisel, *The Canadian General Election of 1957*.
162	23		Interview with Mrs. Ann Sugarman.
164	13	ff	*Trade and Commerce*, Jan. 1959.
	21	ff	*The Globe and Mail*, June 14, 1957.
165	20		*Royal Commission on Energy*, First Report, October 1958, pp. 440, 444.
166	5	ff	*Ibid. Erratum: N.B.* There should be square brackets around the words "the two men."

CHAPTER XII THE GREAT LAKES AFFAIR

174	15		*Report of the commission concerning the sale of the gas network of Hydro-Quebec to the Quebec Natural Gas Corporation*, p. 83.
178	14		F.P.C. examiner Emery Woodhall, quoted in Nesbitt memoir, p. 187.

Note regarding the last page of Chapter Twelve and Reflections: At the time of writing this in 1969 I decided that I could not cover this topic adequately even in a sketchy and opinionated paragraph and still meet publishing and other deadlines. But as of the date of this note (January 20, 1970) it appears all the more important that the whole question of the export of Canadian natural gas to U.S. markets should be examined in the general context of future Canadian energy needs. Obviously any strong continentalist position on this matter raises problems and questions about the very existence of the Canadian nation state.

Index

and Home Oil Company, 12, 159
and Hudson's Bay Oil and Gas, 96,
98, 108, 148-9, 159
and James Kerr, 167-84
and Manning, 90-1, 103, 109
and Montreal area, 58-9
and Northern Natural Gas of Omaha, 25, 27, 28, 57, 86, 106
and Northern Ontario Natural Gas,
139
and press, 69-70, 77-8, 94, 101, 104,
106, 112-13
and Quebec Hydro, 58-9, 87, 143
reflection on, 187-93
and Nathan E. Tanner, 45, 49-50, 56,
57, 58, 63, 72, 75, 82, 84-5, 90, 92-3,
99-100, 107, 109, 126-7, 149-50, 152-
6, 158, 165-6, 175, 178
and Tennessee Gas Transmission, 38-
44, 55, 82, 85-6, 90, 94, 95-9, 100,
107-8, 142, 144, 146-8, 148-9, 158,
159
and Union Gas Company, 57, 60, 64,
139
and U.S. line, 53, 58-9, 169, 174, 177-
84, 187, 192
and Westcoast Transmission, 20-1,
36, 38-9, 61, 105-6, 114, 149, 154-5
and Western Pipe Lines, Introduction, 17, 25-30, 33, 34, 37-8, 41, 42-
4, 52, 59, 96, 143, 187
Trois Rivières, 8-9
Turner Valley, 10-12, 13
Twaits, W.O., 182

Union Gas Company, 57, 60, 64, 139
United Nations, 145-6
United States Steel Corporation, 72,
93, 95, 96, 139, 141, 145

University of Western Ontario Business
School, 37

Van Helmont, Jan. 6-7
Van Horne, William, 24
The Vancouver Province, 137
The Vancouver Sun, 68-9
Vincent, Marcel, 175
Von Humboldt, Alexander, 8

Washington, George, 8
Weeks, Sinclair, 94
Welland County, 9
Westcoast Transmission, 20-1, 36, 38-9,
61, 105-6, 114, 149, 154-5
Western Canadian Coal Operators As-
sociation, 19
Western Pipe Lines Limited, Introduc-
tion, 17, 25-30, 33, 34, 36-7, 41, 42-4,
52, 59, 96, 143, 175, 187, 192
wet gas, 16
White, Weld and Company, 97-8, 141-3
Whiteford, William, 74, 85
Williamson, Alan, 36-7, 41, 44, 56-7, 61,
63, 64, 65-8, 70-1, 72-9, 138
Wilson, Charles, 86
Winch, Harold, 68-9
Windsor, Frederic Albert, 5
Winnipeg and Central Gas Company,
60, 99
Winnipeg Free Press, 125, 126, 134-5
Wood, Gundy, Introduction, 25, 44, 79,
110
Woodsworth, Rev. J.S., 122
Wrong, Hume, 38-9

Young, Brigham, 45, 46
Young, Cyril, 53-4

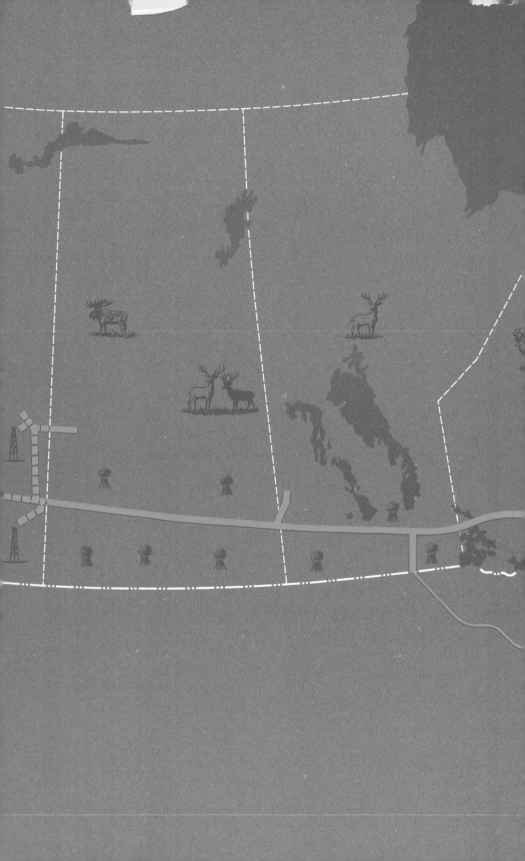